LANDSCAPES
OF THE WYE TOUR

LANDSCAPES
OF THE WYE TOUR

by
Susan Peterken

Logaston Press

LOGASTON PRESS
Little Logaston, Woonton, Almeley
Herefordshire HR3 6QH
logastonpress.co.uk

First published by Logaston Press 2008

ISBN 978 1904396 89 5

Set in Times New Roman by Logaston Press
and printed in Great Britain by
Bell & Bain ltd, Glasgow

Front cover: *River Wye – Tintern Abbey from the Devil's Pulpit*
by David Prentice in watercolour and reed pen

Contents

Acknowledgements

This book would never have been written if the Wye Tour Exhibition had not taken place, so I would first like to thank all the artists who submitted pictures and the many members of the Wye Valley Art Society who helped to mount, move and steward the exhibition. I am particularly indebted to the members involved, with me, in the long planning stage; David Young, Stephen Curtis, Dick Ray and Roger Spragg.

Secondly I am grateful to all the artists who agreed to let me reproduce their pictures from the Wye Tour exhibition and for providing their comments for the captions. Mari Roberts took the photographs of all the paintings in the exhibition on behalf of adventa and the exhibition organisers. David Prentice has given me great encouragement to write this book and kindly allowed me to reproduce his picture on the front cover, which was not submitted for the exhibition.

I greatly enjoyed my visits to museums to choose 18th- and 19th-century pictures to include in the book and would like to thank the following people, who enthusiastically showed me some of their collections and gave permission for me to reproduce the ones I selected: Catherine Willson from the Hereford Museum and Art Gallery, Andrew Helme from the Nelson Museum Monmouth, Anne Rainsbury at Chepstow Museum, and Paul Joyner, Lona Mason and Sion Jobbins at the National Library of Wales. Sue Middleton and Mark Bristow from the Wye Valley AONB provided me with information about their Overlooking the Wye Project.

Many of the books I consulted were in the reference library at the Nelson Museum, but I am grateful to others who lent me books, including Hazel Pickering, Beth Davis, and April Tremlett, who has a collection of late 19th- and early 20th-century Wye guidebooks. Simon Clarke kindly showed me his guidebooks on Ross, and Liz Pitman her extracts from unpublished Wye Tour diaries.

Andy Johnson and Karen Stout have meticulously edited and designed the book, and dealt patiently with all my queries.

Lastly and most importantly I need to thank my husband George for suggesting the theme for the exhibition in the first place and for helping, encouraging and occasionally goading me throughout the process of producing this book. Apart from much help with organising the content, improving the style, drawing the map and manipulating the pictures, he allowed me to use his collection of Wye books and even his computer.

Frontispiece. Artist unknown
The Wye, from Chepstow Castle *Wood engraving 1880*
A rare example of a picture of a Wye tourist drawing a scene on the Wye.
The artist has used the picturesque device of framing the view with a dark
toned foreground to give a sense of depth, though the viewpoint is quite high for
picturesque tastes (Picturesque Europe)

Chapter 1
A new look at the Wye Tour

On a grey Saturday morning in January 2006, ten members of the Wye Valley Art Society gathered in Whitchurch village hall. We had spent the previous eighteen months organising the Society's Wye Tour landscape painting competition, and were now waiting to receive the entries. We were apprehensive, as well as excited, for we had no idea how many of the promised paintings would actually be submitted or what the artistic standards would be, but in the event, no less than 82 artists arrived bearing 223 paintings in an impressive variety of styles. By the end of the day, 69 paintings had been chosen for exhibition and the judges had agreed which should be awarded the prizes.

During the winter and spring the Society organised the selected paintings into an exhibition, which itself went on a Wye Tour from May to September 2006, to Hereford at the Shire Hall, Monmouth at the Nelson Museum and Chepstow in St Mary's Church. It opened in combination with the Wye Valley Area of Outstanding Natural Beauty's 35th anniversary celebrations in the concert hall at Wyastone Leys, when Sir Roy Strong gave a speech and presented the prizes. The exhibition displayed not only the modern paintings, but also a selection of paintings and prints from the 18th and 19th centuries, produced by artists and travellers during the heyday of the Wye Tour, 200 years ago. Throughout the summer visitors to the exhibition could thus make a direct comparison between artistic styles then and now.

The Wye Tour

What was the Wye Tour? On a wet day in the summer of 1770, the Reverend William Gilpin, head-master of Cheam School, stepped into a rowing boat on the River Wye at Ross. As he was carried down river to Chepstow, he made sketches, took notes and later enlarged these into *Observations on the*

River Wye and several Parts of South Wales etc., relative chiefly to Picturesque Beauty; made in the summer of the Year 1770. He was clearly impressed by the valley. On returning home he wrote to a friend: 'If you have never navigated the Wye, you have seen nothing. Besides three or four capital views upon it, the whole is such a display of picturesque scenery that it is beyond any commendation.'

Gilpin first circulated his account in manuscript, but it was eventually published in 1782 and became an instant success, with five editions by 1800. Possibly the first British guidebook, it vividly described his voyage and explained the principles of picturesque beauty in forthright, even pedantic, terms. In the introduction, he suggested a new purpose for travel, which became the basis for the development of picturesque tourism in Britain:

> We travel for various purposes – to explore the culture of soils – to view the curiosities of art – to survey the beauties of nature – and to learn the manners of men; their different polities, and modes of life. The following little work proposes a new object of pursuit; that of examining the face of a country by the rules of picturesque beauty ...

The key word in Gilpin's book was 'picturesque', which was a fashionable idea in the late 18th century. At its simplest it meant 'like a picture', but Gilpin developed the idea into a complicated many-stranded concept, so much so that he became known in some circles as the 'priest of the cult of the picturesque'. Gilpin's publication was particularly well-timed, for it coincided with restrictions on foreign travel during the French Revolution (1789) and the Napoleonic Wars from 1792 to 1815, and also with the period when wild landscapes were becoming increasingly appreciated.

Gilpin was one of the earlier participants in the Wye Tour, a two-day boat journey of 40 miles from Ross down the gorges of the lower Wye to Chepstow, stopping overnight in Monmouth. The map, Plate 1, shows this section of the river and the main sites which excited the tourists. Operating from the mid 18th century until well into the 20th century, the Tour enabled travellers to relax as local boatmen rowed them gently with the current and poled them over the shallows 'in perfect beauty, perfect ease, the awning trembled in the breeze', as the poet Robert Bloomfield expressed it. The tourists glided by awe-inspiring and ever-changing scenes, made sketches and wrote their diaries, leaving for us today a remarkably detailed record of life on the Wye. The Tour attracted not only J.M.W. Turner, William Wordsworth and many other notable artists and poets, but also royalty and thousands of the increasingly wealthy middle classes.

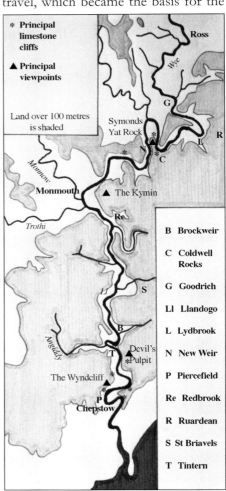

Plate 1. Map of Wye Tour sites
The course of the Wye between Ross and Chepstow is shown, indicating the main Wye Tour sites, with the land above 100m shaded to indicate the gorges. The high land to the left is Trellech Plateau and that to the right Dean Plateau

The Lower Wye was not the only popular tourist destination in the 18th century, for picturesque tours developed in the Lake District, Snowdonia and the Scottish Highlands as well. It was however distinctive, for Wye tourists viewed the valley from a gliding boat, not a jolting carriage, and experienced the gradually changing shapes of the hills, river and cliffs as a theatrical performance with moving stage sets. Significantly, at least four of the artists who visited the Wye in the 18th or early 19th centuries had careers as stage designers or scene-painters.

By the mid 19th century, the Tour was famous and was attracting thousands of people every year. Even in the 18th century, tourists often left the river to make some of the journey on horseback or on foot, and from the 1870s the new railway provided an alternative, and faster, means of viewing the valley. Nevertheless, the Tour continued to attract visitors until the First World War, after which it declined to a few short boat trips or a tour by charabanc or car. Today it is largely forgotten, even by people who live in the Wye Valley.

The Wye Tour exhibition

What prompted the exhibition? In 2004, the Wye Valley Art Society was searching for a theme for an exhibition when my husband George casually wondered why the Society did not take more interest in the Picturesque and suggested that they might reinterpret the scenes made famous 200 years earlier. After a process of rapid learning about Gilpin, picturesque ideas and the Wye Tour, the committee agreed to organise an open exhibition around this theme. Artists from the Wye Valley and surrounding areas were invited to produce paintings based on twelve of the sites between Ross and Chepstow popularized by the Wye tourists, including several viewpoints on or near the river: Goodrich Castle, Ruardean Church, Lydbrook, Coldwell Rocks and New Weir in the gorge above Monmouth, and Tintern Abbey, Piercefield Park and Chepstow Castle in the lower gorge. These were supplemented by several elevated viewpoints: Symonds Yat Rock, which is still a tourist honeypot, the Kymin, overlooking Monmouth, the Devil's Pulpit above Tintern Abbey and the Wyndcliff, which looks down on Piercefield and across to the Severn.

From the outset the Society was keen to encourage artists to produce a set of paintings that would express their interest in, and response to, their selected sites. The aim was not a topographical record. Rather, artists were told: 'We will be looking for paintings which depict these sites in a modern and personal style, reflecting your thoughts and reactions to the sites. You could choose to make a feature of the changes that have taken place to the landscapes since the 18th century.' Entries were received from both amateur and professional artists living as far away as Devon, Derbyshire and Cheshire, who submitted pictures in a great range of styles and to a generally high standard. Selection was not simply a matter of choosing the 'best' paintings. First, a panel of four independent judges was asked to choose eight pictures of good standard for each of the twelve sites that collectively represented a variety of styles and media. Then a hanging committee narrowed this down by selecting artistically balanced groups for each site for exhibition.

The exhibition proved to be a very ambitious project for a small art society, involving a vast amount of work for a few members and contributions from many more members during the exhibition itself. Fortunately, participants and visitors alike deemed it to be a great success. Certainly the organizers felt it was well worth the effort.

This book

As one of the main organizers, I found myself looking for 18th- and 19th-century descriptions of the twelve sites and for contemporary prints and paintings for inclusion in the exhibition as a comparison with the modern paintings. Surprisingly, I could find no recent books that solely covered the Wye Tour, although there were many tantalizing glimpses in 20th-century guidebooks. On the other hand, diaries and accounts written by and for the Wye tourists were full of interesting descriptions, and it suddenly occurred to me that I could fill a gap and write about the Tour and the landscapes, illustrated with pictures from the exhibition.

My aims in writing this book are to summarize the history of the Wye Tour, indicate how 18th- and 19th-century artists, poets and tourists recorded their impressions, explain how they thought about the Wye landscape, and identify how perceptions and artistic responses have since changed. Since the idea of the Picturesque was an important factor in encouraging people to travel, Chapter 2 covers the concept's origins and evolution and how it related to the development of landscape painting, and to poetry and garden design. Chapter 3 describes the geology and land forms, relating them to the viewpoints and sites enjoyed by the tourists, and summarizes the industry, trade, and use of the land during the period of the Wye Tour. The growth of picturesque tourism and the rise and decline of the Wye Tour are discussed in Chapter 4, using quotes from diaries and guidebooks that bring alive the tourists' experiences of their voyage. Some of the famous visitors, poets and artists are described, with examples of the poems and pictures they produced. Chapters 5 and 6 recreate a tour down the river from Ross to Chepstow, visualizing the landscape in words and pictures from the 18th and 19th centuries, alongside the modern paintings from the exhibition, noting what has changed in the last 200 years. The final chapter considers how landscape images have proliferated since the 18th century, how travel has developed, and whether these changes are reflected in the differences between the Wye Tour pictures and those from the 2006 exhibition.

As an artist, I found the process of selecting pictures for this book fascinating. My choice of 32 paintings by 21 artists from the exhibition reflects my personal taste, covers the range of selected entries for each site and hopefully represents the work of 21st-century landscape painters. At my request, artists commented on their pictures, but they were offered no restrictions on what they might say, so the comments (which have been included in the captions) are as diverse as the artists themselves, giving everything from practical details to their emotional reactions to the landscape. The selected artists range from David Prentice, one of the best known landscape artists in Britain, to artists who claim only to have taken up painting in their retirement.

In order to represent the artistic output of the 18th- and 19th-century Wye tourists I have selected 28 prints, drawings and paintings. These were chosen mainly from the collections of the National Library of Wales, Aberystwyth; the Nelson Museum, Monmouth; Chepstow Museum; and Hereford Museum and Art Gallery. My selection, which was influenced by the knowledge that nearly one third of the illustrations in this book had to be in black and white, is biased towards sketches, drawings, engravings and lithographs. The artists range from the most famous, J.M.W. Turner, to John Arthur Evans, who trained as an artist, but spent a large part of his life running a confectionery shop in Monmouth. Gilpin was an uninspiring artist, but he produced some pen and wash sketches of the Wye which were published as aquatints, and seven of these from the second edition are reproduced here at the head of each chapter.

Chapter 2
The Cult of the Picturesque

Like or having the elements of a picture; fit to be the subject of a striking or effective picture; possessing pleasing and interesting qualities of form and colour but not implying the highest beauty or sublimity: said of landscape, buildings, costume, scenes of diversified action etc. also of circumstances, situations, fancies, ideas and the like.
Picturesque gardening; the arrangement of a garden so as to make it a pretty picture; the romantic style of gardening aiming at irregular and rugged beauty.
Of language, narrative etc: strikingly graphic or vivid; sometimes implying a disregard of fact in the effort for effect.

The Oxford English Dictionary

In order to understand the motivation of the picturesque tourists and the attitude of the artists to the landscapes they painted, we should first consider what the Picturesque meant to 18th-century travellers and how its meaning evolved. This chapter describes the many strands of the Picturesque, firstly summarizing their development, then enlarging on particular aspects. The Picturesque is a difficult idea to define. Today it is usually taken to mean little more than 'looks attractive', though the OED definition above shows that discriminating usage neatly retains most elements of 18th-century ideas.

Stages of the Picturesque

The long development of 'picturesque' as a concept is simplified here into six stages. Each has a clear identity and is associated with a particular period, but none is sharply defined, for the component ideas overlap and interweave and at various periods several stages ran in parallel. They provide a guide to the rapidly changing attitudes to landscape in 17th- and 18th-century Britain, and the associated influences on – and from – poetry, prose, painting and garden design. Subsequent sections provide detail on some aspects.

Stage 1: Fusion of styles in 17th-century Italy
Artists from the Low Countries, Germany and France, who had developed a realistic and expressionistic style for painting landscapes, travelled to Rome. Their ideas fused with those of Italian neo-classical painters, who painted landscapes as backgrounds to Arcadian themes. Claude and Poussin, who were the principal exponents of this fusion, painted, within precise rules of composition, subjects in which the idealized pastoral landscape became an important component, a style which became the foundation of the 'Classical Picturesque'. In contrast, Salvator Rosa rejected the idea of improving on nature and painted wild mountainous landscapes imparting a sense of awe or terror: this style later became known as the 'Sublime Picturesque'.

Stage 2: Italian ideas spread to Britain in the mid 18th century
Ideas of the Picturesque arrived in Britain by several routes. Richard Wilson returned from studies in Rome to paint British landscapes in a Claudian style; his paintings later inspired Turner. Independently in the 1760s, Gainsborough, influenced by Dutch landscape painting, adopted a picturesque style well before the full development of picturesque theory. Demand for prints of Italian and Dutch landscapes rose, whilst Grand Tourists returned with paintings by Claude and Rosa, and Edmund Burke developed his ideas on the sublime and the beautiful. Wild landscapes were increasingly appreciated throughout the century,

Stage 3: Formalizing the Picturesque in late 18th- and early 19th-century Britain
In the 1780s, William Gilpin, who was particularly interested in natural landscapes, formulated his rules of composition, including low viewpoints, sidescreens, variety and roughness. Uvedale Price and Richard Payne Knight introduced picturesque principles into landscape design, but their ideas differed from those of Gilpin. Topographical artists produced picturesque prints of British landscapes, with Paul Sandby bridging the gap between topographical and landscape art. Later, Turner painted in topographical and picturesque styles. The professional middle classes toured Britain, appreciating landscapes according to picturesque rules.

Stage 4: Disenchantment, parody and the early 19th-century rise of the Romantic Movement
The Picturesque degenerated into a morass of rules which excluded most landscapes as 'not picturesque'. Criticism and ridicule was heaped on Gilpin and his acolytes. A 'Picturesque Genre' style evolved, depicting hovels, peasants, emaciated animals and blasted oaks. The Romantic Movement developed to fill the gap left by the decline of Rationalism and Christianity: both Constable and Wordsworth rejected rigid rules and expressed their passion for nature freely. Turner developed beyond picturesque rules to embrace Burke's ideas on the Sublime, with colour and light becoming his subject matter.

Stage 5: Picturesque eclipsed: mid 19th century

Numerous social and technical developments overtook picturesque styles of painting and associated tourism. Railways altered the pattern of tourism, and travel on the Continent became easier. Photography began to replace topographical drawing and painting as a record of what tourists saw and experienced. Influenced by Turner and Constable, the Impressionists developed a new art, based on an increasingly scientific understanding of light. The Picturesque declined into a vague idealization of the countryside by an increasingly urban population.

Stage 6: Picturesque diffused: 20th century

A predominantly urban population gained increasing access to the countryside for relaxation. Photography became a popular record and art form, though landscape photographs were often composed according to the old rules of the Picturesque. Landscape design was extended from large rural estates and country houses, to become a technique for managing rural 'amenity' and 'natural landscapes'. Nature conservation developed, based on an appreciation of wild nature. 'Picturesque' became a vague word applied indiscriminately to landscapes, language and behaviour.

Changing attitudes to wild and cultivated landscapes

The development of the ideas on the Picturesque took place during a period of rapid change in the way different types of landscape were appreciated. Throughout the 16th and 17th centuries agriculturalists believed that all land should be cultivated. A tamed and productive landscape was considered not only more useful than a wild one, but also more beautiful, and moreover cultivation was simply right and in accordance with scriptural directives. Thus, straight lines – plough furrows, rows of planted trees in orchards and plantations – were admired because they demonstrated that nature had been brought under control.

Towards the end of the 17th century 'men of taste' were beginning to lose their sense of disgust at the sight of barren, useless mountains and to experience them with a sense of pleasant horror. They began to appreciate that mountains should be enjoyed for their pure air and far-reaching views. In about 1739, Thomas Gray and Horace Walpole, acting under the influence of the new engravings of mountain paintings by the 17th-century Italian artist Salvator Rosa, visited the Alps and produced possibly the first account of mountains as sublime entities, fully 20 years before the concept became fashionable, declaring: 'Not a precipice, not a torrent, nor a cliff but is pregnant with religion and poetry'. An appreciation of wild nature became almost a religious act – awe and reverence was being transferred from God to nature. Attitudes to wild landscapes were still changing when Thomas Hardy wrote in the opening chapter of *The Return of the Native* (1878):

> The time seems near, if it has not actually arrived, when the chastened sublimity of a moor, a sea, or a mountain will be all of nature that is absolutely in keeping with the moods of the more thinking among mankind. And ultimately, to the commonest tourist, spots like Iceland may become what the vineyards and myrtle-gardens of South Europe are to him now; and Heidelberg and Baden be passed unheeded as he hastens from the Alps to the sand-dunes of Scheveningen.

Plate 2. C.J. Greenwood View from the Windcliff Monmouthshire *Lithograph by R.S. Groom* c.*1845*
Three tourists viewing the horseshoe bend round the Lancaut Peninsula, a typical Wye entrenched meander, backed
by Piercefield Cliff, with Chepstow Castle, the mouth of the Wye and the Severn beyond. The cliffs appear more
conspicuous than they are today, possibly because the trees were not so tall. The treatment of the foreground trees and the
clouds is particularly free and lively for the period. One tourist appears to be lecturing the others on picturesque principles

The Lower Wye Valley became appreciated for the contrast between neat regulated fields and sublime rocky cliffs as seen in Plate 2.

These changes were reinforced during the 18th century by enormous changes in the appearance of the landscape brought about by enclosure and 'improvements' in agriculture. Between 1760 and 1820 two million more acres of land were brought into cultivation, and a further two and a half million acres were enclosed in small hedged fields. Inevitably, this led to a reaction against straight lines. Gilpin was disgusted – he thought geometric fields were very unpicturesque – and, as landowners felt the need to improve their estates by making a contrast with the surrounding land, landscape gardeners turned to natural-looking forms, with curves rather than straight lines. Elsewhere in Europe the circumstances were quite different: there was less cultivation, so managed estates with formal designs were perceived as oases in a sea of wilderness. In the less prosperous areas of Britain, characterised by subsistence farming, the idea of creating artificial wildernesses seemed absurd.

Early in the 19th century the growing appreciation of wild landscapes combined with a reaction against the increasing intensity of agriculture, with its regulated landscape, and the artificiality of landscape gardening to generate a movement to protect wild landscapes as a spiritual resource. In a country with increasing industrialization and an expanding population, wild open spaces were seen as a symbol of human freedom. Solitude, once regarded as a distressing state, was increasingly appreciated as an opportunity for spiritual renewal, alone with nature, as described by John Stuart Mill in 1848:

> Solitude ... is essential to any depth of meditation or of character ... Solitude in the presence of natural beauty and grandeur is the cradle of thoughts and aspirations which are not only good for the individual, but which society could ill do without.

European landscape painting and the start of the Picturesque

The origins of the Picturesque lie in changes in artistic taste during the Renaissance and the religious conflicts of the Reformation. Renaissance artists introduced landscapes into the background of paintings whose primary subjects were classical and religious. By the 16th century Venetian artists such as Giorgione (1477?-1510) and Titian (1487-1576) were creating Arcadian landscapes based around the myth of the Golden Age, where colour and light unified the landscape to invoke a mood of poetic melancholy. At the same time, northern artists developed the new technique of painting in oils, which allowed them to portray greater naturalism and more subtle effects of light. The fresco paintings of Italy, in contrast, had to be painted rapidly onto wet plaster.

As the Reformation developed in northern Europe, the demand for religious paintings declined and the interest in landscape painting correspondingly increased. The Calvinists even banned religious, pagan and classical subjects in art, and when the Spanish attempted to impose the Inquisition on the Low Countries in the 17th century, the Dutch broke away from Spain and developed a pure realistic landscape art. Many rich middle-class merchants sought accurate pictures of their surroundings, not obscured by classical or religious myth, and so the story-telling element disappeared from Dutch paintings about a century before those in the rest of Europe. Among the many artists in these developments, Pieter Bruegel the Elder (1525-1569) in Flanders famously depicted the relationship of man to nature and the effects of the seasons and weather on rural tasks. Near the end of his life, Peter Paul Rubens (1577-1640) produced pure landscapes for his own pleasure, in which he showed a delight in the details of nature and glowing atmospheric effects, and these pictures had an important influence in England after the Restoration in 1660. Significantly, the word 'landscape' was derived from the Dutch 'landschap', which was in use by 1597 and became the English 'lantskip' by 1606.

A different theme developed in German landscape art, which combined a mystical attitude to nature alongside accurate observations. As a broad generalization, northern artists used nature to express emotions, while classical artists in Italy expressed ideas. By removing story-telling and human figures from landscape painting, northern artists could select and distort colours to express emotions, creating, like music, poetic and romantic moods. An early influence was Albrecht Dürer (1471-1528), who in 1494 produced what has been called the first traveller's sketchbook of watercolours when he toured the Tyrolean Alps.

Northern expressionism and southern neo-classical idealism came together in the 17th century, when Flemish, German and French artists flocked to Rome. They developed a style of painting that became the fashion for the next 150 years and became the foundation of the 'Classical Picturesque'. The three artists whose work was most influential were Poussin, Claude and Dughet.

Nicolas Poussin (1594-1665) had an intellectual interest in the relationship between man and nature, and tried to give his landscapes a feeling of order and timelessness by constructing strongly architectural compositions and filling his pictures with symbols. The paintings of his brother-in-law, Gaspard Dughet (1615-1675), combined a similar sense of order with greater naturalism and romanticism and were probably of more influence in the development of the Picturesque in 18th-century Britain. Confusingly, Gaspard also took the name Poussin, and references to Poussin during the period of picturesque tourism are more likely to refer to him than to Nicolas.

Gellée Claude (1600-1682), known as Claude Lorraine, had a more decorative, less structural approach and became the best-known artist depicting idealized or beautiful landscapes. His influence was still strongly felt in 18th-century England by artists, landscape designers and tourists – if a landscape did not look like a Claude painting it was not worth looking at. Claude painted a blaze of golden light in a similar way to Giorgione, and by ordering his pictures into a series of planes, carefully controlling tones and inserting visual links such as bridges and rivers between the planes, gave them a sense of space and a dream-like quality. A typical Claude picture had a strongly-lit middle ground framed by a darkened foreground of trees, ruins or mountains. Human figures remained small and the classical myths they portrayed were chosen carefully to convey a poetic melancholy and the transitory nature of life.

In Naples during the same period, Salvator Rosa (1615-73) was producing landscape paintings with the full drama of the Baroque. He opposed the idea that nature could be 'improved', and instead of painting peaceful pastoral landscapes, he expressed his feelings about wild and savage nature in scenes of rocks, cliffs, mountains, waterfalls and storms, all peopled with bandits and gypsies. This romantic style later became known as the 'Sublime Picturesque' after Burke published his essay on beauty and the sublime. Rosa became a cult figure in England, greatly influencing 18th-century landscape painting and helping to popularize the mountainous scenery which the Grand Tourists encountered in the Alps.

By 1748 the influence of these artists in Britain is evident from the often quoted lines of James Thomson from *The Castle of Indolence*:

> Now the black tempest strikes the astonished eyes;
> Now down the steep the flashing torrent flies;
> The trembling sun now plays o'er ocean blue;
> And now rude mountains frown amid the skies;
> Whate'er Lorrain light-touched with softening hue
> Or savage Rosa dashed, or learnèd Poussin drew.

British topographical drawing and painting

Images of the landscape were produced not only as landscape paintings, but also as topographical pictures. The latter, however, were judged by landscape artists and critics to be inferior. If a landscape was not romantic or classical it was contemptible, mere topography; landscape painting should not stoop to feature real places. This attitude was perpetuated in modern times in the division between artists and illustrators. The same distinction was recognised by Edward Dayes, who was well known for his criticism of fellow artists, when he wrote about Joseph Farington around 1804:

When an artist gives a representation of some local spot, we feel obliged by his extending our topographical knowledge; but if, in his fancy pictures, we are ever presented with common-place stuff, such as might ouze out of any futile pate, we feel disgusted, and turn away dissatisfied and uninformed.

From Tudor times onwards, landowners could provide a good living for topographical draughtsmen by commissioning detailed and accurate pictures of their country estates. They took the artist to a high viewpoint, offering in effect a map of their land. Then from the late 17th century, the middle classes began to collect landscape prints, most of which were realistic Dutch and idealistic Italian landscapes. After the introduction of aquatints around 1775 and the development of cheaper steel engraving in 1810, the demand increased and shifted to prints of British landscapes. Topographical artists rapidly supplied the demand for prints in guidebooks and tourist albums. Released by this alternative market from the patronage of landowners, draughtsmen could lower their viewpoints in accordance with picturesque taste and concentrate on details in the fore-ground, as demonstrated in an engraving after William Bartlett (Plate 3). These pictures were

Plate 3. After W.H. Bartlett, Coldwell Rocks on the Wye *Lithograph by T.M. Baynes c.1840*
David Cox drew this view a few years earlier (Plate 9) and the composition is very similar, but Bartlett, unlike Cox, chose to include the trees on the skyline, perhaps producing a less dramatic effect. Bartlett, in contrast, excludes the lime kilns, though he does show smoke from a cottage, and depicts trows, not a tour boat (Chepstow Museum)

usually inhabited by people, to give a sense of scale, animate the scene and help to explain the context. For example, a dignified figure pointing to a ruin set in a wild landscape indicated that this was a well-known antiquity, while an artist painting in the foreground showed that this view was worthy of a picture.

The early topographical pictures were tinted drawings – a series of grey washes to give tone and a few touches of pale colour. Perhaps the most artistic topographical painter was Paul Sandby (1730-1809), who started his career by training as a military draughtsman, where accurate drawing was essential, but later found inspiration in Windsor Great Park, where he painted gnarled and twisted trees in the picturesque manner, developing rich colour washes and reducing the outlines. He was very influential as a founder member of the Royal Academy and was one of the earliest artists to visit the Wye in 1770, exploiting the new technique of aquatints in his published *Views of Wales* (Plate 56). In *Masters of British Landscapes* Laure Meyer described him as the father of British landscape painting, for he bridged the divide between topographical and fine art landscape painting, looked on nature as poetry, and showed subtleties of colour and atmosphere. Gainsborough praised Sandby in a letter to Lord Hardwick, written about 1764 in the third person:

> ... but with respect to real Views from Nature in this Country he [Gainsborough] has never seen any Place that affords a Subject equal to the poorest imitations of Gaspard or Claude. Paul Sandby is the only Man of Genius, he believes, who had employ'd his Pencil that way.

Picturesque and Romantic painting in Britain

Picturesque art was brought to Britain in the mid 18th century by the tens of thousands of English gentlemen who undertook the Grand Tour. Many brought back paintings by Claude and Rosa for their country houses, as well as more topographical works such as the pictures of Antonio Canaletto, and by the 19th century there were eighty Claudes and a hundred Rosas in English collections. The flow was temporarily staunched by 1793, however, when the war with France restricted travel in Continental Europe, and in response artists in search of the Sublime and the Picturesque turned to the wild landscapes of Britain.

The leading landscape painters in 18th-century Britain were Richard Wilson and Thomas Gainsborough. Wilson (1714-1782) was born in Wales, but spent six years in Italy, taking up the dying ideas of the Classical Picturesque, which by then had been reduced to a set of formulae designed to produce a standard arrangement of mountains, trees, waterfalls and ruined towers. When he returned home in about 1755 he introduced the technique of sketching in oils and painted landscapes in a Claudean style: the centre of his pictures was always light and the whole landscape expressed a single mood. Vying with Paul Sandby, he was, according to R.H. Wilenski in *English Painting*, the father of British landscape painting. They were both founder members of the Royal Academy, which opened in 1768 and later provided Wilson with an income by creating the post of Librarian, topographical work being considered demeaning for an artist of his stature.

Thomas Gainsborough (1727-1788) produced paintings that anticipated the theories of the Picturesque by 30 years, a good example being *Sunset: Carthorses Drinking at a Stream*, painted in 1760-65, in which the scene is framed by a gnarled hollow oak to the right and a clump of trees to the left, which combined to create a darkened foreground. Gainsborough was much influenced by Rubens at this period, and also by the French Rococo, but the composition is closer to classical Claude. The fashion of the time, however, was for portraiture and Italian landscapes, not picturesque British compositions, and both Gainsborough and Wilson had difficulty selling their pictures, though Wilson found he could double the price of a picture by including a human figure.

The academic theorists and art critics of this period condemned picturesque landscape painting because they thought it could not improve the mind and did not excite noble sentiments. Romantic landscape painting, which developed alongside the Picturesque in the late 18th century, eventually attracted more acclaim for its greater emotional content, and in due course it climbed to the top of the hierarchy of genres. The Romantics, in contrast to the picturesque theorists, thought that any 'improvements' to nature destroyed the spirit of place, though they were not above moving elements around to improve a picture. The greatest British exponents in the Romantic Movement were Turner and Constable, who expressed the same passion for nature as the poet William Wordsworth.

Joseph Mallord William Turner (1775-1851) spanned the gulf between the 18th-century topographical painters and the art of today. He painted across the range of topographical, classical picturesque, sublime, naturalistic and romantic styles and developed a style of his own which led the way towards abstraction. According to Kenneth Clark in *Landscape into Art*, Turner's greatest achievement was to lighten the tones of his colours so that his pictures not only represented light but symbolized it. His early travels in Wales, with its varied landscapes and changeable weather, greatly influenced his development, and by the early 1790s he was producing watercolours in the topographical tradition. He was also greatly influenced by Richard Wilson, who showed him how the exhausted Classical Picturesque tradition could be revitalized with heightened effect by adapting the styles of Claude and Poussin: Plate 48 demonstrates his use of a Claudean composition. He began rearranging the features in his landscapes to fit with his ideas of picturesque composition, which do not seem to bear much relation to Gilpin's rules. He usually drew buildings accurately, however – his Tintern Abbey pictures are fine architectural studies. By 1795, Turner had absorbed Burke's ideas to the extent that he painted storms and mountains in a sublime manner, with light, colour and spirit of place becoming increasingly important. According to Joseph Farington: 'Turner has no settled process, but drives the colours abt. till he has expressed the idea in his mind.'

Turner's patrons were the new middle classes, not the traditional connoisseurs, and he tried to satisfy all their tastes by painting in a variety of styles. Like many landscape painters of the period, he increased his popularity by producing several series of engravings, which he also felt would leave a more important legacy than his paintings. After his death, Turner influenced some of the Impressionist painters in France, for Claude Monet and Camille Pissarro visited London in 1870-1871 and saw some of his work. His oil painting of 1845, *The Junction of the Severn and Wye*, certainly the most modern painting to come out of the Wye Tour, was based on the mezzotint of 1811 (Plate 48), and now hangs in the Louvre. It focuses on the two rivers, leaving out most of the detail; the trees on the left and the castle have gone and the figure is a dark streak. It was exhibited in Paris in 1887 at the Ecole des Beaux-Arts, and according to Ian Warrell, in Katherine Lochran's *Turner Whistler Monet*, 'made a huge impact on those who saw it, for its dream-like distillation of light and form, appealing alike to those steeped in the impressionist aesthetic, as well as symbolists ...'.

The other great romantic painters of the period were Thomas Girtin (1775-1802) and John Constable (1776-1837), but the former died tragically young and it is Constable who is remembered. An admirer of Claude and Gainsborough in his early life, and much influenced by Dutch realistic landscape painters, particularly Rubens, Constable tried all his life to be a 'natural' painter. At the age of 19 he described his teacher, Joseph Farington, as his master and nature as his mistress. He tried not to develop mannerisms, and in 1836 said: 'When I sit down to make a sketch from nature, the first thing I do is to forget that I have ever seen a picture.' However, near the end of his life, according to Geoffrey Grigson in *Britain Observed*, he thought he might have 'preferred the picturesque to the beautiful – which I hope will account for the broken ruggedness of my style', and feared that he had fallen under the influence of fashions in landscape painting that had been prevalent in his early life. He did indeed paint in a consciously picturesque style in the late 1820s, with sandy lanes, donkeys, dead trees and texture, probably in a bid to make his pictures more saleable. Constable influenced few British artists in his lifetime, but his work was immediately appreciated in France and influenced the French Romantic and Impressionist Movements.

Poetry and the Picturesque

From the 15th to the 19th centuries, poetry, prose and landscape painting all influenced land management and attitudes to landscape. A literary education was considered essential to appreciate nature. Many people found an interest in landscape by reading rather than looking at paintings. I have a childhood memory of reading a vivid description of limestone country in Charles Kingsley's *The Water Babies* (1863) and being conscious of forming a visual image of a landscape I had never experienced. Wordsworth considered that an appreciation of wild mountainous landscape was not inbuilt, but needed to be acquired by aesthetic education, and this idea was perpetuated in novels. Walter Hartwright, the drawing master in Wilkie Collins' novel *The Woman in White* (1859-60), even suggests that admiration of beautiful landscapes needs to be learnt:

> Admiration of those beauties of the inanimate world which modern poetry so largely and so eloquently describes, is not, even in the best of us, one of the original instincts of our nature. As children we possess none of it ... No uninstructed man or woman possesses it ... Our capacity of appreciating the beauties of the earth we live on is, in truth, one of the civilised accomplishments which we all learn as an Art.

During the Renaissance, there was renewed interest in the Augustan poets, Virgil and Horace, who exhorted farmers to manage their land intensively, as shown in Virgil's (70-19BC) *Georgics*:

> Come, farmers then, and learn the form of tendance
> Each kind of tree requires; domesticate
> The wild by culture. Do not let your land
> Lie idle ...   The moral is
> That every tree needs labour, all must be
> Forced into furrows, tamed at any cost.

John Milton's (1608-1674) description of Eden in *Paradise Lost* had a considerable influence on ideas of the Picturesque with his, and a line from his poem *L'Allegro* was quoted by Gilpin and other Wye tourists on first sighting Goodrich Castle – 'Boosom'd high in Tufted Trees'. This extract seems to suggest an early enjoyment of the visual aspects of landscape:

Streit mine eye hath caught new pleasures
Whilst the Lantskip round it measures,
Russet Lawns and Fallows Gray,
Where the nibbling flocks do stray,
Mountains on whose barren brest
The labouring clouds do often rest:
Meadows trim with Daisies pide,
Shallow Brooks, and Rivers wide.
Towers, and Battlements it sees
Boosom'd high in Tufted Trees
Where perhaps some beauty lies.

Alexander Pope (1688-1744), who wrote about landscapes as if they were pictures, was very influential in the development of pure landscape painting. Michael Rosenthal, in *Constable the Painter and his Landscapes*, suggested that the following lines from the poem *Windsor-Forest* describe a landscape from foreground to background, as if it was a Claude composition:

Here waving groves a chequer'd scene display
And part admit, and part exclude the day;
As some coy nymph her lover's warm address
Not quite indulges, or can quite repress.
There, interspers'd in lawns and op'ning glades,
Thin trees arise that shun each other's shades.
Here in full light the russet plains extend:
There wrapt in clouds the blueish hills ascend.

By the 18th century many poets were looking beyond Greek and Roman poetry by using Gothic and Celtic themes and trying to develop a British flavour to their work. James Thomson's (1700-1748) poem *The Seasons*, written in 1730, became very popular – by 1750 it had run to 300 editions – and helped to develop an appreciation of British landscapes. Until that time landscapes had been regarded as a background to man's activities, but for Thomson, the landscape and the effects of the seasons on nature were the central subjects, which he described in terms of pictures. This extract from *The Seasons* might be describing the Wye:

Wide o'er the Brim, with many a Torrent swell'd,
And the mix'd Ruin of its Banks o'erspread,
At last the rous'd-up River pours along:
Resistless, roaring, dreadful down it comes,
From the rude Mountain, and the mossy Wild,
Tumbling thro' Rocks abrupt, and sounding far;
Then o'er the sanded Valley floating spreads,
Calm, sluggish, silent; till again constrain'd
Between two meeting Hills it bursts a Way,
Where Rocks and Woods o'erhang the turbid Stream;
There gathering triple Force, rapid and deep,
It boils, and wheels, and foams, and thunders' thro'.

According to Konstantin Bazarov in *Landscape Painting*, a chain of connections can be demonstrated between poetry and painting, from Virgil's poetry via Claude's paintings and Thomson's poem, to Wilson's and Gainsborough's paintings. Although landscape painting seemed to have had little influence on poetry during the early 18th century, the landscape poetry of this period raised the status of British landscapes, laid the foundation for picturesque ideas and encouraged tourism.

Thomas Gray's (1716-1771) *Elegy in a Country Churchyard*, the most-read poem of the mid 18th century, formed part of what became known as the 'graveyard' school of poetry. Gray was trying to revive an older British tradition, the poetry of Shakespeare and Milton, and some of the early lines do have a Shakespearean air and give the landscape a definite atmosphere:

> Now fades the glimmering landscape on the sight,
> And all the air a solemn stillness holds,
> Save where the beetle wheels his droning flight,
> And drowsy tinklings lull the distant folds:
>
> Save that from yonder ivy-mantled tower
> The moping owl does to the moon complain
> Of such as, wand'ring near her secret bow'r,
> Molest her ancient solitary reign.

William Wordsworth (1770-1850) is, of course, the poet most often associated with the Wye. His *Lines written a few miles above Tintern Abbey* (1798) had a great influence on later tourists. Much of it concerns his memories on returning to the Wye and his changing relationship with the natural world: indeed, he declared that he was a 'worshipper of nature', and his general aim was to show that 'the passions of man are incorporated with the beautiful and permanent forms of nature'. This poem marks the start of the romantic worship of nature, which rejects the Picturesque as a shallow and superficial pleasure in the appearance of nature. Part of the poem is quoted in chapter 4, but the following extract conveys the effects of landscapes on his feelings:

> ... And I have felt
> A presence that disturbs me with the joy
> Of elevated thoughts; a sense sublime
> Of something far more deeply interfused,
> Whose dwelling is the light of setting suns,
> And the round ocean, and the living air,
> And the blue sky, and in the mind of man,
> A motion and a spirit, that impels
> All thinking things, all objects of all thought,
> And rolls through all things. Therefore am I still
> A lover of the meadows and the woods,
> And mountains; and of all that we behold
> From this green earth; of all the mighty world
> Of eye and ear, both what they half-create,
> And what perceive; well pleased to recognize
> In nature and the language of the sense,

The anchor of my purest thoughts, the nurse,
The guide, the guardian of my heart, and soul
Of all my moral being.

Beauty and the Sublime

In the 1850s the growth of a new class of travellers created a demand for instruction in how to appreciate art and landscapes, which led to the publication of several aesthetic theories. In 1853 William Hogarth published *The Analysis of Beauty*, which was the first attempt in Europe to make formal values, such as fitness, variety, line, and proportion, the basis of a definition of beauty, though he mainly analysed the human form. Hogarth's 'line of beauty' underpinned Capability Brown's style of landscape gardening, and his belief that novelty and variety formed a foil or contrast to the Beautiful became the basis of the Picturesque when applied to landscape.

The *Analysis* was eclipsed three years later by Edmund Burke's essay *A Philosophical Enquiry into the Origin of our ideas of the Sublime and the Beautiful*. Sublime was defined as a special sort of beauty, both awe-inspiring and fearsome, eliciting emotion and passion and allowing the viewer to use his imagination. Beauty was equated with delicate qualities – smallness, smoothness and pale colours – whereas the sublime evoked pain, danger and terror. According to Charles Heath in his guidebook, there may be a direct connection between the Wye Valley and the development of Burke's ideas:

> The late Edmund Burke esq. resided for some time at Monmouth, before he entered on the Public Theatre of Life. It has been mentioned, that during his stay here, the fine scenes at New Wear, and other places in the neighbourhood, produced his Work on the "Sublime and Beautiful...

Picturesque theory in the 18th century

At the time it evolved, the Picturesque was regarded as a middle ground between the tyranny of Beauty, as Gilpin saw it, and the chaos of the Sublime, and was an objective aesthetic, allowing judgement to be made on the visual value of a landscape regardless of its content. In his book, *The Picturesque: Studies in a Point of View* (1927), Christopher Hussey considered the Picturesque to be a phase or movement which linked the neo-classical movement of 17th-century Italy to the Romantic period of the 19th century. He thought the Picturesque 'was necessary in order to enable the imagination to form the habit of feeling through the eyes ... It occurred at the point when art shifted its appeal from the reason to the imagination.' Malcolm Andrews, however, in *The search for the Picturesque* (1989), the most significant book on the subject in the later 20th century, argued that the Picturesque embodied elements of both neo-classical and romantic art, and thus that it was not a distinct phase between the two. Alternatively, it seems to me that the Picturesque was a blend of the Neo-classical and the Sublime, and that the Romantic Movement took elements from all three. The word 'picturesque' is derived from the French *pittoresque* and the Italian *pittoresco*, which came into use in the early 18th century. However their meanings were not the same as that of 'picturesque': *pittoresco* translates as 'in the manner of painters', implying a connection with painters' methods, whereas the English word means 'like a picture'.

The two main picturesque theorists of the late 18th century were William Gilpin and Uvedale Price. Their views differed considerably, however. Price was a landowner who applied picturesque ideas to designing his estate, whereas Gilpin was responding to wild landscapes and his books helped readers to see nature as an artist sees it and provided rules for judging the value of a view.

William Gilpin (1724-1804) was a pioneering educationalist and headmaster of Cheam School (1750-1777) before he became vicar at Boldre in the New Forest, where he set up a school for local children. An author of many religious and biographical books, and well known as an artist and critic, he started thinking about the Picturesque in the 1740s when he was a student at Oxford. His views developed around a neo-classical appreciation of Claude and Poussin and the manner in which they composed pictures, with a frame of trees, towers, hills, or an archway that concentrated attention on the view and accentuated the depth of field. In 1768, Gilpin published *An Essay upon Prints; containing some remarks upon Picturesque Beauty* and attempted to define the word, which was then in common use. From 1764, he visited various parts of Britain, and by 1770, when he visited the Wye Valley, he had much to say about what constitutes a picturesque view:

> ... Every view on a river, thus circumstanced, is composed of four grand parts; the area, which is the river itself; the two side screens, which are the opposite banks, and mark the perspective; and

Plate 4. After Edward Dayes View of the Doward rocks on the Wye *Engraved by F. Jukes 1790s*
This may be a rare depiction of the Seven Sisters rocks, though equally it could be upstream at New Weir.
It demonstrates picturesque elements of a low viewpoint, side screens, detailed foreground, variety and roughness. The
trow must be empty, for the bow hauliers do not seem to be exerting themselves
(Herefordshire Heritage Services, Herefordshire Council)

the front-screen, which points out the winding of the river ... But when we introduce a scene on canvas – when the eye it to be confined within the frame of a picture, and can no longer range among the varieties of nature; the aids of art become more necessary; and we want the castle, or the abbey, to give consequence to the scene. Indeed the landscape-painter seldom thinks his view perfect, without characterising it by some object of this kind.

The engraving after Edward Dayes (Plate 4) exemplifies a picturesque view, with the winding river and sidescreens, drawn from a low viewpoint.

In 1792 Gilpin published *Three Essays:- on Picturesque Beauty, on Picturesque Travel; and on sketching landscape*, in which he said that beauty in real objects comes from neatness and smoothness, which on their own can never please in representation. He thought that a rugged outline and a rough surface formed the essential difference between the Picturesque and the Beautiful. In considering Capability Brown's gardens he commented:

> Turn the lawn into a piece of broken ground; plant rugged oaks instead of flowering shrubs; break the edges of the walk; give it the rudeness of a road; mark it with wheel-tracks; and scatter a few stones, and brushwood; in a word, instead of making the whole *smooth*, make it rough; and you make it also *picturesque*.

Gilpin also praised the idea of variety, which had been championed by the poet Thomson: 'This country exceeds most countries in the variety of its picturesque beauties.' Despite his rules, Gilpin felt that the main pleasure in picturesque travel was not a careful analysis of a landscape but an aesthetic response: 'We rather feel than survey it.' This epitomised the general decline in rationalism, which was replaced during the 18th century by an increase in 'sensibility' and eventually led to 19th-century sentimentalism.

Picturesque painting differed from neo-classical styles by adopting a low viewpoint. This was also reflected in landscape design, for 17th-century prospects were replaced by gardens into which viewers were invited to walk and examine the detail. Looking at a view from the bottom of a valley rather than the top of a hill made foregrounds more important and lent more height and drama to a hilly landscape. Gilpin's opinion in his *Three Essays* was that 'the foreground is the basis, and foundation of the whole picture', and in his Wye book, he often dismissed views as not picturesque because the viewpoint was too high:

> Ross stands high, and commands many distant views; but that from the churchyard is the most admired, and is indeed very amusing. It consists of an early sweep of the Wye; and of an extensive country beyond it. But it is not picturesque. It is marked by no characteristic objects: it is broken into too many parts; and it is seen from too high a point.

The success of Gilpin's Wye book can be partly explained by the fact that he gave advice to amateur artists on how they could achieve picturesque compositions:

> Nature is always great in design. She is an admirable colourist also; and harmonizes tints with infinite variety and beauty. But she is seldom so correct in composition, as to produce an harmonious whole. Either the foreground, or the background, is disproportioned: or some

awkward line runs across the piece: or a tree is ill-placed: or a bank is formal: or something or other is not exactly what it should be. The case is, the immensity of nature is beyond human comprehension. She works on a vast scale; and no doubt, harmoniously, if her schemes could be comprehended. The artist in the mean time, is confined to a span; and lays down his little rules, which he calls the principles of picturesque beauty, merely to adapt such diminutive parts of nature's surfaces to his own eye, as come within it's scope. Hence therefore, the painter, who adheres strictly to the composition of nature, will rarely make a good picture. His picture must contain a whole; his archetype is but a part. In general however he may obtain views of such parts of nature, as with the addition of a few trees; or a little alteration in the foreground, (which is a liberty, that must always be allowed) may be adapted to his rules; though he is rarely so fortunate as to find a landscape completely satisfactory to him ... The complex scenes of nature are generally those which the artist finds most refractory to his rules of composition.

Uvedale Price (1747-1829) in his youth came under the influence of Gainsborough, who was a friend of his grandfather. His ideas were also moulded by his father Robert, who in 1741 was one of the first travellers to visit the glaciers near Mont Blanc, and to make a drawing on the spot. Robert bought topographical prints in Paris, collected Dutch landscapes and started the improvements to his estate (Foxley, close to the middle Wye in Herefordshire) that his son was to continue. Uvedale published his *Essays on the Picturesque* in 1794, around the time that he undertook the Wye Tour. He was not interested in composition, but in the details of picturesque landscapes. Beautiful and sublime landscapes could be immediately appreciated by anyone, but:

> A scene may, and often does exist, in which the qualities of the picturesque, almost exclusively of those of grandeur and beauty, prevail; and ... persons unacquainted with pictures, either take no interest in such scenes, or even think them ugly, while painters, and lovers of paintings, study and admire them ...

Price differed from Gilpin in his attitude to cottages and labourers. Gilpin liked to include castles and churches to give consequence to a picture, but shunned the inclusion of peasants because this raised uncomfortable moral questions. Price thought that 'the lover of painting considers dwellings, the inhabitants and the marks of their intercourse as ornaments to the landscape'. In his opinion hovels, cottages, dilapidated mills, interiors of old barns, disturbed surfaces of water, certain kinds of tree (oaks, elms, and especially storm-shattered trees), shaggy goats and sheep, gypsies and beggars were all suitable subjects. The landscape was merely a backdrop to the detail.

As a landowner, Price was more interested in agricultural landscapes than Gilpin:

> The usual features of a cultivated country are the accidental mixtures of meadows, woods, pastures, and cornfields, interspersed with farm houses, cottages, mills, &c. and I do not know in this country that better materials for middle grounds and distances can be obtained, or are to be wished for ...
>
> Pastures with cattle, horses or sheep grazing in them, and enriched with good trees, will always afford picturesque compositions; and enclosures of arable are never completely ugly, unless when lying in fallow.

Price also believed that some objects and scenes had innate picturesque qualities, but this was in direct opposition to the ideas of another Herefordshire landowner, Sir Richard Payne Knight (1750-1824). Knight published *The Landscape, a didactic poem* in the same year that Price published his essay, Knight arguing that objects were not intrinsically picturesque but that it was the manner of representation or the way of seeing that was picturesque. Eventually, after publishing their arguments over several years, the two friends fell out.

Mocking the Picturesque

It was very easy to mock the earnestness of those who followed the picturesque rules. Indeed, Gilpin was satirised by William Coombes in *The Tour of Dr Syntax in search of the Picturesque*, published in 1809 with wicked illustrations by Thomas Rowlandson:

> I'll make a TOUR – and then I'll WRITE IT,
> You well know what my pen can do, and I'll employ my pencil too:
> I'll ride and write and sketch and print, and thus create a real mint:
> I'll prose it here, I'll verse it there, and Picturesque it everywhere:
> I'll make this flat a shaggy ridge and o'er the water throw a bridge.
> I'll do as other sketchers do, put anything into the view.
> Thus I (which few, I think, can boast) have made a landscape of a post ...

During his tour Dr Syntax gets drunk and falls in the river, is tied to a tree by a highwayman and is charged by a bull.

Likewise, Edward Clarke in *A Tour through the South of England, Wales and parts of Ireland in 1791* was also obviously referring to Gilpin:

> It appears to me that the world is weary of that word picturesque, it is forced in upon every occasion; nay, one gentleman, the grand master of landscape, has contrived with the aid of a few muddy sketches, to swell that word to a volume.

Edward Dayes, who considered himself to be a picturesque painter, reacted against the more grotesque aspects of the later Picturesque. As quoted in Jane Munro's *British Landscape Watercolours*:

> We must give up our understanding [of the picturesque] if we call that landscape *fine* which represents dirty rugged grounds, scrubby bushes, poor scraggy and ill-formed trees, shapeless lumps of antiquity, and muddy pools; dirty beggars, clothed with rags, their heads decorated with filthy drapery, skins like tanned leather, and their employ disgusting; and these accompanied with poor and old cattle, or nasty swine on filthy dunghills.

Even Jane Austen was moved to write with tongue in cheek about picturesque rules in *Northanger Abbey* (1798):

> He [Henry Tilney] talked of fore-ground, distances and second distances – side screens and perspective – lights and shades; – and Catherine was so hopeful a scholar that when they reached the top of Beechen Cliff, she voluntarily rejected the whole city of Bath, as unworthy to make part of a landscape.

Picturesque gardens and landscape design

Picturesque ideas remained alive during the 20th century mainly in relation to the study and appreciation of garden and estate design, and today the word is associated with this rather than with pictures or wild landscapes. Garden design changed dramatically in the 18th century from the formal, symmetrical, stiff and unnatural forms of the previous century to more informal, apparently natural arrangements. The impetus came from the increasing enclosure of the countryside and the requirement that gardens and parks should contrast with their surroundings. Furthermore, park and countryside had to be viewed from the house, and the house had to be seen in a grand setting, so garden walls were replaced by ha-has, flowers and vegetables were moved to unobtrusive walled gardens, and avenues and canals were replaced by lawns, groves and parks embellished with sinuous lakes and clumps of trees. Such designs made Capability Brown famous in the 1750s to 1770s: his contrived naturalness was disconnected from the surrounding landscape and sought to show the wealth and power of the landowners.

Pre-picturesque gardens were seen from a single viewpoint, either the elevated prospect of the 17th century or the great house in the 18th century, but picturesque gardens were designed to be seen as visitors moved down and through the garden to witness close-up detail, shrubberies and artificial wildernesses. Moreover, long views may have been screened off so that visitors did not have to look too far ahead. Prospects implied considerable confidence in the future, but by the late 18th century, farmers and landowners feared that the French Revolution might spread to Britain. Pessimism was understandable, for Britain declared war on France in 1793. When in 1797 French soldiers landed in Pembrokeshire, the gentry panicked, fearing that their own labourers would attack them.

The reaction against Capability Brown's smooth bare landscapes led to increasingly intricate and picturesque designs for gardens and parks. Uvedale Price in his essay said: 'He therefore, in my mind, will shew most art in improving, who *leaves* (a very material point) or who creates the greatest variety of landscapes.' Humphrey Repton (1752-1818), who became the most influential landscaper after Brown, created landscapes that appeared more natural and diverse. In the 1790s he toured the lower Wye with Uvedale Price, and their joint experience evidently influenced their work. Richard Payne Knight criticised Brown's landscapes and argued in his poem *The Landscape* (1794) for local distinctiveness and a more sensitive management of the land. Picturesque landscapes were judged to be successful if they showed no obvious signs of management, though usually the impression of neglect was carefully contrived:

> How best to bid the verdant Landscape rise,
> To please the fancy, and delight the eyes;
> Its various parts in harmony to join
> With art clandestine, and conceal'd design;
> T'adorn, arrange; - to sep'rate, and select
> With secret skill, and counterfeit neglect;
> I sing.

Landscape designers needed to know both landscape paintings and descriptions of landscape in poetry. In fact, gardens were seen as a series of landscape paintings: Horace Walpole said that 'every journey is made through a succession of pictures'. Even colours and tones in the gardens were influenced by paintings. Andrews quotes Henry Hoare (1739):

The greens should be ranged together in large masses as the shades are in painting ... The lights and shades in gardening are managed by disposing the thick grove work, the thin, and the openings in a proper manner; of which the eye generally is the properest judge.

The Piercefield Walks, described more fully in Chapter 6, are an important example of an early picturesque designed landscape. They were constructed in the 1750s, with every viewpoint planned as a Claudian painting. Turner's mezzotint, *Junction of the Severn and Wye,* shows one of these views (Plate 48). The park at Piercefield, on the other hand was laid out in the style of Capability Brown and can be seen in **Plate 54**.

Attitudes to ruins

The increasing complexity of ideas in the Picturesque can be traced through the changing attitude to ruins and particularly the use of them in gardens. In the early 18th century only antiquarians had been interested in ruins, but as Arcadian ideals were rejected, the prevailing religious awe of ruins was replaced by a feeling of pleasing melancholy or agreeable horror. Indeed, the desire to experience this melancholy was the main reason for the popularity of visits to ruined abbeys, which symbolized the end of Popery, and ruined castles, which symbolized the end of Gothic feudalism. This mood fitted the times: more people had sedentary jobs, the diet was very rich and the suicide rate was rising fast. Moreover, according to Andrews, a yearning for melancholy was reinforced by a damp climate, and the Wye Valley is particularly damp! Gilpin referred to Cromwell as 'that picturesque genius who omitted no opportunity of adorning the countries ... with noble ruins', and Uvedale Price thought:

The ruins of these once magnificent edifices are the pride and boast of this island; we may well be proud of them; not merely in a picturesque point of view; we may glory that the abodes of tyranny and superstition are in ruins.

Later enthusiasts appreciated the mood, colour and composition of ruins, whereas visitors before 1760 were more interested in their political and moral aspects. Plate 5 demonstrates how the growth of vegetation on a ruin can enhance its mood. Agreeable melancholy was evoked not just by ruins, but also by buildings in use. For example, in Jane Austen's *Mansfield Park* (1814), Fanny, when shown the

Plate 5. Joshua Cristall Goodrich Castle *Pencil sketch with wash
The date of this sketch is uncertain. Joshua Cristall took the Wye Tour
with his friend Cornelius Varley in 1803, so it could be contemporary
with Plate 17. Alternatively, it could have been executed after
Cristall came to live at Goodrich in 1823
(Herefordshire Heritage Services, Herefordshire Council)*

chapel at Sotherton, exclaimed 'I am disappointed ... This is not my idea of a chapel. There is nothing awful here, nothing melancholy, nothing grand. Here are no aisles, no arches, no inscriptions, no banners.'

When classical and gothic buildings were built in country parks and gardens to lend a picturesque focus, some were built as perfect structures, but increasingly the fashion was for contrived ruins, with Tintern Abbey held up as a model. Real ruins, in contrast, could be groomed too much – Francis Grose commented on Tintern Abbey: '... the ground is covered over with a turf as even and trim as that of a Bowling-green, which gives the building more the air of an artificial Ruin in a Garden, than that of an ancient decayed Abbey.'

Eventually, many people had wearied of ruins, as this extract from the Somerset House Gazette of 1824, quoted by Munro, shows:

> We had begun to tire of the endless repetitions of Tintern Abbey from within, and Tintern Abbey from without, and the same by moonlight, and twilight, and every other light in which taste and talent could compose variations to the worn-out theme.

The growth of picturesque tourism

The home life of the middle classes had become increasingly comfortable by the mid 18th century. Time and money for travel were available and an element of danger could be enjoyed on holiday as a contrast to home life. Snowdonia became a paradise in their minds, and by 1744 Cader Idris was being regularly climbed, albeit with a guide. By the 1760s, the first visitors were also reaching the Lake District, the Wye Valley, and the Scottish Highlands, and these areas began to be considered as common property, existing to supply picturesque or sublime landscapes. Travel by road improved with the development of turnpikes, comfortable new designs of carriage, better maps and increasing numbers of sign posts. The early tourists were more interested in wild picturesque landscapes than the land-owning gentry, but also relished the contrast between wild scenery and the smoke and noise of industry, where many of them were employed.

As tourism expanded, the number of areas which were regarded as picturesque increased. Thus, the Yorkshire Dales, the Peak District (especially around Matlock), the Northumbrian coast, the Isle of Wight, the Devon coasts, Bristol Gorge, Norwich and the middle reaches of the Thames all became popular and by 1798, according to Andrews, picturesque travel had reached its heyday. Robert Southey, the poet, exclaimed in 1807:

> Within the last thirty years a taste for the picturesque has sprung up; and a course of summer travelling is now looked upon to be ... essential ... they study the picturesque, a new science for which a new language has been formed, and for which the English have discovered a new sense in themselves.

The moderate scale and relative accessibility of the Lower Wye landscape provided a particularly suitable introduction to sublime scenery for middle-class visitors, most of whom had been brought up with the idea of pastoral landscapes as the height of rural beauty, and few of whom had ever seen a mountain. The view from Symonds Yat Rock was one of many on the Wye Tour combining the pastoral with the sublime – meadows contrasted with relatively small rocky cliffs as seen in Plate 26

– which would have been far less of a culture shock than a trip to North Wales or the Lakes. The tour allowed the passengers to see the landscape in terms of gradually changing compositions. Travelling southwards, they generally faced into the sun and experienced the scenery as a Claude painting, with dark foregrounds and lighter, sunlit middlegrounds.

Picturesque rules and the Wye Tour

The steep-sided Wye Valley was particularly suited to Gilpin's rules of the Picturesque, for it restricted the view and presented scenes that conformed in all respects, with sidescreens, detailed foregrounds, and only limited distant views. Moreover, travel by boat achieved the low viewpoints and upward-looking perspectives which picturesque rules required. In his book, Gilpin was careful to explain at the outset why he considered the scenes on the river to be picturesque:

> It flows in a gentle, uninterrupted stream; and adorns, through it's various reaches, a succession of the most picturesque scenes. The beauty of these scenes arises chiefly from two circum-stances – the lofty banks of the river, and it's mazy course ... the views it exhibits are of the most beautiful kind of perspective; free from the formality of lines.

These views were varied by the 'contrast of the screens' and by the 'folding of the side-screens over each other ... Plain banks will admit of all the variations ... but when this plainness is adorned, a thousand other varieties arise'.

Gilpin considered that there were four different kinds of 'ornaments' of the Wye – ground (i.e. land forms), woods, rocks and buildings – each of which made its particular contribution and suffered from certain limitations. The ground varied from the 'steepest precipice to the flattest meadow' and could be broken by losing its turf and showing the naked soil of various colours. Gilpin became a little defensive at this point:

> Nor let the fastidious reader think, these remarks descend too much into detail. Where an exten-sive distance is described ... it would be trifling to mark these minute circumstances. But here the hills around exhibit little, except foregrounds; and it is necessary, where we have no distance, to be more exact in finishing objects at hand.

He continued more positively by describing the other 'ornaments' which create the great variety of Wye landscapes:

> The woods themselves possess little beauty, and less grandeur; yet, when we consider them as the ornamental, not as the essential parts, of a scene; the eye must not examine them with exactness; but compound them for a general effect.
>
> Some objects, are beautiful in themselves ... But the rock, bleak, naked and unadorned, seems scarcely to deserve a place among them, tint it with mosses, and lichens of various hues, and you give it a degree of beauty. Adorn it with shrubs and hanging herbage, and you still make it more picturesque. Connect it with wood, and water, and broken ground; and you make it in the highest degree interesting ...
>
> Abbeys, castles, villages, spires, forges, mills and bridges ... characterise almost every scene. These works of art are however of much greater use in artificial, than in natural landscape. In

pursuing the beauties of nature, we range at large among forests, lakes, rocks, and mountains. ... And tho the works of art may often give animation and contrast to these scenes, yet still they are not necessary.

Chapter 3
The Lower Wye Landscape

The Wye Tour prospered not only because William Gilpin, Thomas Gray and other well-known visitors promoted it, but also because the valley was easy to reach from centres of population and distinctive in character. Juxtaposing the deep, twisting, wooded gorge and precipitous rocky cliffs with peaceful agricultural views and small pockets of industry, it is outstanding in lowland Britain in combining pastoral and sublime scenery, both of which were elements in the Picturesque. The only comparable districts are the Severn Gorge at Coalbrookdale, the Derbyshire Peak and the Middle Clyde valley, and these, too, became popular destinations.

The river and its landforms
The Wye rises very close to the source of the Severn on Plynlimon, 24km east of Aberystwyth, and flows 248km to the Severn estuary. Unusually for a British river, it does not flow through a major industrial area, so it has remained relatively unpolluted. The river runs conventionally in an ever-broadening valley through the old counties of Montgomeryshire, Radnorshire and Breconshire, then sweeps in great meanders across the Herefordshire Plain as far as Ross. Below Ross it changes entirely. At Goodrich it plunges into high ground through a deeply incised valley, loops back out onto the plain below Symonds Yat Rock, then returns to the high ground at New Weir, and continues through a gorge until it reaches the Severn just below Chepstow. This strange behaviour is mapped in Plate 1. Below New Weir Herefordshire lies to the right, and below Redbrook Gloucestershire lies to the left, with Monmouthshire on the right, but between the Biblins Bridge and Redbrook Monmouthshire extends to the left bank.

The Wye has clearly carved its way down through 180m of limestone and Sandstone, but at least two hypotheses have been advanced to explain its present form. At its simplest, the Wye is regarded as an example of superimposed drainage. The course established in the early Pleistocene (1.6 million years ago), when the river supposedly meandered over a wide plain 180m above its present level, has been retained whilst the river, rejuvenated by a fall in the sea level relative to the land, eroded the various rock types at different rates. The Old Red Sandstone under the Plain of Hereford is relatively soft, so eroded more rapidly than the harder rocks of the Dean and Trellech plateaux. The Dean Plateau is a downfold of rocks with an upper layer of Coal Measures, around which layers of Carboniferous Limestone, Tintern Sandstone and Quartz Conglomerate, formed 250 to 300 million years ago, outcrop like a stack of bowls inside a bowl of older Lower Devonian Sandstone laid down 350 million years ago. Alternatively, a more complex evolution has recently been suggested, which has the original Wye flowing east from Hereford to join the Severn, leaving the Monnow as the original river that formed much of the lower gorge. This drainage pattern was supposedly altered during successive ice ages when meltwater lakes were forced over a col on the edge of the Dean into the Monnow and carved out the upper gorge in a gigantic rush of ice and water.

However it was formed, the convoluted course of the Wye always impressed visitors. Louisa Ann Twamley, in her 1839 *Ramble on the Wye*, described the river as tortuous:

> It is worthy of remark, how suddenly the banks of the WYE acquire their fine picturesque outline, when the river enters the *Mountain Lime*. The abrupt eminences which are the constant features of that formation, here twist and drive the bed of the river into the most tortuous windings, and coop it up like a prisoner between their craggy walls; but it no sooner turns into the adjacent *Red sand-stone*, than it goes on its way more evenly, and spreads out within its gently-sloping boundaries, apparently glad of more room and sunshine.

In their guidebook of 1861, Mr and Mrs Hall described the course of the river in similar terms:

> We make acquaintance with the peculiarities of the Wye. Its 'winding bounds' are so remarkable that frequently after the boat has floated four or five miles, we find ourselves within gun-shot of the place from which we started. ... On quitting the level ground, the varied and broken scenery on either side suggests a vague, though irresistible impression, that the craggy precipices, rocky ascents, and isolated plateaux, between which the stream takes its tortuous way ... were the boundaries of a river always, in a word, that the Wye is a river designed by Nature itself.

The geography of Wye Tour locations

The places the Wye tourists found so exciting were formed by the interaction between the river and the geology over millions of years. After meandering within a wide flood plain, the Wye passes Ross, which is built on a Brownstone bluff (part of the Old Red Sandstone) created by erosion (and accentuated by road-building) on the outside of an ancient meander. The river once flowed round Chase Wood and Penyard Park, 30m above its present level, from a point north of Ross, and returned just to the south of the town, a giant meander that was breached relatively recently in geological terms. A few miles south, Goodrich Castle, the first site of interest to the tourists, also stands on a Brownstone bluff: the castle was built partly from the local stone hacked out to form the moat, so the ramparts and walls appear to grow out of the rock, as seen in Plate 16.

Near Bishopswood, the surrounding land rises up to 200m above the river. Here the Wye has incised deeply through a hard band of Quartz Conglomerate and Lower Carboniferous Limestone, yet still bends smoothly round Courtfield and Coppet Hill, passing Rosemary Topping and the limestone crags of Coldwell Rocks on its left. The long reach below the scrubby slopes and miniature Quartz Conglomerate cliffs of Coppet Hill takes the river out on a 6.5km loop into the lowlands close to Goodrich, before it curves right round and returns to the high ground at Symonds Yat. At this point the Wye is just 400m away from where it was 6.5km earlier, the neck in between being the famous and enduringly popular Yat Rock. This is a promontory of Carboniferous Limestone, laid down 350 million years ago, with cliffs and rock towers on each side at Coldwell Rocks and around the Longstone above New Weir. Rocks that fell from the cliffs litter the slopes and river bed below and force the Wye into rapids, but have also helped silt to accumulate behind an island of quarrying spoil. Looking north from the top of Yat Rock, visitors can see both the outcrops of Quartz Conglomerate on Huntsham Hill and Coppet Hill and the fallen blocks in the fields and river below. Plates 4, 9, 26 and 29 give a good idea of the landforms in this area.

Below Symonds Yat the river winds gently below the steep limestone cliffs of the Great Doward, which include the magnificent sequence of bluffs known as the Seven Sisters (Plate 4). Above these cliffs is the famous King Arthur's Cave, where important remains of Ice Age mammals and early man were excavated in the 1870s. Further on, below Little Doward, another small island was formed from collapsed pillars of limestone. The Wye then passes into gentler country at Hadnock on the margins of the Dean Plateau until Monmouth, where it is joined by the Monnow and Trothy. At this point the Brownstone scarp and the Quartz Conglomerate outcrop lie just to the east, rising nearly 250m to the Kymin, topped by the Round House, a famous viewpoint 200 years ago, and a conspicuous modern landmark. Plate 38 shows the westward view from the tower.

Beyond Monmouth, the river breaks through the Brownstone scarp, which stretches away past Mitchel Troy to the west, and continues in a deep, sinuous valley between the Dean and Trellech plateaux. From here to Tintern the Wye has cut down to the relatively soft Lower Devonian Sandstone, so the valley sides are merely steep, not precipitous. Quartz Conglomerate or pudding stone outcrops high on the valley sides, but its cliffs are now hidden in the trees. Along this reach, the valley sides rise 150m above the Wye, and the river has descended almost to sea level. At Redbrook the Wye once flowed 115m above its present level out to Newland – the largest abandoned meander on the Wye – but its passage is now marked by two small streams running in disproportionately large valleys. The other abandoned meander is the great amphitheatre below St Briavels. Here the Wye was a mere 30m above the present river, showing that it was cut off much later than the meander at Redbrook.

Bigsweir Bridge marks the high point of the tides. Immediately below it, as the river leaves the ancient St Briavels meander, the valley narrows and the sides become steeper. Above Llandogo a small stream descends over Conglomerate outcrops as Cleddon Shoots, a series of waterfalls that become very impressive after long periods of rain. Folds and faults in the Upper Devonian rock around Brockweir, here known as Tintern Sandstone, have formed somewhat gentler slopes, and these lead down to Tintern Abbey. South from Brockweir the Wye again enters the Carboniferous Limestone: this has been hard enough to resist any breaching of meander necks, so the Wye forms grand, sweeping curves below ever steeper slopes as it passes below the great limestone exposures of Shorn Cliff and Banygor Rocks. Opposite Tintern, an eminence known as the Devil's Pulpit forms another of the famous viewpoints affording panoramas over the whole 'Vale of Tintern', as seen in the engraving after William Bartlett (Plate 6). On the right bank, the Black Cliff rises 210m above the ancient rubble of the largest landslide in the valley. Beyond is the Wyndcliff, 230m high, from the top of which is an extensive view, lyrically described by the Wye tourists, over the fields of the Lancaut peninsula, the great horseshoe meander where the Wye flows between tidal mud flats below precipitous woods, and the passage past Chepstow to join the Severn. Plate 2 gives some idea of this view. The Piercefield Cliffs, of limestone capped with Sandstone, stand 70m above the river: from their base a stream flows from a remarkable series of caves beneath the Chepstow racecourse. At the far end, on the inside of the bend, is a strange curved spit of low land, best seen from the higher cliffs on the left bank. The Wye finally passes Chepstow Castle, which rises directly from riverside limestone cliffs, and passes under three generations of Chepstow bridges before flowing past salt marsh and into the Severn.

Weather

The Wye Gorge and the high ground to east and west enjoy an oceanic climate. The average annual rainfall of 1020mm falling on about 200 rain days is typical of most of upland Britain outside the

Plate 6. W.H. Bartlett The Vale of Tintern from the Devils Pulpit *Engraved on steel 1845*
One of the most prolific of the later topographical painters, W.H. Bartlett had many of his watercolours engraved.
This view of Tintern Abbey was included in The Castles and Abbeys of England *by W Beattie and clearly*
shows the pulpit from which the devil is said to have taunted the monks
(Llyfrgell Genedlaethol Cymru/National Library of Wales)

more mountainous districts. As several tourists discovered, south and south-west winds frequently generate low cloud, drizzle and veils of mist that can hide one side of the valley from the other. By contrast, Ross on the Hereford plain is on the edge of the relatively continental climate of central England, where the annual rainfall is less than 760mm, and around Chepstow the proximity to the coast brings more sun and less rain. The start and finish of a Wye Tour was thus always likely to be drier and sunnier than the passage through the gorge.

Several Wye tourists got soaked, though most carried on regardless. 1770 was a particularly wet year, with damaged harvests and floods, but Gilpin tried to make the best of it, though he used rain as his excuse for not climbing up to Goodrich Castle or to Symonds Yat:

> Having seen [the bank] under the circumstances of a continued rain; which began early in the day, before one third of our voyage was performed ... Even the rain gave a gloomy grandeur to many of the scenes; and by throwing a veil of obscurity over the removed banks of the river, introduced, now and then, something like a pleasing distance. Yet still it hid great beauties; and we could not help regretting the loss of those broad lights, and deep shadows, which would have given so much lustre to the whole.

On the following day he was lucky: 'The weather was now serene: the sun shone; and we saw enough of the effect of light, in the exhibitions of this day, to regret the want of it the day before.' For some, it was just cold and windy. Henry Skrine in 1798 recorded:

> The water at times so rough from strong gusts of wind, that we found it difficult to proceed ... our boatmen were fatigued with their exertion against the wind – Unfurling our canvass awning, we enclosed ourselves in the boat, and excluded all objects during the time of dinner, to protect ourselves from the cold.

Fortunately, many tourists enjoyed warmth and sunshine. William Coxe noted at Coldwell Rocks that:

> The weather was peculiarly favourable, the sky clear and serene, the sun shone in full splendour, illumined the projecting faces of the rock, and deepened the shade of the impervious woods, which mantle the opposite bank.

Louisa Twamley, describing the view from Symonds Yat Rock, was clearly influenced by the weather: '... and all this lit up gloriously by real sunshine, not the counterfeit usually seen in our cloudy land, but clear, laughing cheerful sunshine!' L. Valentine in *Picturesque England* was equally enthusiastic:

> It was one of those brilliant days that sometimes close September, when the air has a clearness we never see in summer, without much warmth, but is fresh and exhilarating, and the tints around us, though beautiful and rich, are very different from the colours of July. The sky was far off, of a most celestial blue. A few tiny white clouds floated gently over it, even as we floated on the clear blue-tinted, or here and there, brown-hued water of the stream.

Woodland and agriculture

After the dramatic landforms, the second feature which strikes a visitor to the Lower Wye is the great abundance of mainly native, deciduous ('natural') woodland on the steep slopes – Wordsworth's 'sylvan Wye' (Plates 19 and 29). Although they have been exploited for millennia, many of the gorge woodlands are ancient, and have survived in various forms continuously since the Mesolithic. Now the lower Wye is recognised as one of the most important areas for native woodland in Britain, dominated by beech, oak, ash, wych elm, field maple, wild cherry, alder, hazel, holly, yew, whitebeam and, notably, a large concentration of small-leaved and large-leaved limes, the forest dominants of the late Mesolithic. Interestingly, the valleys of the Middle Clyde, Severn Gorge and the Matlock area of the Peak District, which all have an early industrial history, also support high densities of similar woodland.

When the Wye Tour was at its height the woods were intensively managed as coppices, cut down every 12-30 years and made into charcoal for the local metal industries. Gilpin records the smoke from the charcoal hearths as he passed through the upper gorge:

> The smoke, which is frequently seen issuing from the sides of the hills; and spreading its thin veil over a part of them, beautifully breaks their lines, and unites them with the sky.

Charles Heath, in a footnote in his guidebook, described the impact of coppicing on the scenery:

> This is the general complexion of the adjacent country: – for every ten or twelve years, the woods, are cropped quite close to the ground, principally to supply the forges and furnaces with charcoal, &c and as they sprout again, this delightful verdure appears scarce distinguishable at some distance, from the most luxuriant crops. As in other spots their vigour is increased, or come to full growth, different tints and shades are seen, which constitute the wonderful variety so peculiar to these scenes.

The Wye industries declined during the 19th century and ceased altogether in the mid 20th century, and by this time most coppicing had also ceased. In the absence of cutting, the woods have grown tall, so the patchwork of freshly felled coppices that confronted the Wye tourists has now been replaced by unbroken, apparently natural woods. Since many of the small fields have also reverted to woodland in the last 200 years, it is no surprise that both prints and paintings from the Wye Tour period and early picture postcards frequently show bare hillsides and prominent rock outcrops where today we see mostly trees. Indeed, many of the viewpoints enjoyed by the Wye tourists, particularly those at Piercefield, are now so overgrown that the view is blocked. Conifers were planted in the 19th and 20th centuries, and although they add some variety to the landscape, they are now gradually being felled and replaced by native trees. Reverend Fosbroke would have approved: in his guidebook of 1818 he asked: 'Will it never be known that firs in a group are like plumes on the graves of the Picturesque?'

Although woodland is prominent, much of the land is and was used for agriculture. The Dean Plateau was intensively cultivated; the steep upper slopes had a small-scale mosaic of pasture, woodland and orchards; the lower slopes had larger fields, except the steepest, which remained wooded; and the narrow flood plain was used as meadow and pasture. Ancient wooded commons on the Doward, Hudnalls and elsewhere were being settled by squatters in the 18th and early 19th centuries, leaving a scatter of stone cottages amongst very small fields and remnant woodland. West of the

Wye, the Trellech Plateau had extensive heaths, but these were enclosed in 1810 to become a mixture of farmland, smallholdings, pasture, rough grassland and plantation. Today some bilberry heath is recovering where the plantation trees have been removed. To the north, the Herefordshire Plain of Old Red Sandstone enriched with alluvium, is intensive arable farmland, at one time covered with extensive orchards and rich pasture for Hereford cattle.

In the 18th century, William Gilpin appreciated the large amount of pasture in the area:

> During the whole course of our voyage from Ross, we had scarce seen one corn-field. The banks of the Wye consist, almost entirely either of wood, or of pasturage; which I mention as a circumstance of peculiar value in landscape. Furrowed-lands, and waving-corn, however charming in pastoral poetry, are ill-accommodated to painting ... Pasturage not only presents an agreeable surface: but the cattle, which graze it, add great variety, and animation to the scene. The meadows, below Monmouth, which ran shelving from the hills to the water-side, were particularly beautiful, and well-inhabited. Flocks of sheep were every where hanging on their green steeps; and herds of cattle occupying the lower grounds. We often sailed past groups of them laving their sides in the water: or retiring from the heat under sheltered banks.

Charles Heath also commented on the cattle and on the orchards at Llandogo:

> These dwellings are surrounded by abundance of the choicest of fruit trees, which produce a great quantity of cider in a favourable season, while valuable herds of fine cattle are seen grazing in the vale below. In short, the dairies of these and the adjoining farms on the banks of the river, are not surpassed in any part of the country.

For William Coxe, it was the natural aspects that stood out:

> The general character of the scenery, however is wildness and solitude; and if we except the populous district of Monmouth, no river perhaps flows for so long a course through a well cultivated country, the banks of which exhibit so few habitations.

Industries on the river

The Lower Wye was an industrial centre from at least the 16th century. The river provided transport; the steep side-streams supplied water power; woods provided charcoal and timber; and enough coal and iron ore was available locally to initiate the industries. Many Wye tourists relished the contrast between the busy, noisy forges and the quiet calm of the river, fields and woodland. At Redbrook, Mr and Mrs Hall noted:

> There are quays here: we note the bustle of commerce, – other life than that of the stream and the forests. The masts of many barges rise from the river: they are loading or unloading. It is the manufactory of tin – or, rather, of tin in combination with iron – that gathers a population here, and breaks, pleasantly or unpleasantly, according to the mood of the wanderer, the sameness and solitude of the banks of the Wye.

At Ross two foundries made agricultural tools and machinery, using coal imported from Lydbrook, itself an important industrial village, with furnaces, forges, chemical works, tinplate works, cable works and rolling mills, and the first commercially successful blast furnace in the Forest of Dean, built in 1608. Just upriver at Bishopswood, an iron works was started in the 17th century, with quarrying and lime-burning nearby.

One of the earliest iron mills on the river was at New Weir. In 1770, Thomas Whateley described the effect of the industry in the dark tree-covered chasm:

> In the midst of all this gloom is an iron forge, covered with a black cloud of smoak, and surrounded with half burned ore, with coal, and with cinders; the fuel for it is brought down a path, worn into steps narrow and steep, and winding among precipices; and near it is an open space of barren moor, about which are scattered the huts of the workmen. It stands close to the cascade of the Weir, where the agitation of the current is encreased by large fragments of rocks which have been swept down by the floods from the banks, or shivered by tempests from the brow; and this sullen sound, at stated intervals from the strokes of the great hammers in the forge, deadens the roar of the water-fall.

Above the forge, the Great Doward was covered in quarries and lime kilns, fed by the coal brought by mules over Symonds Yat Rock. Limestone towers were quarried, leaving only the Longstone. As Fosbroke recorded with regret, they:

> ... were standing sixty years ago, insulated from the main wall of rock but now either fallen or gormandized by the ravenous lime-kiln, that regardless of the beauty of the Wye, 'in grim repose expects its evening prey'.

Charles Heath described another local industry just south of Monmouth, at Penallt: 'Very excellent mill-stones are cut in dove-tailed burrs, which millers pronounce equal to the valuable French stones, and the surrounding counties are also supplied with cider-mills.' The millstones were shaped high up on the hillside where the Quartz Conglomerate outcrops, and slid down the hill in channels to the river for export.

At Redbrook two copper works operated from 1692 to 1730, with 26 and 16 furnaces respectively, the first commercial copper smelting in Britain. Ore was imported up the Wye from Cornwall and the works were said to be 'managed by Swedes and other foreigners'. Copper smelting later moved to Swansea when coal became the preferred fuel. In the 17th century iron forges were established, initially using local iron, with two charcoal-powered blast furnaces. Two tinplate works were built in 1790, of which the lower one (Plate 7) continued in production until 1961. In 1799, Coxe thought that the iron and tin works here 'gave animation to the romantic scenery'.

Downriver, Whitebrook supported a branch of the Tintern wireworks from 1606 to 1720, but from 1760 the mills were converted to paper making, which continued into the 19th century. High quality paper, including bank notes, was exported by barge to Bristol, using rags as the raw material initially, but later esparto grass was imported up the Wye.

The wireworks industry at Tintern started in the 16th century, and was soon taken over by the Company of the Mineral and Battery Works, which was set up by the Government to license manufacturing. It imposed a monopoly on wiremaking in Britain for over 60 years, allowing the branch wireworks to be built at Whitebrook. Most wire was made into carders for combing wool before spinning, but some became fish hooks and pins. At least eight separate wire factories were spread

Plate 7. Artist unknown Industry at Redbrook *Engraved on wood* c. *1860*
One of the very few depictions of industry on the Wye, this engraving shows the lower tin plate works in full production and belching out smoke. Several boats at the quay include a trow with its mast folded down to allow it to pass under a bridge. In the foreground is a Wye Tour boat with canopy and two pairs of oars (Nelson Museum Monmouth)

up the steep-sided Angiddy valley, including one next to the abbey, as well as several water-powered corn mills. By 1820 twenty waterwheels were operating, including a tide-powered wheel at the mouth of the Angiddy. In 1781 John Byng was told by the agent that 1500 workmen were paid from 18s to 20s a week.

According to H.G. Nicholls' *Forest of Dean*, David Mushet recorded in the 1720s that:

> When in full work, Tintern Abbey charcoal furnace made weekly from twenty-eight to thirty tons of charcoal forge pig iron, and consumed forty dozen sacks of charcoal; so that sixteen sacks of charcoal were consumed in making one ton of pigs.

Mushet also claimed this was: 'the first charcoal furnace which in this country was blown with air compressed in iron cylinders'. Francis Grose in 1775 looked out of the window of The Beaufort Arms and saw:

A kind of Fireworks occasion'd by the Sparks which ascended from the Forges, which having a high dark mountain for a Back Ground and the Night being rather cloudy exhibited a pleasing Appearance.

Boats and trade

After improvements for navigation in 1696, the Wye became a very important trading route. The peak period for carrying cargo was the 18th century and the first half of the 19th, when there were 26 wharves between Hereford and Chepstow. Hereford was a centre for the distribution of agricultural produce — wool, corn and cider — and from Ross downwards there was much traffic of raw materials and finished products from the various industries. Some 16,000 tons of goods were brought up the Wye in 1790.

The Wye is tidal up to Bigsweir, so even the larger sea-going trows of 50 tons could get to Llandogo on a spring tide. Trows were sailing ships with flat bottoms, designed for working the Severn and Lower Wye, one of which is shown in Samuel Ireland's picture of Llandogo (Plate 8). Boats were built in several places along the river, and many under 100 tons were built at Brockweir, a

Plate 8. After Samuel Ireland Llandogo *Sepia aquatint by C Apostool 1797*
A Wye Tour boat with curved canopy, a limp sail and apparently only one oar lies in front of a much larger trow with furled sail at Llandogo. The extremely large trees partly hide the steep hills behind. Ireland wrote 'Here the river forms a smooth and glassy bay, through which the white sailed vessel is seen constantly gliding, or lying moored on the shore to take in her freight.' (Chepstow Museum)

practice that continued right up to 1925. In 1824, thirteen boats were launched here, and in the same year a much larger ship was launched at Monmouth, followed by several barques and brigantines of over 500 tons.

At Brockweir goods were transferred to smaller barges – upriver trows – which were then hauled up the river by teams of men. At one haulier for each ton of cargo, a heavy coal barge needed 20 bow-hauliers, and up to 30 were needed to drag the boats over the shallows, a task which Heath thought 'none but British hearts would have the courage to call forth and persevere in'. In the 1860s the Rev Keene Mottram Pitt, quoted in Colin Green's *Severn Traders*, recorded:

> Hauling a loaded barge upstream was no light task and at a rapid it was desperate work, the advance being made only foot by foot. The men bent forward and sometimes, if the barge happened to give a sheer in a stream, they almost lay on the ground and waited until she could recover herself.

Teams of bow hauliers are depicted in Michael 'Angelo' Rooker's painting of New Weir, and the print after Edward Dayes of the Doward Rocks, though these ones appear to be taking the strain with ease (Plates 4 and 33). Conditions started to improve in 1808 however, when a tow path was built between Lydbrook and Hereford, so that two horses could pull each coal barge.

Gilpin recorded some of the river traffic he passed:

> In this part of the river also, which now begins to widen, we were often entertained with light vessels gliding past us. Their white sails passing along the sides of woodland hills were very picturesque ... In many places the views are varied by the prospect of bays, and harbours in miniature; where little barks lie moored, taking in wood and other commodities, from the mountains. These vessels, designed plainly for rougher water, than they at present incountered, shewed us, without any geographical knowledge, that we approached the sea.

Leith Ritchie, in *The Wye and its Associations: a Picturesque Ramble*, approved of the trows:

> But even the coasting barge, with her blackened sails, and sixty tons of cargo, is not here 'a jarring and a dissonant thing'. Creeping with the tide along these solemn banks, she acquires a portion of their solemnity, floating silently through those pastoral veils, she is invested, for the time being, with their simplicity.

Coracles were common on the Lower Wye, where they were used for salmon fishing. Mr and Mrs Hall left a fine description:

> The coracle, which boatmen and fishermen use today on the Wye, differs little from that in which their forefathers floated when the Romans were rulers on its banks. In shape it resembles the half of a walnut-shell; some laths, or rude sticks, laid cross-wise form the skeleton; that is covered with canvas – zinc, however, has been lately adopted for the purpose ... A plank across the middle makes the seat; a small paddle is used for directing its movements; it is so light, and draws so little water, as to be very easily upset ... they are so light that the boatmen carry them on their backs.

Great quantities of bark – another product of the coppice woods – were exported for tanning from Monmouth, Llandogo and Brockweir. In the late 18th century Chepstow handled up to 5,000 tons of bark each year, mainly exporting it to Ireland. On their return trip the ships brought iron ore from Cumberland and Lancashire for the iron works at Tintern. The trees were stripped of their bark while still standing – 'flayed alive' – then left to die during the summer. Timber was required for pit props in the Forest of Dean coal mines, but most of the timber exported from Chepstow between 1750 and 1850 was sent to the naval dockyards for ship building, the peak coming during the Napoleonic Wars.

Chepstow, the largest port on the Lower Wye, was well known for importing fine wines. William Coxe listed the goods handled here in 1801, as told him by the Customs Officer. Timber, grain, pig, wrought, and bar iron, wire, tin plates, coal, tar, grind and mill stones, paper, cider and oak bark were exported, while shop goods, furniture, iron ore from Lancashire, linen from Ireland, cloth, wine, beer and a 'few commodities for interior consumption' and Baltic deals, hemp, iron, pitch, tar and tallow were all imported. Tar seems to have been imported and exported.

Transportation of goods changed considerably in the mid 19th century. A canal was built between Gloucester and Hereford in 1845, which rendered the Lydbrook to Hereford tow path obsolete. The canal itself was superseded ten years later, when the railway from Gloucester to Hereford was opened and, with the opening of the Ross to Monmouth and Monmouth to Chepstow lines in 1874 and 1876, river traffic declined. Some trows lingered on into the 20th century and were fitted with engines after the First World War, finally dying out in the 1960s.

Chapter 4
Wye tourists and the Wye Tour industry

After a slow start in the mid 18th century the Wye Tour increased in popularity until, at its peak in the 1860s, thousands of visitors took part each year. Initially, artists, aristocrats and men of letters favoured the Tour, but as the number of visitors grew, so their class – as the British would put it – declined: tourists were replaced by trippers. While it prospered, the Tour provided work for boat proprietors and their boatmen, innkeepers and other providers of lodgings, guides and those who maintained the castles and abbey, coachmen and train drivers, not to mention publishers and writers of guidebooks, and presumably these jobs took up some of the employment slack from the simultaneous slow decline of the metal industries. This chapter describes how the Tours were organized and introduces some of the important tourists.

The rise and decline of the Wye Tour

The first Wye tours began in 1745, when John Egerton, Rector of Ross, took his friends and relatives down the river. Many of the early tourists were noble, as Egerton was the grandson of the Earl of Bridgewater. In his guidebook of 1799, Charles Heath recorded Egerton's role:

> Under his auspices the Excursion was first founded, which has since arisen to be of so much importance in the world of Fashion and Pleasure, – and we must not withhold from the Honourable Prelate the title of 'Father of the Voyage down the Wye'. Soon after taking possession of this his first benefice, he caused to be built a commodious Pleasure Boat, for the purpose of taking excursions on this river; and whenever any of his friends visited him in the summer, an excursion down the Wye formed always a part of their amusement ... For some years afterwards,

a single boat was sufficient to convey the company down the Wye, but since the pleasure of the excursion has been made known, and its scenery illustrated by the engraver, they have increased to the number of EIGHT, and MORE are sometimes wanted, to accommodate the company.

The earliest known description of a Wye Tour was written in 1754 by Sir Roger Newdigate of Arbury Hall, Warwickshire. The Tour had not caught on at this date, but two who undertook the tour in 1770 were influential enough to increase its popularity. One, Thomas Gray, the poet, published a series of letters about his journey and described his experiences to friends in London. One letter to William Mason in 1771 declared:

> Its banks are a succession of nameless beauties … Monmouth, a town I never heard mentioned, lies on the same river; in a vale, that is the delight of my eyes, and the very seat of pleasure.

The other influential visitor was William Gilpin, who visited the Wye a few weeks later and produced a manuscript account incorporating rough sketches and his developing ideas and rules on the Picturesque. He showed it to Gray, who urged him to publish it, but publication was delayed until 1783 owing to the lack of a satisfactory method of reproducing the watercolours developed from his sketches. In due course the pictures in the first edition were reproduced by a combination of the new aquatint method and etching, but the second edition in 1789 used pure aquatints, which Gilpin felt were more satisfactory. His pictures were so generalized that they frequently confused the tourists. According to Gilpin's biographer, C.P. Barbier, William Mason wrote to Gilpin in 1784: 'If a voyager down the Wye takes out your Book, his very Boatman crys out, "nay Sir you may look in vain there no body can find one Picture in it the least like."'

Earlier, in 1775, Paul Sandby published his first set of aquatints of the Wye, including Chepstow Castle (Plate 56), and these also attracted many early tourists. A later publication which must have increased the popularity of the Wye Tour, particularly for those outside the wealthy classes (who rarely bought books), was an eight-page illustrated guide to the Wye Valley, including a description of the Wye Tour, which appeared in the *Penny Magazine* of 31 August 1835, a publication of the Society for the Diffusion of Useful Knowledge, which claimed to have a circulation of 200,000. It describes the landscapes seen on the tour and gives an account of its development, even suggesting that the tour nearly died out before Gilpin and Gray popularized it, and that Gray had attracted more tourists than Gilpin:

> To this end Dr. Egerton built a pleasure-boat; and year after year excursions were made, until it became fashionable in a certain high class of society to visit the Wye; but when the doctor was removed to the see of Durham, his boat was left to rot on the banks, the voyage becoming less and less frequent. Mr. Whately, a writer on landscape gardening, and an exquisite critic, directed attention to the New Weir, Tintern Abbey, and one or two other scenes on its banks; and in 1770, the Wye was visited by the Rev. William Gilpin, who, though somewhat of a pedant in art, and not over-correct in his descriptions, did good service to taste and the lovers of nature, by publishing the account of his tour. The same year a greater name connected itself with the Wye, for it was visited by the immortal author of the 'Elegy in a Country Churchyard.' ... It may almost be said that the last happy moments Gray knew in this world were spent upon the Wye; for a

few months after we find him a prey to ill health and despondence, complaining of an incurable cough, of the irksomeness of his employment at Cambridge, and of 'mechanical low spirits',and he died in the course of the following summer. The publication of Gray's correspondence probably attracted more tourists than Gilpin's book, and yet, for some years afterwards, a single boat was all that was required to convey the company down the Wye.

The comment about the single boat may not be correct, as Pat Hughes and Heather Hurley state in *The Story of Ross* that the first boats were let out to hire in 1760. The *Penny Magazine* continues:

> At present there are several pleasure-boats in pretty constant employment during the fine season, and these are to be hired for private parties. ... Last summer, however, a large vessel, something like a city barge, was started at Ross, and the passage per head to Chepstow is very reasonable. This fact sufficiently indicates that, like all the best and most intellectual of our pleasures and tastes, the love of travelling and fine scenery is finding its way among the great body of the people. We trust we shall render an acceptable service by pointing out and recommending this excursion in preference to many more distant and expensive tours.

A century after Gilpin, in 1875, J.H. Clarke, a local newspaper publisher, began his small guide book, *Tours from Ross and Monmouth (by rail and water),* by adapting the famous opening lines of Jane Austen's *Pride and Prejudice:*

> It has long been an admitted fact that the tour of the Wye is unequalled for its beauty in England, whether the traveller be a poet, painter, antiquary, or merely a sight-seer – and almost as rich in historic associations as it is in beauty.

The amount of river traffic generated by the Tour changed over the years. In 1803 Joseph Farington counted five boats moored at Ross and in 1799 Charles Heath claimed a total of eight boats were needed and sometimes more. By 1827, according to Martin Morris's book on Ross, up to eight boats left Ross each day. Assuming a four day turn-around time, this implies a 'fleet' of 32 boats at Ross alone. Even working on a conservative figure of 30 boats in total, and assuming that each boat took six passengers, as many as 6,300 people could take the tour over a summer season of 150 days. In the 1850s, according to Hughes and Hurley, Joseph Evans, basket maker, Post Master and boat proprietor, claimed he had made the boat trip 1,200 times in 40 years. A local tourist website claimed that the Wye Tour peaked in the 1860s, with over 30 boats moored alongside Wye Street in Ross. The information was later withdrawn, but if it was true, there could have been up to 120 boats operating from Ross alone, with more from Monmouth, Hereford and Symonds Yat. However, by this stage many boat trips were very short: even by the 1820s some Wye tourists did not float further than the ale house and pleasure grounds which had grown up at the ferry crossing below Goodrich Castle. Inn 1828, as a further attraction to visitors, Sir Samuel Meyrick built Goodrich Court, a mock medieval castle, on the ridge overlooking the genuine castle, where he housed his famous collection of armour. Other tourists still wanted to experience the Wye Tour, but as quickly as they could, and for a day or two before the full moon it was said to be possible to go from Ross to Chepstow in a single day of ten hours. There are even reports of boat trips taking place by moonlight, as shown in the engraving after David Cox (Plate 9).

Plate 9. After David Cox Coldwell Rocks, on the River Wye *Engraved on steel by W. Radclyffe* c.*1836*
The combination of Cox and Radclyffe is claimed to have produced some of the finest steel engravings. This night
voyage on the Wye has a particularly dramatic atmosphere, with rocks dark against the moonlit sky and smoke from
limekilns breaking the massive growth of woodland. Curiously, the fully-laden tour boat seems to be rowing upstream
(Nelson Museum Monmouth)

When the Hereford, Ross and Gloucester railway opened in 1855, the Ross to Monmouth railway in 1874 and the Wye Valley line from Monmouth to Chepstow in 1876, there was an initial surge in the number of visitors taking the Wye Tour, but this surge soon died down as tourists began to realize they could travel greater distances more easily and visit distant regions. The *Ross Gazette* reported the opening of the Monmouth to Ross line: 'The line of the railway runs by the side of the River Wye nearly all the way, and thus the advantages of the "Wye Tour" are partially secured to the railway passengers.' However, J.A. Stratford, in his book *The Wye Tour* of 1896, suggested:

> Nothing should tempt the tourist to give up the water for the shorter trip, because the charm of the river scenery cannot be fully witnessed from the land, or sufficiently realised during the speedy transit of a railway journey.

The number of day excursions by train to popular sites such as Tintern and Symonds Yat, from Bath, Bristol, Newport, Cardiff, Cheltenham and Gloucester increased steadily. In the 1880s train-loads of a thousand people would come on September evenings to view the harvest moon rising through the abbey windows. As many as 1,300 people packed the train by 1900 and until at least 1917, the 'harvest moon special' was the most popular excursion on the railway. Charles Heath may have been the first to record the effect of the moon:

> At that part of the year, when the HEAVENS are lighted up in the fullness of their glory, by what we name the HARVEST MOON, the Abbey then presents itself in grandeur beyond the power of my abilities to express. Rising, as she generally does in a southwardly direction, her influence is rendered inimitably fine on that part of the building; for the window, which is of considerable size, being almost screened by a curtain of the most exquisite drapery, formed by the Hand of Nature, her lustre becomes finely chastened, and serves to heighten, if possible, the grandeur and solemnity of the scene.

The Wye Tour continued for some time after the advent of trains. Mr and Mrs Hall's guidebook of 1861 describes travelling to Chepstow by train, then to Ross, presumably by road, before taking a boat downriver. In 1880, H. Shutz Wilson, writing in *Picturesque Europe*, said that 'the tour of the Wye is one of the loveliest of river-trips in England'. However, Clarke, in his 1875 guidebook, suggests that visitor numbers had declined:

> The bosom of the lovely Wye is sometimes enlivened by boats containing pleasure parties from Monmouth and Ross, but this 'descent of the Wye' does not frequently occur, on account of the difficulty in getting the wherries back again.

Even so, the book does contain an advertisement for boats:

BOATS. BOATS.

T. FULLER, BOAT PROPRIETOR, WYE BRIDGE, MONMOUTH,

Begs to inform Tourists and Families desirous of travelling over any part of the beautiful Wye between Ross and Chepstow, that he supplies BOATS and trustworthy men, on the shortest possible notice. Boats kept waiting for every train from Ross. Parties desirous of making the entire tour by water, from Ross to Chepstow, would oblige by giving one day's notice by post to the above address.

As late as 1905, Baedeker's *Great Britain Guide Book* gave a brief description of the Wye Tour with detailed prices of boat hire, but by 1910, A.G. Bradley, in his book *The Wye*, stated that Ross is: 'the place where the oarsman, intent on rowing down what the outside world generally understands by the Wye, hires his boat', which implies that by this date, if you wanted to experience a Wye Tour, you had to row yourself. This DIY approach had been around for some time. A recently published journal, *Camping on The Wye*, written in 1892, amusingly describes a trip by four undergraduates in a 'Salter's Randan' boat. They descended from Whitney, below Hay on Wye, to Chepstow, sleeping in a large bell tent wherever they landed each evening, even camping in Goodrich Castle.

Nevertheless, hired boatmen did survive for some time: a 1920s guidebook, *The Official Guide of the City Council and Chamber of Commerce, Hereford, the Centre for the Wye Valley* stated:

> Visitors who wish to make a trip on the Wye may apply to Mr R Jordan, Wye Bridge, Hereford, close to the bridge, where boats may be hired at reasonable charges, with experienced boatmen, if desired, by the hour, day, or week.

In the same period, Henry Dowell and Sons of Ross were advertising day trips to Monmouth, with passengers leaving Ross at 10.30am, stopping for one hour at Goodrich, lunching at Lydbrook, walking up to Symonds Yat Rock and reaching Monmouth at 5pm.

The end of the Wye Tour as a commercial enterprise came in 1912, according to Keith Kissack in *The River Wye*, when the *Wilton Castle* steamship was abandoned due to lack of trade. Hughes and Hurley suggest that by 1914 the term Wye Tour had been replaced in guidebooks by 'Boating on the Wye'. However, a small guidebook to Ross, published by the Chamber of Commerce about 1936, stated that 'boats may be hired of Messrs. Dowell and Sons, The Docks, who also, if desired, provide skilled boatmen for those who wish to take an extended river trip'. The guide's section on the Wye Tour starts:

> The journey by boat down the Wye is one of the most memorable experiences in the life of those who have had the good fortune to undertake it. The scenery it presents is unquestionably unique, and must be seen to be fully appreciated. The rapid stream carries the boat along through a veritable fairyland of transcendent beauty.

Some short rowing-boat trips continued even later. An article in the *Forest and Wye Valley Review* of 25 August 2006 showed a photograph (possibly an old picture postcard) of Mr Pickering, a river boatman, seen through an arch at Tintern Abbey: he evidently continued to take trippers downstream to view the abbey from various angles until 1940. The 1936 Official Guide of the Monmouth Chamber of Commerce, grandly entitled *Monmouth The Touring Centre for the Far-Famed Wye Valley*, described the country between Monmouth and Ross as the English Rhineland, and advised that 'some of the principal gems of the Wye Valley scenery may be viewed more intimately by taking a boat at Symond's Yat ferry and proceeding back to Monmouth by river'. But in 1942, in *Coming down the Wye*, Robert Gibbings stated:

> I had hoped to find a boat at Hay, a boat that would carry me, at leisure and in comfort, to the sea. But at Hay they referred me to Hereford, and at Hereford they suggested Ross. At Ross they were unable to help.

By 1951, Gordon Cooper's *A fortnight in the Wye Valley*, published in London, commented that 'in the latter part of the eighteenth century the "Wye Tour" became fashionable ... but with the advent of the internal combustion engine this practice appears to have fallen into disuse'.

Even now, there are still popular boat trips on the river – Kingfisher Cruises have large, covered, flat-bottomed boats, as seen in Susanna Birley's watercolour (Plate 32), which make short trips upstream from Symonds Yat in summer, and there are at least three centres where canoes can be hired. Longer tours of the Wye can be experienced by walkers using the many public footpaths and the Wye Valley Walk and Offa's Dyke Path long distance trails.

Wye Tour boats and boatmen

The first tour boats were small and simple, but by the late 1780s, a few years after Gilpin's book was published, boats had become very sophisticated. Gilpin does not say how many passengers his boat took, simply that: 'at Ross, we planned our voyage down the Wye to Monmouth; and provided a covered-boat, navigated by three men. Less strength would have carried us down; but the labour is in rowing back'.

John Byng described his boat from Monmouth on his second visit (1787): 'Our galley was well fitted up, with a carpet, wooden sides and awning, and lockers surrounding a table, at which fourteen people might commodiously dine.' By 1793, some of the boats had grown even larger: In *Monmouth: the Making of a County Town*, Keith Kissack quotes an advertisement in the *Hereford Journal*:

A Pleasure Boat for sale, easy draught of water, adapted for rowing or sailing; holding 20 persons. Awning with checked curtains, full suit of colours, mainmast, mizzenmast, bowsprit, two pairs of oars, all sails and rigging; at Hereford.

William Coxe described a smaller boat in 1801:

We embarked at seven in the morning in a convenient vessel, capable of containing eight persons besides the boatman, and provided with an awning, which, as the weather was unclouded and sultry, we found a good defence against the rays of an August sun.

Typical boats with flat-topped canopies are seen in the engravings of Coldwell Rocks and of Redbrook (Plates 7 and 9). Samuel Ireland's picture of Llandogo (Plate 8) shows a boat with a curved-top canopy and a small limp sail which does not look large enough to be of much use, even when the wind was in the right direction. The masts, incidentally, were hinged to allow the boats under bridges. Canopies must have considerably restricted the views of the tops of the hills, especially in the narrower parts of the gorge, but I have found no record of tourists' frustration on this point, perhaps because awnings were usually removed from the framework when it was fine. In very windy weather, when it was most needed, the awning often had to be removed, presumably because it flapped too much and made the boat difficult to steer. Some boats in contrast, had a hard canopy: Nicholas Pocock's picture of 1791, in the Castle Museum Norwich, shows tourists or boatmen sitting and standing on the roof.

Charles Heath assured the tourists that: 'the proprietor of the vessel accompanies them so that the ear is not pained with a coarseness of language too frequently heard from the navigators of public rivers'. The boatmen may also on occasion have been a little drunk, as Joseph Farington implied in his diary of 1803:

We breakfasted, and at a quarter before 9 went on board our Boat. The Boatmen told us they had never known the water so low as at present, thought one of them had been employed on the River 30 years ... A little way beyond the Bridge, we had proof of the difficulty we had to encounter from the river being so shallow; The Boatmen were obliged to go into the water and to force the Boat along by dragging and lifting. This they did and with much good humour. One of them entertained the others by saying 'it was like pulling a pig to market'.

But the pleasure we had in viewing the scenery was frequently interrupted by the difficulty of getting our Boat over passages so shallow that it seemed almost impossible to force it forward. It was frequently obliged to be lifted with poles by the men standing in the water, & in one part it required that the Boats should be lightened, accordingly Hoppner & Mr Evans Junr. were carried on shore by the men who took them on their Backs but unfortunately one of these assistants had by too repeated an application to his Bottle become a little unsteady & giving way under the weight of Mr Evans he was dropt into the water and with a narrow escape of falling upon his back into it.

In 1835, the *Penny Magazine* mentions a large vessel like a city barge being used. Indeed, around this time, some boats were described as house boats, with tourists spending the night on board at Monmouth. Robert Bloomfield, the poet, wrote about his experience of waking up on the river:

> The boat was moor'd upon the strand,
> The wakeful steersman ready lay
> To rouse us at the break of day.
> It came – how soon! And what a sky
> To cheer the bounding traveller's eye,
> To make him spurn his couch of rest
> To shout upon the river's breast.
> On upland farm and airy height,
> Swept by the breeze and clothed in light,
> The reapers, early from their beds
> Perhaps were singing o'er our heads.

Louisa Twamley and Thomas Roscoe both describe their boats as a type of gondola, with a clear division into parts. Twamley also appreciated the boatmen:

> We soon embarked in a boat, which looked as if it wished to be taken for a gondola's fifteenth cousin, or thereabouts; just like enough to be thought one of the family; – with commodious seats round the 'company' end, and a table in the midst. A keen, honest and intelligent old man was our 'skipper' and his two 'helps' were as strong, stout young Welshmen as need be.

Roscoe was more interested in the awning:

> My 'light bark' was not much unlike a gondola, when its tarpauling cover was spread over the framework; but being favoured by a randomly bright morning, I preferred sitting under the skeleton and enjoying the charming scenes around me. A table in the centre of the part allotted to passengers, and cushioned seats around, made this small floating parlour a most commodious conveyance.

Mr and Mrs Hall informed readers in 1861 that 'Excellent boats, well and carefully manned, are to be obtained either at Hereford, Ross, or Monmouth ... When the lighter boat is used, the boatman finds it easier to bring it back by land, on a truck, the distance being only ten miles.' Since the Ross to Chepstow lines were not open at this date, this might refer to a railway truck taking the boats from Ross back to Hereford.

Some tourists became very aware of the dangers of their boat trip. Describing a trip from Whitchurch over the rapids at New Weir, L. Valentine in *Picturesque England* (1894) said:

> As the boat was not yet up, we waited for it in the churchyard close by. The inspection of the tombstones was not encouraging for intending Wye voyagers, for nearly half or more of the inscriptions recorded that the deceased was drowned on the Wye! We were glad to be relieved from such dismal suggestions by the appearance of our stalwart boatman, and were soon seated with our escort in his boat ... Then came our first rapid – the first we had ever crossed – for

though accustomed to oceans, we had never before rowed on a river except the Thames. How lovely the water looks as it plays over the little rocks, sparkling and babbling as it dances by them! Yet boats are sometimes, as we have seen, upset in these picturesque spots, and then if a strong swimmer could reach the shore, it is most frequently an impregnable wall of rock he would find before him. But our boatman was skilful, and we passed them well.

Steamships may have been a safer alternative and several operated on the Wye in the 19th century, but it is not clear how much they affected the number of rowing boats, which would have appealed to a different type of tourist. Keith Kissack records that a steam ship, the *Paul Pry*, was launched in 1827, but, despite the cheap fares, it was (according to Pat Hughes and Heather Hurley) re-equipped the next year as a steam tow-boat for towing barges up to Hereford. Later, the well-known *Water Witch*, an 80-foot-long steamship, took passengers, and in 1836 the *Man of Ross* ran day trips down to Chepstow. Colin Green, in *Severn Traders*, suggests that some of the old trows may also have been used as pleasure boats at the end of the 19th century, though he does not say whether they were converted to steam. In 1902, a stern-wheel, flat-bottomed paddle steamer, the *Wilton Castle*, which could carry up to a hundred people at 8 knots, was launched at Ross. At 65 feet long and 10 feet in beam, this was said to be the largest pleasure boat on the Wye at the time. Unfortunately, with the decrease of the commercial traffic, the Wye started silting up, and the *Wilton Castle* could not take visitors very far. The cruises ended in 1912.

The cost of the Tour

The cost of hiring a boat hardly changed throughout the early decades of the Tour then decreased substantially until about 1860, due partly to general deflation but also to increased competition arising from an oversupply of boats. Gilpin does not mention a cost, but John Byng, staying at the Beaufort Arms in Monmouth in 1781 reported that: 'The Landlord (who seems tolerably intelligent) tells me to my sorrow, that a boat to Chepstow will cost one guinea and a half; and that I had better ride and save my money.' Farington's trip in 1803 cost £4 4s, which was relatively expensive – the equivalent of well over £200 today:

> In the evening we hired a boat to take us to Monmouth. The fare is one guinea and a half for the boat, and half a guinea to the Boatmen, three in number, one to steer and two to row – We were informed that the passage from Monmouth to Chepstow is made upon the same terms. It is also usual to take a basket of provisions from Ross to eat in the boat at such a place on the passage as may be preferred.

A Ross guidebook of 1827 advertised a trip from Ross to Monmouth for £1 11s 6d and from Ross to Chepstow for £3 3s. In 1836 the *Man of Ross* steam boat was running trips from Ross to Chepstow in one day for a mere 10s. An advertisement for the Wye Tour in the *Ross and Archenfield Gazette* of 9 June 1855 states:

> Tour of the Wye. THE PUBLIC BOAT to GOODRICH COURT and CASTLE will sail from Ross daily, at Twelve o-clock (Sundays excepted). Fares 1s each. Applications to secure places to be made to Joseph Evans, Pleasure-Boat Proprietor, Post Office, Ross.

In 1859 Evans was advertising trips to Monmouth for five shillings and to Chepstow for ten shillings, but in 1861 Mr and Mrs Hall seem to have picked a more expensive boat, for the cost was 15s for a boat with one man from Ross to Monmouth, or 30s for a larger boat with two men. Baedeker's 1905 *Great Britain Guidebook* quoted: 'A boat with one boatman from Ross to Goodrich Castle costs 6s; to Symond's Yat 10s; to Monmouth 15s; to Tintern 25s, to Chepstow 30s, with two men about one half more.'

At the end of the 19th century, the cost of the tour included within a 'package' was almost negligible. The Great Western Railway offered Londoners a 3rd class return ticket for 27/-, which included a rail journey from Paddington to Hereford, the boat trip from Hereford to Chepstow, and the return from Chepstow by train. Breaks could be made anywhere along the river to extend the trip. The *Ward Lock* guide of 1897 advertised three-day, 64 mile boat trips (with boatmen) on any day in the summer from Hereford to Chepstow for £3 15s 0d. Alternatively, the tour could take four days for an extra 7s 6d. In the 1920s, Henry Dowell of Ross was taking day trips to Monmouth by rowing boat for 8 shillings per passenger.

Food and accommodation

The majority of the tourists ate at recognised stops. On the first day many breakfasted at the Goodrich ferry, lunched with a picnic at the foot of Coldwell Rocks ('the Halfway Point'), then climbed up to Yat Rock. Tintern Abbey provided a popular breakfast or lunch stop on the second day. Most boats were hired inclusive of provisions, but there was obviously competition to provide more food. Thus, John Byng, on his second visit in 1787, went aboard at Monmouth at 2pm with three boatmen and two servants:

> ... ladened with baggage (like a Calais embarkation) ... We saw several salmon fishers and purchased of them a fresh caught botcher of 3 or 4 pounds weight to add to the quantity of provisions we were cajoled to send aboard for ourselves and our crew. This, with their charge, the beer etc., etc., makes water travelling shamefully expensive; but the boatmen pretend the great difficulty and tediousness of returning against the stream.

Joseph Farington ate a meal at Piercefield provided by his Inn in Chepstow: 'Having brought provisions with us we dined at the entrance of a subterranean passage cut through the rock. Not having knives and forks and glasses we sent to Piercefield House and were furnished with them.' John Byng proposed a picnic at Tintern Abbey:

> Bring wines, cold meat, with corn for the horses; (bread, beer, cyder and commonly salmon may be had at the Beaufort Arms), spread your table in the ruins; and possibly a Welsh harper may be procured from Chepstow.

At Piercefield he suggested 'In these shades one might pass a happy day, and dine as I had before proposed in Tintern Abbey; for there is a well near the Elm Walk, that would serve to cool wine in, and the grotto or cave will protect from bad or sultry weather.'

The number and size of the hotels to accommodate the Wye tourists increased rapidly in response to demand. By the early 19th century, the Beaufort Hotel, the main coaching inn in

Monmouth, had according to Kissack in *Monmouth and its Buildings* expanded to 36 bedrooms, and the Kings Head, also a posting inn, had 18 bedrooms. This increase mirrors the growth of stage-coach travel. A regular service from London to Ross and Monmouth started in the 1770s and reached a peak around 1820, when competition from the railways began to take effect.

Some of the diarists felt strongly about accommodation. For example, John Byng described his experience in 1781:

> I arriv'd at the Beaufort Arms, Monmouth, this evening, rather tired; and am now sitting in a mean room at this bad inn; which may be the best for here. The stables are new and good, that's a comfort; for if my horse does not fare and sleep well, why there wou'd be an end of my travel.

The situation deteriorated the next day:

> I slept very ill last night. It is a plague to be in an inn with troops, for the officers employ, and occupy the whole house; on this account the landlord oppresses the traveller, and the officer, from remembrance, takes pleasure in eating up a landlord.

Likewise, Joseph Farington was not impressed by his inn at Ross: 'At 5 oClock we dined & were not very pleased with our entertainment. The fowls were tough, and the wine very bad … At Ross our dinners were charged 2s 6d each, Wine 4s 6d a bottle, – brandy 6s a bottle. Breakfasts 1s 3d – Beds 1s each. The Landlord never made his appearance to us, and on the whole we were glad to shift our quarters.' Monmouth, however, met with his approval – the landlord must have changed since Byng's visit: 'we soon joined our friends at the Beaufort Arms the principal Inn at Monmouth. Here the accommodations were in all respects very good, the wine remarkably so.'

Charles Heath listed the inns of Ross – The Swan, the King's Head, The George and Excise Office, and at Monmouth, The Beaufort Arms, The Kings Head, and the Crown and Thistle:

> Parties making the Excursion down the Wye, may be provided by Pleasure Boats at each of the above Houses: – cold collation, the best Wines, and every other necessary Refreshment for the Voyage.

The tourist trade at Tintern was established well before the Wye Tour became popular, and by the middle of the 18th century, there were very few buildings in Tintern which were not taking in lodgers. Accommodation was upgraded for the Wye tourists, as shown by Charles Heath's comments on improvements to the Beaufort Arms, which had been: 'fitted up in a neat and commodious manner' and several new rooms had been added, furnished with new beds and bedding. There was a 'fresh stock of good liquors laid in their cellars'. Thomas Roscoe was not impressed, however:

> It is to be regretted that there are not better accommodations for visitors at Tintern. The Beaufort Arms' Inn is the best house, but it is small and inconvenient. I heard when I was there some talk respecting the erection of a new and splendid hotel, similar to that at Llanberis, in Caernarvonshire.

Later, Mr and Mrs Hall seemed satisfied with the Inn, though also called it small:

Several neat, though small, houses are let as lodgings; and besides the comfortable little inn, 'The Beaufort Arms', there are two other inns, with fair promise of 'entertainment'. The accommodation they afford, however, is by no means adequate to the demand in the season', but that is no great evil, inasmuch as Tinterne is but five miles from Chepstow, and ten miles from Monmouth – both places abounding in hotels.

Guides to sites and sights

Tintern Abbey was notorious during the early Wye Tour for the large number of beggars who waited at the landing stage to offer themselves as guides. Indeed, some visitors found them as interesting as the ruins. For example, John Byng commented:

> I enter'd the abbey accompanied by a boy who knew nothing, and by a very old man who had forgotten everything; but I kept him with me, as his venerable grey beard, and locks, added dignity to my thoughts; and I fancied him the hermit of the place.

Gilpin was more concerned about their pitiful state:

> Among other things in this scene of desolation, the poverty and wretchedness of the inhabitants were remarkable. They occupy little huts, raised among the ruins of the monastery; and seem to have no employment, but begging: as if a place, once devoted to indolence, could never again become the seat of industry. As we left the abbey, we found the whole hamlet at the gate, either openly soliciting alms; or covertly, under the pretence of carrying us to some part of the ruins, which each could shew; and which was far superior to any thing, which could be shewn by any one else. The most lucrative occasion could not have excited more jealousy and contention.

The beggars had all been swept away by the time Mr and Mrs Hall toured in 1861, but they did note guides at other places. At Wyndcliff 'the carriage stops at the Moss House ... in which resides the caretaker of the hill, who will accompany you if you please; but his companionship is not needed, for on its summit, where the 'views' are, you will find an old soldier stationed – to direct your notice to such places as have names.' Earlier, on their climb up to Symonds Yat:

> We shall first rest at the neat and 'cozy' cottage of the guide; if it be spring, we may scent the blossoms of an abundant orchard; and if autumn, we can taste its fruit; at any season, a draught of home-made cider is sure to be offered to the tourist by the civil and obliging woman who keeps the house, and who will presently walk with us through the close underwood that may confuse our path, if unattended. She will draw attention to a little bubbling rivulet, that here divides Herefordshire from Gloucestershire; point out a pretty infant-school ... She will show you other objects that greet the eye as you ascend; and will soon place you – and leave you – on a broad platform.

This may have been the same guide who had earlier accompanied Louisa Twamley:

A few pale autumn flowers delighted me exceedingly, and as I was gathering sprays of each, the good woman who acted as guide, exclaimed regretfully, 'Ah Ma'am, you should come here in summer, we've hall the Horchises!'

At Goodrich Castle the Halls describe:

A venerable chatelaine – one Titus Morgan – who makes shoes in the village, and who has had the place in charge during forty-nine years, succeeding his father in the office, is an excellent and very communicative usher to its attractions; or his aides-de-camp, two agreeable daughters, are as ready and as skilful as himself in greeting and in guiding visitors.

Guidebooks and Tour accounts

By 1850 more than 20 guidebooks had been published and hundreds more unpublished journals and tour accounts produced, which are now mostly stored in public record offices. Guidebooks often plagiarized passages from previous guides without acknowledgement and usually without quotation marks, so quotes and misquotes, especially from Gilpin's book, became embedded in more modern observations. The combination of material from various guides was proposed by an anonymous reviewer in *The Topographer* of 1789, quoted by Andrews, to save the tourists from having to carry several guidebooks around with them.

Samuel Ireland, like Gilpin, wrote many accounts of his tours in picturesque regions of Britain, including the whole length of the Wye from Plynlimon down. His *Picturesque Views on the Wye* (1797) is illustrated with sepia aquatints taken from his sketches, such as Plate 8, enlivened by simple and direct descriptions. He hoped: 'that his drawings should, like the transparent mirror of his stream, truly reflect the landscape that exists around, as well as the objects that decorate its banks'.

Most guidebooks were written by visitors, who spent only a few days in the area, but two were written by local residents with a detailed knowledge of the Wye Valley. Charles Heath, who published and sold books in Monmouth, produced a guide to the Wye which incorporated many quotes from Gilpin. First published in 1799, numerous editions followed until the 1880s, each with different combinations of material. The long title page of the 1808 edition was characteristic of the time:

The Excursion down the Wye from Ross to Monmouth comprehending historical and descriptive accounts of Wilton and Goodrich Castles also of Court Field, the nursery of King Henry the Fifth; New Wear, with other public objects on the voyage; and throughout the whole are interspersed, a variety of amusing and interesting circumstances, never before collected: – particularly Memoirs and Anecdotes of the life of John Kyrle, esq. rendered immortal by the muse of Pope, under the character of The Man of Ross, 'But all our PRAISES why should LORDS engross? Rise honest MUSE. And sing the MAN OF ROSS' By Charles Heath, Monmouth. Printed and sold by him, in the market-place; sold also by D Roberts Ross and at all towns in the county.

The other resident guidebook writer, the Reverend Thomas Dudley Fosbroke, lived at Walford. A well-respected scholar, antiquary and local historian, his *The Wye Tour, or Gilpin on the Wye, with historical and archaeological additions,* first published in 1811, compared the Wye Valley with the Vale of Tempe in Greece, a place of legendary beauty. Wordsworth was said to have owned a copy.

Archdeacon William Coxe of Salisbury was considered by later writers to be, like Gilpin, one of the authorities on the Wye. His *A Historical Tour in Monmouthshire* (1801) included two chapters on the Wye Tour, with engraved views by his fellow traveller, Sir Richard Colt Hoare. Coxe had a pedantic interest in exact measurements. For example: 'The serpentine course is so considerable, that the distance from Ross to Chepstow, which in a direct line is not more than sixteen miles and four furlongs, is thirty seven miles and seven furlongs by water.' Occasionally, however, he exaggerated: he claimed that Symonds Yat Rock was 2,000 feet high!

Two books published in the 1830s included engravings by William Radclyffe from paintings by David Cox, which are considered to be amongst the best engraved topographical works (Plate 9). Thomas Roscoe was possibly the first traveller to mention trains, but his colourful descriptions in *Wanderings in South Wales, including the River Wye* (1836) were written well before the Wye Valley line was built. An early user of Ordnance Survey maps, he was amused, when talking to local people, by: 'the utter astonishment manifested by my honest friends at my accurate knowledge of each locality, although now traversing the district for the first time'. Louisa Anne Twamley did not take the standard Tour, but came instead by steamer from Bristol to Chepstow, travelled up the valley as far as Monmouth, then, unusually, took a boat upriver to Ross. Her cheerful and vivid style in *An Autumn Ramble on the Wye* (1839) often emphasized the effects of light on the landscape, and revealed her interest in plants. She went on to lead an exciting life as Tasmania's leading botanist.

Two years later, Leith Ritchie also used 'ramble' in his title, *The Wye and its Associations, A Picturesque Ramble*: perhaps the word 'tour' was going out of fashion. Ritchie felt that the picturesque character of the Wye should be evaluated in: 'winter, when the Wye and its ruins are stripped of the adjuncts of foliage, which in the imagination of common travellers is inseparably connected with ideas of the picturesque or beautiful in natural scenery', and only after seeing the other rivers of Europe.

The Book of the Wye, South Wales and the Coast of 1861 by Mr and Mrs S.C. Hall was planned as a rail trip covering most of South Wales, with a detour to take the Wye Tour by boat. It is a thorough, occasionally tedious account, containing much detail on churches and castles, and extensive quotes from Gilpin, Coxe and others. Although a variety of well-known and local artists are listed at the front of the book, frustratingly, the many fine wood engravings are rarely attributed to a particular artist.

Of those Tour journals that languish unpublished in public record offices, some are dry topographical and antiquarian records, while others are personal accounts and diaries of the tourist's experiences, containing lively descriptions of the boats and boatmen, tour guides, food, accommodation and weather. As they tried to outshine the guidebooks or to link the scene to the work of particular artists or poets, so their descriptions of views and buildings became ever more strained and elaborate. One exception, the diary of John Byng, later Fifth Viscount Torrington (published and edited by C. Bruyn Andrews in 1934 as *The Torrington Diaries*) was a forthright and lively account of his visits in 1781 and 1787. Another, Joseph Farington's journal of 1803, was lost for many years until it was discovered by chance in Hereford Museum and published with a commentary by E. Newby in 1998. The diary is a strange, jumbled mixture of irrelevant stories about various acquaintances, combined with opinionated comments on politics, and his accommodation, food and costs. He does however make useful practical comments on the landscape from the point of view of an artist, and produced some sketches which can be related to diary entries (Plate 10).

Plate 10. Joseph Farington Chepstow Castle on the River Wye *Pencil sketch 1803*
Farington records in his diary for 19 September that, after spending four hours on a drawing from the bridge, he
'passed the remainder of the day in making another drawing of the chapel of the Castle where it is the principal
feature of a wood scene'. Since he started at 9am and dined at 5pm, this drawing could also have taken him four
hours to complete. The Great Tower was often known as the chapel at this time
(Herefordshire Heritage Services, Herefordshire Council)

Aids to viewing and recording landscapes

Picturesque tourists described their journeys in pictures and words, and this helped them appreciate the landscapes – the frontispiece shows a Wye Tourist at Chepstow Castle recording the view through a doorway. Gilpin was the first to show aspiring artists how easy it was to record their experiences as paintings, advising them to use a soft black-lead pencil for sketches: 'Nothing glides so volubly over paper, and executes an idea more quickly.' He suggested that pen outlines and ink washes could be added to give a tonal composition from which a watercolour could be produced later. In a picturesque view, Gilpin ruled that the shaded areas should be greater than the light areas, and that it was easiest to draw at 'sight size', which means that an inch measured along a pencil held at arm's length against an object in the view could be represented by an inch-long line on the paper.

Aspiring artists were also helped by the profusion of picturesque prints which became available in specialist print shops during the 1790s, when the Continent was inaccessible. Seventy-nine prints of Tintern Abbey were produced between 1730 and 1850, according to Isaac Williams' (1926) catalogue in the National Museum of Wales. In the top ten places listed, Tintern came second and Chepstow Castle fourth with 68 prints. Tourists took prints with them to help find the 'best' viewpoints, but as picturesque rules demanded that artists 'corrected' the view, frustrated visitors could not always identify the site. Familiarity with poetry and 17th-century European painting helped them to recognise and describe certain types of landscapes as pictures, so they quoted Thomson and Milton, or made comparisons with Claude, Rosa or Poussin when their own words failed them. On many picturesque tours, particularly those through the Lakes and North Wales, tourists were helped to produce a well-composed drawing or painting by numbered stations listed in guide books, accompanied by instructions on exactly where to stand and what to include.

Various other aids helped tourists to 'capture' a view and idealize the composition. The Claude glass was a convex mirror, oval or rectangular, backed with black foil, which gave a small, simplified reflection of the landscape when the artist stood with his back to the view and angled the glass over his shoulder. The reflection took out most of the colour, leaving a tonal composition, and distorted shapes to some extent, making the foreground more important and the background more distant. Coloured glass lenses were also available, which miniaturized the view, and gave a more harmonious colour scheme – a dawn glass would give a golden glow to the whole of the landscape even at midday, while a dark glass gave a moonlight effect. Telescopes helped tourists to pick out distant detail: one was mounted on the flat roof of the Round House on the Kymin. These aids allowed the viewer to use his imagination and become detached from the physical reality of the landscape.

Some artists used a *camera obscura* to help them achieve an accurate composition. This was a darkened box which allowed in light through a double convex lens and projected an image of an external scene onto paper or a glass screen. According to Ronald Russell in *Guide to British Topographical Prints*, John Britton, at the start of his artistic career, undertook a three month tour costing £11 16s 9d, which included a walk from Ross to Chepstow, during which he carried maps, compass, books, umbrella and underwear, as well as a *camera obscura*.

Famous visitors to the Lower Wye

By far the most popular and fêted celebrity to take part in the Wye Tour was Admiral Lord Nelson, who in 1802 floated down the river with Lady Hamilton as crowds cheered them on from the banks and cannons fired from the Kymin. Nelson stayed in the Beaufort Arms, Monmouth, breakfasted on the Kymin with local dignitaries, and was awarded the Freedom of the Borough. He later also inspected the Naval Temple, which had been constructed to commemorate his victory at the Battle of the Nile in 1798. Nelson's visit still leaves its mark: a collection of Nelson memorabilia was left to the town in 1924 and now forms an important part of the Nelson Museum, Monmouth.

Royalty, Prime Ministers and Presidents all flocked to the Wye. George IV is said to have visited, Lord North, then Prime Minister, brought his family, and Queen Victoria put up at the Royal Hotel, Ross with Princess Mary. American tourists were mentioned at Tintern and Chepstow in *Camping on the Wye* in 1892, and much later a guidebook of about 1936, *Ross, The Gateway of the Wye Valley*, boasted that the President of the United States, Woodrow Wilson, said 'Yesterday I rode for nearly twenty miles beside the Wye, and of all the parts of England I have seen, it has most won my heart.' Prince Arthur, third son of Queen Victoria, rowed nearly all the way from Ross to Chepstow in torrential rain in 1863, when he was 13, and there is an account of the boat trip taken by Princess Victoria May of Teck, later Queen Mary, and her brother Prince Alexander George in 1891. They arrived in

Ross in a carriage drawn by four grey horses and were escorted through the town by the Shropshire Yeomanry and the Ross Brass Band. At the Dock, the party embarked in three boats, with boatmen wearing scarlet jerseys, white flannel trousers and white straw hats with scarlet bands. They lunched at Goodrich Court and then floated to Symonds Yat, where 16 decorated boats formed a guard of honour. Foreign royalty also visited the area: Thomas Morgan, a boat proprietor in Monmouth, advertised his boats as 'Patronised by HRH the Crown Prince of Siam'.

Many famous writers came to the Wye valley, including Charles Dickens, who met his friend and biographer John Forster at the Royal Hotel, Ross. George Bernard Shaw visited the Argoed, near Penallt, for meetings of the Fabian Society, and praised the area to Ellen Terry. Some claim that Henry Fielding wrote his famous novel *Tom Jones* while staying at Tintern Manor House in the first half of the 18th century, and William Makepeace Thackeray, a later visitor to Tintern, wrote: 'There is almost every kind of natural beauty to be found among this little tract of country. The rocks are as tall, the fields as green, the woods as rich, the river as meandering as the heart can desire.'

Poets on the Wye

Poets and poetry attracted just as many visitors to the Wye valley as artists, paintings and prints. Thomas Gray (1716-1771), for example, visited the Wye in 1770: sadly, he left no poem – he fell ill soon after and died the following year – but, as has been shown, his letters influenced many others to visit the Wye. Over 20 years later, William Wordsworth (1770-1850) crossed from Bristol in 1793 and walked up the Wye to Goodrich where he met the little girl he immortalized in *We are seven*. Returning in 1798 with his sister Dorothy, he composed *Lines written a few miles above Tintern Abbey*, probably the greatest and certainly the most quoted poem about the Lower Wye. He walked from Tintern up the Gloucestershire side of the river to Goodrich, walked back to Chepstow next day, returned by boat to Tintern and finally crossed the Severn back to Bristol. The poem, which he claimed was written entirely in his head, was completed only as he walked into Bristol and was never subsequently revised. Published immediately, it not only helped to popularize the Wye Tour but also stimulated the growth of the whole Romantic Movement. The extract in Chapter 2 illustrates Wordsworth's attitude to nature, whilst the following extract brings out the harmony in the Wye landscape, where pastoral beauty merges with wild sublimity:

> Five years have passed; five summers, with the length
> Of five long winters, and again I hear
> These waters, rolling from their mountain-springs
> With a sweet inland murmur. Once again
> Do I behold these steep and lofty cliffs,
> Which on a wild secluded scene impress
> Thoughts of more deep seclusion, and connect
> The landscape with the quiet of the sky.
> The day is come when I again repose
> Here, under this dark sycamore, and view
> These plots of cottage-grounds, these orchard-tufts,
> Which, at this season, with their unripe fruits,
> Among the woods and copses lose themselves,
> Nor, with their green and simple hue, disturb

> The wild green landscape. Once again I see
> Those hedge-rows, hardly hedge-rows, little lines
> Of sportive wood run wild; these pastoral farms
> Green to the very door ...   How oft
> In darkness and amid the many shapes
> Or joyless daylight, when the fretful stir
> Unprofitable and the fever of the world
> Have hung upon the beatings of my heart,
> How oft in spirit have I turned to thee,
> O Sylvan Wye, thou wanderer through the woods,
> How often has my spirit turned to thee.

Other, no less famous poets also wrote about the Wye, but none has had quite the same enduring impact as Wordsworth. Samuel Taylor Coleridge (1772-1834) visited the area several times and accompanied the Wordsworths in 1798. His *Reflections on having left a place of retirement,* published in 1796, includes his reaction to the view from the Wyndcliff:

> But the time, when first
> From that low Dell, steep up the stony Mount
> I climb'd with perilous toil and reach'd the top.
> Oh! what a goodly scene! Here the bleak mount,
> The bare bleak mountain speckled thin with sheep;
> Grey clouds, that shadowing spot the sunny fields;
> And river, now with bushy rocks o'erbrow'd,
> Now winding bright and full, with naked banks;
> And seats, and lawns, the Abbey and the wood,
> And cots, and hamlets, and faint city-spire;
> The Channel there, the Islands and white sails,
> Dim coasts, and cloud-like hills, and shoreless Ocean –
> It seem'd like Omnipresence! God, methought,
> Had built him there a Temple: the whole World
> Seem'd imag'd in its vast circumference:
> No wish profan'd my overwhelmed heart.
> Blest hour! It was a luxury, – to be!

Much later, Alfred Lord Tennyson (1809-1892) inserted this stanza in his long poem *In Memoriam* (1833):

> There twice a day the Severn fills,
> The salt seawater passes by
> And hushes half the babbling Wye,
> And makes a silence in the hills.

Two poets linked the personalities of famous people to the river. Thus, Alexander Pope (1688-1744), who frequently visited Holme Lacy higher up the Wye, described the Wye as he immortalized John Kyrle, the Man of Ross, in his *Epistle to Bathurst* (1733):

Rise, honest Muse, and sing the Man of Ross,
Pleas'd Vaga echoes thro' its winding bounds,
And rapid Severn hoarse applause resounds.
Who hung with woods yon mountain's sultry brow?
From the dry rock who bade the waters flow?
Not to the skies in useless columns tossed,
Or in proud falls magnificently lost,
But clear and artless, pouring through the plain,
Health to the sick, and solace to the swain.

Robert Southey (1774-1843) contrasted the long incarceration in Chepstow Castle of Henry Marten, one of the signatories to the death warrant of Charles I, with the freedom of the Wye at the foot of the castle walls:

For thirty years, secluded from mankind,
Here Marten lingered. Often have these walls
Echoed his footsteps, as with even tread
He paced around his prison. Not to him
Did nature's fair varieties exist;
He never saw the sun's delightful beams,
Save when through yon high bars he poured a sad
And broken splendour.

Gilpin quoted Pope's line 'Pleas'd Vaga echoes through its winding bounds' in his book, and Southey, according to Mr and Mrs Hall, was quoted by every visitor to Chepstow Castle – though the Halls pointed out smugly that most of the facts about Marten were wrong. Other poets evidently made less impact, but made more effort to describe the landscape in picturesque terms. For example, as early as 1745, the Revered Sneyd Davies (1731-1802) published *A Voyage to Tintern Abbey*:

The crooked bank still winds to something new,
Oars, scarcely turned, diversify the view;
Of trees and stone an intermingled scene,
The shady precipice and rocky green.
Nature behold, to please and to surprise,
Swell into bastions, or in columns rise:
Here sinking spaces with dark boughs o'ergrown,
And there the naked quarries look a town.
At length our pilgrimage's home appears,
Tintern her venerable fabric rears,
While the sun, mildly glancing in decline,
With his last gilding beautifies the shrine:
Enter with reverence her hallowed gate,
And trace the glorious relics of her state;
The meeting arches, pillared walks admire,
Or, musing, hearken to the silenced choir.
Encircling groves diffuse a solemn grace,

> And dimly fill th' historic window's place;
> While pitying shrubs on the bare summit try
> To give the roofless pile a canopy.
> Here, O my friends, along the mossy dome
> In pleasurable sadness let me roam:
> Look back upon the world in haven safe,
> Weep o'er its ruins, at its follies laugh.

Edward Davies, a Chepstow poet, who also wrote vividly about Tintern was inspired as much by the industry as the abbey. His *Poetical Description of Tintern Abbey* was included in Heath's guidebook:

> Here, now no bell calls monks to morning prayer,
> Daws only chant their early matins there,
> Black forges smoke, and noisy hammers beat
> Where sooty Cyclops puffing, drink and sweat;
> Confront the curling flame, nor back retire,
> But live like salamanders in the fire.

The peasant poet, Robert Bloomfield (1776-1823), who is principally remembered for *A Farmer's Boy*, visited the Wye in 1811 and produced an interminable poem in a picturesque and unpretentious style, *The Banks of the Wye*, which ran to no less than four volumes. This extract gives a flavour of his work:

> Enough, for WIND-CLIFF still was found
> To hail us as we doubled round
> Bold in primeval strength he stood;
> His rocky brow, all shagg'd with wood,
> O'er-look'd his base, where, doubling strong,
> The inward torrent pours along;
> Then ebbing turns, and turns again,
> To meet the Severn and the Main,
> Beneath the dark shade sweeping round,
> Of beetling PERSFIELD'S fairy ground,
> By buttresses of rock upborne,
> The rude APOSTLES all unshorn.

Artists in the Wye Valley

Finally, we come to the several hundred professional artists who visited the Wye in the 18th and 19th centuries. The artists selected here were either well-known in their day, or influential in establishing the popularity of the Wye Tour, or have one of their pictures included in the book.

Of all the artists who came to the valley, the one whose reputation today stands way above the others is, of course, Joseph Mallord William Turner (1775-1851). He visited the Wye in the 1790s, but continued to produce pictures from the sketches he made then for another 50 years. In 1792, aged only 17, he crossed from Bristol, travelled up the Wye to Monmouth, and completed mainly architectural sketches. From these he produced several watercolours, including two of Tintern Abbey in 1794, drawn from a low angle to dramatise the soaring arches, and one of Chepstow Castle in 1793 taken from river level, with the old timber bridge in the foreground and the keep of the Castle jutting into the sky. Turner returned in 1798 and produced two South Wales sketch books with pencil drawings of Ross, Goodrich Castle, Monmouth and three views on the Wye with rocky or wooded cliffs, one with a watermill and one with a boat carrying cattle. He planned his sketching itineraries meticulously, noting castles, churches, abbeys and bridges that would be worth drawing, and the mileages involved. His early Welsh pictures were described by Andrew Wilton in *Turner in Wales* as: 'works of richness and vitality, a readiness of inspiration and a fecundity of technical invention, that rival those of any other period of his life, and [which] must count among the most intense of all romantic landscapes'. In 1811, Turner produced a mezzotint of the *Junction of the Severn and Wye* as seen from Piercefield Park (Plate 48), which was included in his *Liber Studiorum*. The last picture that he produced from his Wye sketches was an oil painting based on this view, painted as late as 1845, which was much more abstract and atmospheric. The trees on the right are still recognisable and the light shining in the water of the two rivers is interpreted as two white streaks in a haze of burnt sienna. When exhibited in France, this picture is said to have amazed Pissarro with its opalescent layering of glazes.

At least seven well-known artists came to the Wye before Turner. In 1757, well before the Wye Tour became popular, John Inigo Richards (1731-1810) produced a painting of Chepstow Castle, looking across the river in a classical Claudean composition. He was a well-known scene painter in London and became a founder member of the Royal Academy, and later its secretary. Paul Sandby (1730-1809) took part in the Wye Tour in 1770 and published some of the first British aquatints, including a view of Chepstow Castle in 1775 (Plate 37), which started to popularise the area before Gilpin's book appeared. He is said by Russell to have travelled to Wales when it was 'an unknown land to ordinary Englishmen ... No-one ever thought of travelling in Wales for pleasure only'. Thomas Jones (1742-1803), a student of his fellow Welshman, Richard Wilson, painted views on the Wye in 1772, including one north of Monmouth, possibly at Symonds Yat. Four years after Sandby, Samuel Hieronymus Grimm (1733-1794) toured Wales with Henry Wyndham. Known as the illustrator for Gilbert White's *Natural History of Selborne* (1789), he was born in Switzerland, but settled in England in 1768, producing clear pen and wash drawings, lightly coloured, including one of Tintern Abbey (Plate 41). Engravings from his drawings were published in Wyndham's *A Gentleman's Tour through Monmouthshire and Wales* in 1775. Another foreigner, Philippe de Loutherbourg (1740-1812), who came from Strasbourg to England in 1771, became a set-designer and scene-painter at Drury Lane, where he replaced set designs depicting buildings with picturesque and sublime landscapes, producing effects suggesting fire, sun, moonlight and volcanic eruptions. He exhibited dramatically-lit paintings, such as the famous *Coalbrookdale by night*, at the Royal Academy. After he visited the Wye around 1787, he produced a sensitive watercolour sketch of Chepstow Castle (Plate 11) and in 1805 painted *The River Wye at Tintern Abbey*, with the abbey right at the side and cattle and sheep in the river. Another theatre scene-painter, this time at The Haymarket, Michael 'Angelo' Rooker (1746-1813), once a student of Paul Sandby, painted picturesque ruins and cottages in a sublime, melancholic style. He produced various Wye pictures, including Tintern Abbey with haymakers in the foreground; New Weir with a trow and the team of bow hauliers (Plate 33); Coldwell Rocks; and the Monnow Bridge at Monmouth. Finally, John 'Warwick' Smith (1749-1831), the son of a

Plate 11. Philippe de Loutherbourg Chepstow Castle *Watercolour sketch 1786-88*
De Loutherbourg was a stage and set designer at Drury Lane and this elongated watercolour sketch does have a
slightly theatrical feel. Drawn from the opposite bank, rather than the more usual oblique view, it shows the various
ages of the buildings strung out along the cliffs, dominated by the Great Tower
(Llyfrgell Genedlaethol Cymru/National Library of Wales)

gardener of the Gilpin family, accompanied William on some of his sketching trips in the 1770s, and studied under his father and brother. He painted Tintern Abbey by moonlight in 1789 (Plate 40) and a view of the abbey from the village, dominated by a large modern house.

In 1794, two years after Turner's first visit, Thomas Hearne (1744-1817), one of the leading anti-quarian topographical draughtsmen of his time, who was thought to have influenced Turner, toured the Wye with George Beaumont. Between 1786 and 1806 he published, with William Byrne, engravings of Tintern, including one of the forge, in *Antiquities of Great Britain*. His *Goodrich Castle on the Wye* views the castle from the river, showing tourist boats in the foreground and smoke from charcoal hearths rising above the trees. Joseph Farington (1747-1821) thought Hearne's drawing of the south window at Tintern Abbey was the finest he had seen. Farington, a founder member of the Royal Academy, was known as a great string-puller. A pupil of Richard Wilson, he produced traditional picturesque land-scapes in ink or muted colours, which were not considered of great significance by his fellow artists. In 1803 he kept a diary of his Wye Tour, and produced a charcoal sketch called *Fish house at New Weir on the River Wye*, and chalk drawings of *Goodrich Castle* and *Chepstow Castle on the River Wye* (Plate 10), among many others. Another visitor, Edward Dayes (1763-1842), was, like Rooker, a pupil of Paul Sandby. He later became an influential teacher of watercolour, and even Turner copied some of his pictures. As a picturesque illustrator of topographical publications, he travelled throughout Britain and worked up sketches of amateur artists. After visiting Wales, he produced some of his best watercolours, notably of Chepstow (1795), Wilton Castle (1797), New Weir and *View of the Doward Rocks* (Plate 4). Dayes had a difficult relationship with his fellow artists and was jealous enough of his pupil, Girtin, to have him imprisoned for unruly behaviour. His malicious commentary in *Professional Sketches of Modern Artists* was published posthumously after he committed suicide.

Samuel Ireland (1725-1800) was an author, print-dealer and engraver, as well as an artist whose pictures were not highly regarded at the time. One of the few topographers to travel the whole length of the river from Plynlimon, he published *Picturesque Views on the River Wye* in 1797, with sepia aqua-tints of his sketches, including *Chepstow &c from Persfield*, *Monmouth from a neighbouring hill*, *Simmonds*

Rock (showing four horses pulling a boat over the New Weir), and a view of Monmouth looking along the river to the bridge. Plate 8 shows his view of Llandogo, with a Wye tour boat. Two other highly respected artists came to the Wye a few years after Ireland, both leading members of the Norwich Society of Artists. John Sell Cotman (1782-1842) was drawing master at Norwich and later at King's College, London. In 1800 he produced a painting of Tintern Abbey at night, with the moon showing through the west window, and a watercolour drawing of Monnow Bridge, later published as an etching in 1838. The same subjects were painted five years later by John Crome (1768-1821), founder of the Norwich School, who was influenced by Dutch genre painting.

In the same period, two London artists toured the Wye together in 1803, both making pencil sketches of Goodrich Castle (Plates 5 and 17). Cornelius Varley (1781-1873) was one of a family of artists, a founder member of the Society of Painters in Water Colour and a member of a winter sketching club called The Society for the study of Epic and Pastoral Design. His interest in light and shadow and cloud formations was expressed in broad watercolours, free from the influence of theories of the ideal or picturesque. His friend Joshua Cristall (1768-1847), also a founder of the Society of Painters in Water Colour, and later its President, read Virgil as a boy and painted nymphs and shepherds in harmony with nature. In 1823, at the climax of his career, he settled in Goodrich, where he produced some of his best work, mainly of peasant girls cutting bracken, but also delicate paintings and drawings of Goodrich Castle and Coldwell Rocks. He joined the committee of the Ross Society for the Encouragement of the Progress of Fine Arts and in 1827, helped to mount an exhibition of 200 paintings, the first art exhibition in Herefordshire and one of the first in England outside the major cities.

In 1821, A.V. Copley Fielding (1787-1855), published his *Illustrations of the River Wye,* with aquatints by his brother of his watercolours. A pupil of John Varley (brother of Cornelius), he later became president of the Old Watercolour Society. Another leading 19th-century watercolourist, Peter de Wint (1784-1849), who painted idealised landscapes ignoring the increasing industrialization, made several tours of Wales in the 1830s, calling it 'a painter's country'. An engraving of Goodrich Castle, with a team of bow hauliers pulling a boat upriver in the foreground, was based on one of his drawings.

Yet another theatrical scene-painter, David Cox (1783-1859), later became a drawing master and exhibited at the Royal Academy from 1805 to 1855. His early work was topographical with a bias towards the picturesque, but later his style became broader. He worked in Hereford for some years, and was considered to be the official painter of Welsh views. His pictures around the Lower Wye include an etching of Monnow Bridge of 1827 and a watercolour overlooking Monmouth (Plate 39). His son, also David Cox, (1809-1855) painted too, and for several years, David Cox senior added the figures to his son's landscapes. The illustrations produced by Radclyffe from paintings by both Coxes in Roscoe (1836) and Twamley (1839), include images of New Weir, Coldwell Rocks by moonlight (Plate 9) and Goodrich Castle. Another Hereford artist was James Wathen (1751-1828). Known locally as 'Jimmy Sketch', he was an amateur who painted many watercolour sketches between 1790 and 1820, for reproduction in guidebooks, including one in 1793 of Capler Wood, one of the few pictures showing the river between Hereford and Ross. He also acted as a guide to the Wye for writers and artists and exchanged sketches with them.

In 1835, Samuel Palmer (1805-1881) became one of the last really great artists to visit the Wye Valley. Arriving after a tour of North Wales, he painted a delicate, unfinished sketch, *Tintern from the Chepstow Road.* In a letter to George Richmond he wrote:

61

We have this evening got into a nook for which I would give all the Welch mountains ... I think of the Abbey – and such an Abbey! The lightest Gothic – trellised with ivy and rising from a wilderness of orchards – and set like a gem amongst the folding of the woody hills'.

Said by Kenneth Clark to be the last painter of Virgilian landscapes, he founded the Shoreham School of Painters (1825) with William Blake, and together they created their own Golden Age, with pictures showing a mystical reverence for nature.

Throughout the 19th century, many minor artists made a living producing pictures of British towns and countryside, mainly for reproduction in guidebooks and folios. One, John Preston Neale (*c.*1771-1847), who started as a post office clerk, exhibited at the Royal Academy. He produced architectural pen drawings tinted with watercolour, included in *Seats of the Nobility and Gentry* 1822-4 and the *Beauties of England and Wales*, and painted the oil *The Wye at Symond's Yat* looking towards Coldwell Rocks (Plate 29). One of the most prolific artists of the period, William Henry Bartlett (1809-1854), produced much brighter watercolours than earlier artists. More steel engravings were made from his work than any other topographical painter; one, *The vale of Tintern from the Devil's Pulpit* (Plate 6), was published in 1845 in W. Beattie's *The Castles and Abbeys of England*. Watercolours he produced for an unknown patron, now in the National Library of Wales, include New Weir (Plate 30), Goodrich Castle, Monmouth and Coldwell Rocks (Plate 3 shows the lithograph). He visited Europe, the Near East and America but died relatively young, from a tropical disease, while returning by boat from a sketching trip in Egypt. William Callow (1812-1908), painted landscapes, buildings and seascapes all over Europe, and produced a watercolour of Wilton Castle and Bridge in 1848 (Plate 13). Known as the Victorian heir of the picturesque, topographical school, he was secretary of the Old Watercolour Society from 1866-1870, exhibiting there for 70 years. Ralph Lucas (1794-1874) painted six watercolours at Piercefield around 1840, including one of Piercefield House (Plate 54). They are identical in composition to the lithographs by George Eyre Brooks, (fl. 1820s-1830s), but it is not known which were produced first. Two lithographs of the view from the Wyndcliff, one by Brooks (Plate 49) and one by C.J. Greenwood (fl. 1840-1852) (Plate 2) show the landscape from slightly different angles, both making a feature of the tourists and the boats on the river below.

Two late 19th- and early 20th-century artists deserve a place in this book. H. Sutton Palmer (1854-1933) studied at the Royal College of Art and was elected to the Royal Institute of Watercolour Painters in 1920. His watercolours for A.G. Bradley's *The Rivers and Streams of England* (1909) and *The Wye* (1910) include Lydbrook (Plate 19) and the view from near Symonds Yat Rock (Plate 26). A Monmouth artist, John Arthur Evans (1854-1936), lived in a cottage on the Kymin and produced some of the few paintings of the place (Plate 35). Many examples of his work are held in the Nelson Museum, Monmouth, but he was better known in the town for boasting that he was the first person in Monmouth to sell hokey-pokey icecream in his confectionery shop. A fashionable flavour in the late 19th and early 20th centuries, this was a plain icecream with added crushed caramel pieces, also known as cinder toffee.

Chapter 5
A journey down the Wye – Ross to Monmouth

This and the following chapter describe the course of a Wye Tour by mixing descriptions left by the original tourists with modern observations. In particular, the intention is to record what our predecessors thought about the scenes on the river and identify the changes they would notice if they could repeat their tour today. In practice, sadly, neither they nor we can repeat their experience, for boats can no longer be hired in Ross and boatmen can no longer be found to guide us gently to Chepstow. We can, of course, canoe safely down to Bigsweir Bridge, but below that the tides are too dangerous for ordinary visitors, and anyway, neither sketching, writing nor indeed photography is compatible with paddling. Public footpaths follow most of the riverbank down to Tintern, so visitors can still see many of the views that inspired the Wye Tourists. This chapter covers the first half of the trip to Monmouth, the distance travelled by most 18th-century tourists on their first day.

Ross to Goodrich Castle

Once they had reached Ross, tourists would find an inn and hire a boat for the following day, then walk past the church to the Prospect, a promontory that overlooks a great bend of the Wye. The experience was described in Clarke's guidebook:

> The Prospect Walk adjoins the churchyard, and lies at the back of the Royal Hotel. It is a quadrangular promenade, containing some noble elms, and surrounded by a dwarf wall and iron palisades. It was laid out by Mr. Kyrle for the benefit of the public ... A most delightful view is obtained from here. The scene embraces the lovely valley of the Wye, with luxuriant woods and beautiful pastures, with glimpses of the castles of Wilton and Bridstow; whilst far in the background is seen the Skirrid, Blorenge, and Sugar-loaf mountains, in the neighbourhood of Abergavenny, and the more distant ridge of the Black mountains as far as the Hay.

Plate 12. Artist unknown View of River Wye from the Prospect at Ross *Lithograph R. Powle, publisher*
Gilpin described this view as 'very amusing' but not picturesque, for 'it is marked by no characteristic objects: it is
broken into too many parts; and it is seen from too high a point'. This lithograph, probably produced at the height of
the Wye Tour, shows two tour boats, with their awnings removed, exposing the hoop framework
(Herefordshire Heritage Services, Herefordshire Council)

Plate 12 shows this view with two Wye Tour boats waiting to depart. Today, the scene has changed little, except that the Wilton-Ross bypass sweeps across the river on an elegant concrete bridge.

John Kyrle, 'The Man of Ross', became famous in 1732 when Alexander Pope's poem *Epistle to Bathurst* described his improvements as poetic gardening. Kyrle was evidently the first person to appreciate the beauties of this part of the Wye. Indeed, he built the Prospect so that the townspeople could learn to love the view. Leith Ritchie considered that 'without the trees planted by John Kyrle, Ross would be nothing, so far as the picturesque is concerned'. Not everyone agreed: Thomas Gray (quoted by Ritchie) said that 'all points that are much elevated spoil the beauty of the valley, and make its parts which are not large, look poor and diminutive'. Kyrle also improved and restored the church, added the 'heaven-directed spire', built a reservoir as a water supply for the town, and rebuilt the causeway over the marsh to Wilton Bridge. The townspeople obviously failed to appreciate what 'The Man' had given them, for by the end of the 18th century, 75 years after Kyrle's death, Charles Heath recorded that his summerhouse was neglected, the churchyard elms had been cut down for fuel, the water supply was broken, the fountain was full of dead animals, and seats on the Prospect had been destroyed.

Once the excitement of embarkation below the Hope and Anchor Inn had receded, the first stretch of the river often proved to be disappointing. As Gilpin remarked:

The first part of the river from Ross, is tame. The banks are low; and there is scarce an object worthy of attention, except the ruins of Wilton-castle, which appear on the left, shrouded with a few trees. But the scene wants accompaniments to give it grandeur.

The watercolour of 1848 by William Callow (Plate 13) shows the castle and the six-arch bridge, built in 1597 to replace a ferry. Mr and Mrs Hall added meticulous details:

> The old bridge, which dates as far back as the reign of Elizabeth, presents some unusual features in the way in which the arch-stones are morticed, and retains marks of the 'breaking down' to arrest the on-march of Cromwell's troops.

Heath agreed that the first part of the voyage lacked excitement:

> From Ross to Goodrich castle, a distance of nearly four miles the river has little interesting, if we except this sinuous course, which plays in the most amusing manner through meadows of the richest verdure, filled with cattle cropping the green herbage.

Cattle still graze some of the meadows, but many fields have been converted to arable, despite being flooded nearly every winter. Away from the river on the left bank is a rapidly expanding sea of polytunnels, a plastic blot on the landscape. A little further on Joseph Farington noted:

> The river passing under a lofty bank, covered with light, beautiful trees, – at the top is a House called Pencraik belonging to a Mr. Robinson, most pleasantly situated, – the effect of the whole was very pleasing; the colour of the wood, sober, dark & varied against a mottled sky.

Plate 13. William Callow Wilton Castle and bridge Watercolour 1848
William Callow was a well-known watercolourist, and considered to be the Victorian heir of the picturesque tradition.
This picture, painted a third of the way through his long life, shows a masterful control of tone and clever composition to include both bridge and castle (Herefordshire Heritage Services, Herefordshire Council)

Plate 14. John Harris Goodrich Castle *Mixed media 2005*
I had painted this view (risking my life on the side of the A40!) several times before. My initial attraction to the scene was its perfect composition with the castle as the focal point. In this particular painting I deliberately strengthened the colours conveying a strong right to left light (Wye Tour Exhibition)

Commentators did not always agree on what exactly was picturesque. According to Leith Ritchie, as the boats approached Goodrich Castle, the scenery changed 'from the gentle, the graceful, the gay' to 'the picturesque, the bold and the grand'. Gilpin had pronounced opinions on the value of this, the 'first grand view':

> After sailing four miles from Ross, we came to Goodrich-castle; where a grand view presented itself; and we rested on our oars to examine it. A reach of the river, forming a noble bay, is spread before the eye. The bank, on the right, is steep, and covered with wood; beyond which a bold promontory shoots out, crowned with a castle, rising among the trees. This view, which is one of the grandest on the river, I should not scruple to call correctly picturesque; which is seldom the character of a purely natural scene.

William Coxe, however, thought the view only became fully picturesque *under* the castle:

> The first view of these ruins, which present themselves at a sudden bend of the river, crowning the summit of an eminence clothed with wood, is extremely grand and interesting; they vanish and reappear at different intervals, and as we passed under them assumed a less majestic, but a more picturesque aspect.

On the other hand, Joseph Farington was moderately impressed with the distant view of the castle, but thought little of it close to:

> The situation of Goodrich Castle is on the whole picturesque, the Hill on which it stands being formed of good lines for a picture; but the Castle itself exhibits no striking features; so that the effect arises from the general form and mass of all the parts collectively and not from the commanding character of any single part.

We can still experience the drama of this scene today if we have a canoe, but access to good views on the banks is more difficult. When my husband and I hired a Canadian canoe and paddled doggedly down from Ross on a very hot day, the castle suddenly appeared as we rounded the bend, so exactly like Gilpin's description that I felt I had been there before. On another occasion I took the footpath from Kerne Bridge on the castle side, once the horse towing path, but ploughed so enthusiastically that the walk was a heavy, muddy slog. Passing beyond the castle and looking back at the towers rising above the winter trees, both the same pinkish grey, I slithered down the bank to river level to get a better angle for a photograph, wishing desperately that I could project my camera out into the centre of the water on a long pole. John Harris claimed to have risked his life photographing the view from the A40 (Plate 14), which gives an unusual angle on the castle and its promontory, and Ann Baxter-Wright has painted the castle from a low viewpoint across the river, with picturesque dead trees in the foreground (Plate 15).

Plate 15. Ann Baxter Wright Goodrich Castle from Walford *Oil 2005*
I've always loved the pink sandstone of Goodrich Castle glowing on the hill. I felt the painting was a bit like the Celestial City from the Slough of Despond!! (Wye Tour Exhibition)

Plate 16. Jennifer Catterall Dark castle *Pastel 2005*
The dark history of the castle influenced my feelings about Goodrich rather
than the romantic ruin on the skyline that can be seen from the river below.
A young girl was incarcerated during the civil war for falling in love and eloping
with a soldier from the attacking forces. My choice of colours was influenced
by this story, particularly the purple and red at the heart of the picture and the
powerful colours of the castle against the drab grey sky
(Wye Tour Exhibition)

Goodrich Castle was built to guard the ford on one of the main Roman routes between England and Wales. Started by Godric Mappeston or Mapsonne, who was mentioned in the Domesday Book, it remains the largest and finest medieval ruin in Herefordshire and a good example of a border castle. The Earl of Derby, the future Henry IV, once feasted here when he heard of the birth of his son at Monmouth. He is said to have been told the news by the ferryman and granted him and his family the rights to the ferry. Jennifer Catterall's romantic painting (Plate 16) reflects her knowledge of the castle's darker history. In 1646 it was amongst the last strongholds to fall during the Civil War. After eighty barrels of powder had been voted by the Commons for use at Goodrich, according to Mr and Mrs Hall, Colonel Birch used a 'battering cannon', 'two monster pieces' and 'six granadoes' for four months until the governor and his troops surrendered and were taken prisoner. Parliament decreed that the castle should be 'totally disgarrisonned and slighted', but despite the battering and the removal of the lead from the roof, the gatehouse, keep and curtain walls remain largely intact.

Most of the tourists made their first stop at Goodrich ferry, then climbed the hill to inspect the castle, though Gilpin excused himself on account of the rain. William Coxe recorded: 'Having breakfasted at a ferry house at the foot of the hill on which the castle is situated, we ascended the steep sides of the acclivity, through rich groves of oak and elm, to the ruins which on our approach reassumed their former grandeur.' Joseph Farington described an 'Ale house kept by the people who have the Care of the Ferry' where he first saw cider being made. He crossed on the ferry to get the best view of the castle, but thought the light would have been better for a sketch if he could have waited until evening. A boy was persuaded to carry Farington's drawing apparatus up the hill, but gave up after a short distance and Farington, obliged to carry the stuff himself, became very hot and regretted leaving the boat, for 'nothing was concealed that on nearer inspection seemed considerable or interesting'. Louisa Anne Twamley was more easily impressed:

> The entrance is very beautiful: you look under a lofty gateway, between towers canopied with ivy, along a gloomy array of portcullises and archways, extending fifty feet; then across the open area, and beyond that through a lofty arch, which gracefully frames the picture of the distant Court.

The Court, incidentally, was Goodrich Court. Built in 1828, in the combined styles of Edward I, II and III, to house a collection of armour, it proved in 1949 to be unsaleable, so the fittings were auctioned off and the building was pulled down.

Ivy and other vegetation once helped to impart an air of gloom and mystery to the castle. An unfinished pencil drawing by Cornelius Varley of 1803 (Plate 17) shows just how prolific the ivy became. Varley may have visited Goodrich with Joshua Cristall (Plate 5): certainly they took the Tour together and their drawings are similar. Ivy still covered the castle in 1910, according to A.G. Bradley, and the moat was choked with ferns and foliage.

Mr and Mrs Hall toured the castle with a guide, and described the view from the keep:

Plate 17. Cornelius Varley Goodrich Castle *Pencil sketch 1803*
This marvellous unfinished sketch, carried out when Cornelius Varley did
the Wye Tour with his friend Joshua Cristall, gives a very good idea of how much the shrubs and the vegetation added
to the romantic or picturesque atmosphere of the castle, and made it seem almost a natural part of the environment
(Herefordshire Heritage Services, Herefordshire Council)

Hills, enclosing fertile vales; dense woods surrounding pasture-fields, dotted with sheep; low meadow lands, on which luxuriate the famous Herefordshire cows, known here and everywhere by their red coats and white face. On one side are the distant Malvern Hills; on another, the hills that look down upon Hereford city. Further off are the Welsh mountains; while, moving southwards, we see the Coldwell rocks, Symond's Yat Rock, and the tall Kymin, that hangs over Monmouth … Doward Hill and Coppett Hill rise above the river, crossed by a bridge, Kerne Bridge, very near to which are the venerable remains of Flanesford … From this spot we best note the singular windings of the Wye: from Goodrich Ferry underneath us to Huntsham Ferry is a distance of only one mile, while by water there is a space of eight miles to be traversed between one ferry and the other.

Today, the view from the keep has hardly changed, though at least 90% of the fields are ploughed. On my December visit sheep grazed the lower slopes of Coppet Hill, and some were folded on arable in two fields nearer the river, but the Herefordshire cattle were nowhere to be seen. Cars passed frequently over Kerne Bridge and the sound of traffic on the A40 was very noticeable. A beech plantation beside the track to the castle now obscures the Halls' view of Coldwell Rocks, but I could just make out the shape of the Kymin through the tops of the bare branches. Turning clockwise, an avenue of hybrid limes on the skyline marks the drive to Goodrich Court, and to the north-west, looking down on the river, the newly-ploughed fields on either side gleam wetly in the furrows. Pylons march in line across the fields to the north and several fields of polytunnels, looking at this distance like rectangular sheets of water, distract the view to the spire of Ross church. Further round, to the north-east, another line of pylons, shining in the sun above the tower of Walford church, follows the line of the old Wye meander round Chase Hill.

Goodrich to Coldwell Rocks

On a rare sunny day in December we set out on a circular ten mile walk from Goodrich, to enjoy the river views and identify the changes in the landscape since the heyday of the Tour. Coming down the road from the village, wisps of mist were rising from the gleaming river, and the dark winter trees were spiky against the fields. Kerne Bridge would not have been seen by the early tourists, as it was built in 1828; it is considered amongst the most beautiful bridges over the Wye. Taking the right-bank footpath downriver, we looked back at Goodrich Castle glowing on the skyline above Flanesford Priory. In 1803, Joseph Farington noted that the Priory had become a farm of 200 acres for which the farmer paid 200 guineas a year. Now it advertises itself as luxury self-catering apartments, for weddings, parties and special occasions.

Reverend T.D. Fosbroke, who lived nearby at Walford, described this stretch of the river:

From hence the Wye takes a bold turn, at which commences the proper introduction of its characteristic scenery, mountainous and rocky banks, here in fine undulating outlines of harmonious curves. Upon the right side is the long steep ridge of Coppet wood, teethed at the beginning with a ledge of rude rocks, ground partly heath, partly wood: upon the left is Bishop's wood, a more gradual ascent, dotted irregularly with cottages, orchards, and patches of wood, all rising in amphitheater above each other.

Coppet Hill Common, now densely wooded, was open pasture in the past, kept open partly by commoners, who cut wood to burn and bracken for bedding. As we proceeded below the hill, several kayaks were launched on the far bank and were rapidly swept downriver in the strong current. 200 years ago the tourists saw coracles instead of canoes, but coracles last bobbed on the Wye in 1910 – at Kerne Bridge. After 1873, tourists would have seen the Ross to Monmouth railway on the left bank, crossing the river diagonally on a girder bridge and running into a tunnel under Coppet Hill before emerging and re-crossing the river, where it joined the Severn and Wye railway at Lydbrook Junction. Both tunnel portals are now hidden in the woods, the tracks and the first bridge were removed in 1964, and the puffs and hoots of the trains have been replaced by the perpetually intrusive noise of traffic on the Lydbrook to Kerne Bridge road. Other modern additions include not only several more houses on the far bank, spruce plantations and wire fences, but also the inevitable plastic bags caught up on branches overhanging the river.

We turned into a straight reach of the river, into the view that Gilpin had described from his boat:

Plate 18. Stephen Curtis Ruardean Church *Oil 2005*
The view exactly epitomizes the terrain along the Wye; high and dense vegetation on one bank and open countryside on the other; huge and exciting strong tonal differential (Wye Tour Exhibition)

> The view at Rure-dean-church unfolds itself next; which is a scene of great grandeur. Here, both sides of the river are steep, and both woody; but in one the woods are intermixed with rocks. The deep umbrage of the forest of Dean occupies the front; and the spire of the church rises among the trees. The reach of the river ... is a noble piece of natural perspective [which] continues some time before the eye: but when the spire comes directly in front, the grandeur of the landscape is gone.

Gilpin's church is the 14th-century St John's, which stands on Ruardean Hill, the highest point in the Forest of Dean. The spire, which reaches to 1,000 feet above sea level, can still be viewed from the river bank, though interrupted repeatedly by large trees overhanging the river. Stephen Curtis's painting, with the spire reflected in the river (Plate 18), is a classic Claudean composition, with dramatic tonal contrasts.

Samuel Ireland described this reach of the river by concentrating on the contrast between the rural and the industrial:

> Its banks are screened on the south, by an extensive coppice wood, and on the north by the fertile meadows rising towards Bishopswood, from which a considerable iron furnace in the vicinity derives its name. From the stone quarries in the neighbourhood the new bridge at Bristol was principally erected.

The spoil heaps of the quarry can still be seen from the footpath, but are now covered in trees. Iron working started at Bishopswood in the 16th century, using charcoal from the nearby coppice woods. In 1810, a tramway was completed to carry the iron to Lydbrook, but four years later the furnace closed. From the opposite bank, all we could see was a group of chalets or (non) mobile homes perched above the river, and on the hill behind, houses stacked up the slope, just as Samuel Rogers described them in 1791:

> Cottages perched one above another, half sheltered with wood, and often discovered only by the blue wreaths of smoke that ascended from them ... a chain of orchards, the apple-trees twisting into a thousand forms.

Little has changed in the last 200 years in the approach to Lydbrook across the floodplain meadows, though the shiny railings, metal tower and CCTV cameras of the water abstraction plant on the left bank create a jarring contrast. Lydbrook, however, is one of several settlements below Ross which have changed dramatically with the death of their industries. Once it was an important industrial centre: the first successful blast furnace in the Forest of Dean was built here (in 1608), and in 1817 it contained three forges, rolling and bar mills and a tin-plate works.

William Gilpin approved of the contrast between industry and its woodland setting:

> At Lidbroke is a large wharf, where coals are shipped for Hereford, and other places ... A road runs diagonally along the bank; and horses and carts appear passing the small vessels, which lie against the wharf, to receive their burdens. Close behind, a rich, woody hill hangs sloping over the wharf, and forms a grand background to the whole. The contrast of all this business, the engines used in lading, and unlading, together with the solemnity of the scene, produce all together a picturesque, assemblage. The sloping hill is the front-screen; the two side screens are low.

Nearly a century later, Mr and Mrs Hall also enjoyed the contrast:

> The village ... presents a busy and bustling scene; the smoke from tall chimneys rising above the foliage, and the boats and barges at the quay forming a picture somewhat singular and striking in this peculiarly rural district. We may, for the moment, fancy ourselves gazing up one of the wooded slopes that borders the busy town of Sheffield.

William Coxe, however, was more interested in the labour involved in hauling the coal than in the visual aspects: 'From Lidbrook large quantities of coal are sent to Ross and Hereford; and we passed several barges towed by ten or eleven men, which by great exertions are drawn to Hereford in two days.' Since a man could pull only one ton, large teams were needed to haul the barges, and even more were needed to drag boats over shallows during periods of low water. In 1808, a horse towing path costing £5,000 was opened between Lydbrook and Hereford, only to be replaced in the 1840s by a canal from Gloucester to Hereford.

No 18th- or 19th-century paintings of Lydbrook's riverside industry have come to light. Sutton Palmer's watercolour of 1910 (Plate 19), looking upriver to Lydbrook, shows a very peaceful scene,

Plate 19. Sutton Palmer Lydbrook *Watercolour 1910*
This idyllic view looking upriver to Lydbrook brings out the slightly hazy appearance often generated on the Lower Wye by the steep-sided, wooded hills and the soft atmosphere. The industry and the railway viaduct have been successfully hidden behind the bank of trees on the right (The Wye A.G. Bradley)

Plate 20. Audrey Hart Lydbrook has a history *Oil 2005*
I have depicted what I feel to be relevant to Lydbrook in 2005 – its
dark past and its equally dark present. I painted this imaginary
picture because I felt so strongly about the situation, and it came together
very quickly, to my satisfaction. I have deliberately lit up the church,
shining out over the dark past and the dark present
(Wye Tour Exhibition)

whereas Audrey Hart in 2005 chose to paint the industrial past of Lydbrook, with the railway viaduct, which crossed the steep side valley (Plate 20). The wharves where coal was loaded onto barges have been transformed into grassy platforms scattered with benches overlooking the river and a large car park downriver. Two paintings of the view upriver from here (Plates 21 and 22) use strong tones to add drama. Anthony Sully's acrylic is the only modern painting to feature people in the foreground. David Prentice made the reflections of the trees his main subject, leaving out the foreground bank.

Continuing our walk towards Coldwell Rocks, we passed Courtfield House high up to our right. Originally a medieval fortified manor house where the future Henry V was reputed to have been nursed, it was rebuilt in 1805 and now sports conspicuous glass-clad 20th century additions. Next we reached Welsh Bicknor church, though not the building visited by many Wye tourists, for the church was completely rebuilt in a striking Italianate style in 1858. The ground below the church, once open, is now partly covered by scrub from which poles rise to support the power supply to the large, old rectory, now a youth hostel.

The old railway bridge, kept as a footbridge, now came into view, with the fast flowing river churning noisily around the supports. On the opposite bank, the abandoned paper mill retains an elegant octagonal brick chimney. Climbing through the woods over a stile and out into a steeply sloping pasture, the dark pointed shape of Rosemary Topping rose on the left and Coldwell Rocks could be seen glimmering pale in a notch ahead. Like the Wye tourists, we were travelling south, looking into the afternoon sun, which made the foreground dark, like a Claude painting.

Plunging again into the woods, we found the tomb of a drowned youth, whose grieving parents left a touching inscription, perhaps the only surviving physical link to an individual Wye tourist. Often described by later visitors, who climbed out of their boats to take in the sad event, the tomb is

Plate 21. Anthony Sully Couple on bench
Acrylic 2005
It was a beautiful day and these two people seemed to soak up the tranquillity of the scenery. I tried to capture the stillness of the water and contrasting shadow and light (Wye Tour Exhibition)

Plate 22. David Prentice River Wye – upstream from Lydbrook *Watercolour & reed pen 2005*
The Wye, like my longstanding work on the Malvern Hills, represents an interest in cultural and geographical edges. My work ranges from on the spot works like this to larger, elevated abstract representations of place (Wye Tour Exhibition)

Plate 23. John Harris Afternoon Light *Watercolour 2005*
My wife and I canoed down the river, sketching on the way. The bend beneath Coldwell Rocks was dramatic but I increased the drama by using strong contrasts and bringing in mist which I had seen elsewhere at times on the Wye (Wye Tour Exhibition)

swathed in stylised stone stalactites, topped with a graceful urn, and surrounded by ornamental iron railings. Obscured and eroded though they are, George could still just decipher the words as I wrote them down:

> Sacred to the memory of JOHN WHITHEAD WARRE who perished near this spot whilst bathing in the River Wye in sight of his parents brothers and sisters on 14th September 1804 in the 16th year of his age. GOD'S WILL BE DONE WHO IN His mercy granted consolation to the parents of the dear departed in the reflection that he possessed truth, innocence, filial piety and fraternal affection in the highest degree……….. THIS MONUMENT is here erected to warn parents and others to be careful how they trust the deceitful stream and particularly to exhort them to learn and observe the directions of the Humane Society for the recovery of persons apparently drowned. Alas! It is with extreme sorrow here commemorated what anguish is felt from the want of this knowledge. The lamented youth swam very well, was endowed with great bodily strength and activity and possibly had proper application been used, might have been saved from his untimely fate.

(Ironically, at this very moment, George lost his balance, fell back and rolled down towards the river bank. The corroded railing which he had been clutching parted from the rest.)

He was born at Oporto in the kingdom of Portugal on the 14th February 1789, third son of James Warre of London and of the County of Somerset, Merchant and Eleanor, daughter of Thomas Greg of Belfast Esq.

Passenger, who ere thou art, spare this tomb. It is erected for the benefit of the surviving, being but a poor record of the grief of those that witnessed the sad occasion of it. God preserve you and yours from such a calamity, should you not require their assistance, that if you unfortunately should, the apparatus with instructions for their application by the Humane Society for the Saving of Persons Apparently Drowned are lodged at the church at Coldwell.

Plate 24. Susan Peterken The Sentinels *Pastel 2005*
Approaching Coldwell Rocks by canoe is far more
awe-inspiring than walking along the bank – the rocks seem to
loom above you. I wanted to accentuate the feeling of the height
of the rocks by the vertical format, and by including reflections
with some vertical lines. I reduced the chaos of the vegetation
to simple shapes to increase the power of the rock shapes – the
colours were inspired by the pinky-grey of the sunlit winter trees
(Wye Tour Exhibition)

Since there is no church at Coldwell, any apparently-drowned tourists would be unwise to rely on these instructions.

The path was now some distance from the road, and as we approached Coldwell Rocks, the only sound was of buzzards calling mournfully overhead. From this point, we left the river and took a path up through woodland onto Coppet Hill and back to Goodrich. The view from above Goodrich is panoramic, but few Wye tourists would have had enough time to see it.

I have twice paddled a canoe below Coldwell Rocks, and have found it to be the most sublime or dramatic section of our trips from Ross to Symonds Yat. John Harris also approached the rocks by canoe but chose a more distant viewpoint for his atmospheric watercolour (Plate 23). Below the rock, the water seems darker; I featured it in my pastel painting (Plate 24) and the Reverend Fosbroke mentioned it 200 years earlier:

The scene at Coldwell, on the left side commences by a grand mass of rock, partially insulated, of rude resemblance to the square keep of a ruined castle … The attitudes of the rocks, though all in fanciful caprice, are of graceful informality, and display irregular outlines, and broad masses, relieved by creeping lichens, and weather stains … The river too is deep, dark, and solemn.

Another Reverend, William Coxe, also noticed the resemblance to castles: 'like the battlements of an immense castle, as much more sublime than Goodrich, as nature is superior to art', and Hazel Pickering's painting suggests castle towers or possibly even lighthouses or modern glass tower blocks (Plate 25). Joseph Farington, however, had a much more practical attitude:

> At this point I decided the preference of the Scenery of the Wye in this part over that of Matlock, to which it bears a nearer general resemblance than to any other that I remember. To speak in the language of the painter, the combination of lines in the scenery here is better than that of Matlock, and the parts are seen to more advantage ... at Matlock, there are very few points where an artist could take a stand to make a picture, the choice in this respect is much greater upon the Wye where the assemblage of objects is frequently so happy as to present a compleat composition.

Plate 25. Hazel Pickering Morning Glow *Acrylic 2005*
The main impression I had was of soaring cliffs on a crisp, bright, early spring day, and listening to the calls of falcon, buzzards and rooks in the surrounding trees. I wanted to show the clear bright sunlight, and the winter season (yellow and blue), and give height and structure to the rocks with the cold clear waters of the river running below (the clean sharp lines), although in reality the colours are greys and browns, the rocks covered in trees, and their outlines indistinct (Wye Tour Exhibition)

The lithograph after William Bartlett shows the whole sweep of Coldwell Rocks, with Symonds Yat Rock on the right (Plate 3). The engraving by D. Radclyffe from a watercolour by David Cox depicts a similar view, made more dramatic by the moonlight, with a Wye Tour boat in the foreground, apparently rowing upriver (Plate 9).

In 1861 Mr and Mrs Hall, as was their custom, embellished their description with facts given to them by their boatman:

> A succession of rocks – bare in parts, and in others clad in green – hanging almost perpendicularly over the river, are separated by deep and narrow clefts, in which grow a variety of trees, some of them rising so high as to be on a level with the hill-top ... As we approach it we see Raven Cliff right before us; presently a pretty peaked rock ... comes in sight, then Symond's Yat; then Vansittart's Rock; then Adare's rock ... These rocks are all on the left bank; on the right bank is a sweep of low-lying meadow land, not unfrequently covered with water.

The rocks were named, around 1800, after a boatload of barristers from the Oxford Circuit who sailed down the Wye to the assizes at Monmouth.

Following breakfast at Goodrich, many Wye tourists took their second meal at the base of the Coldwell Rocks. Robert Bloomfield, who also had a rock named after him, described his languid meal:

> Noon scorched the fields, the boat lay to,
> The dripping oars had naught to do ...
> Here in one gay according mind
> Upon the tranquil stream we din'd
> As shepherds free on mountain heath,
> Free as the fish that watch'd beneath
> For falling crumbs where cooling lay
> The wine that cheer'd us on our way.

The peace we experience today would have been rudely shattered during the middle period of the Wye Tour, for, as Charles Heath recorded:

> The beauty and quiet of this scene has lately received considerable diminution, by the erection of an extensive Lime-Kiln just below [Coldwell Rocks], – the effluvia from which is not only disagreeable in itself, but obscures by its smoke the appearance, in some places of those beautiful greens, with which the rocks are cloathed, and for which they are so peculiarly admired.

However, Leith Ritchie thought:

> The shadowy hollows scooped out of the sides of the precipices, and overhung by foliage, which are nothing more than the sites of lime kilns, are more advantageous to the picture than the finest ruins imaginable.

Tranquillity would have been further eroded when the railway was built along the base of the cliffs. This certainly offered the train passengers a brief sublime experience, but it surely detracted from the atmosphere for tourists in the boats.

At the end of this reach, most tourists climbed up to Yat Rock, thereby gaining a view but missing the four mile loop of the river out into the lowlands. William Coxe, however, decided to stay in the boat: 'I was unwilling to lose the beauties of the ever shifting scenery, and preferred a succession of home views on the banks beneath, to the most boundless expanse of prospects from above.' William Gilpin also declined the climb to the viewpoint because of bad weather:

> The water-views, in this part, were very tame. We left the rocks, and precipices behind; exchanging them for low-banks and sedges. But the grand scenery soon returned. ... Here we sailed through a long reach of hills; whose sloping sides were covered with large, lumpish, detached stones, which seemed, in a course of years, to have rolled from a girdle of rocks, that surrounds the upper regions of these high grounds.

Recent tree felling on Huntsham Hill has again revealed these enormous conglomerate boulders, which must have slid down the hill from the outcrop during distant glaciations.

Plate 26. Sutton Palmer View from Symonds Yat *Watercolour 1910*
It is difficult to understand why Palmer chose to draw this view north from the col
between the Rock and Huntsham Hill, rather than from the top of the Rock itself,
as it lacks the drama of looking straight down onto the river.
This autumnal view depicts the dead bracken on Coppet Hill, the only hill in the
area to show this colour (The Wye A.G. Bradley)

Plate 27. Lindsay Steele Symonds Yat Rock *Mixed media 2006*
This was my first visit to the Wye Valley and I was amazed at the breathtaking
view from Symonds Yat. I took some time sketching it and painted it at home
while the impact was still fresh in my mind. As I was working from a drawing I
was able to take liberties with the colours (Wye Tour Exhibition)

Symonds Yat Rock and New Weir

Symonds Yat Rock is now by far the most popular viewpoint on the Lower Wye, with coach-loads and car-loads of tourists arriving every day at the vast Forestry Commission car park. The view northwards is included in every guide book, leaflet, calendar and poster, although surprisingly I have been unable to find any 18th- or 19th- century pictures – the watercolour by Sutton Palmer (Plate 26) is early 20th century. The mixed media picture (Plate 27) by Lindsay Steele and my pastel (Plate 28) are both very personal interpretations, exploring the use of colour and texture to flatten the view into a pattern. Many visitors come to watch the peregrines, which returned to nest on Coldwell Rocks in 1981 after an absence of 30 years: the view south-eastwards towards the nest site was painted by John Preston Neale (Plate 29). The popularity of Yat Rock as a viewpoint must lie partly in the surprising behaviour of the river, which was clearly expressed by A.G. Bradley in 1910:

Here, bewilderment is always blended with admiration. For the three reaches of the Wye that glimmer in various directions so far below may well be, as in truth they are, the despair of the uninitiated as to whither they go and whence they come. It is one thing to look at the flat surface of a map, but quite another to stand up here for the first time, as thousands do, with no particular topographical notion of the district at command, and be immediately challenged, as it were, by the river to explain its strange contortions.

Today there is little sense of achievement in reaching Yat Rock. After leaving the car park, visitors saunter up a gently sloping path cut through the banks and ditches of an Iron Age Fort, past a café and gift shop, over a footbridge high above the road to Huntsham Bridge, through a tunnel of trees, and suddenly arrive on a rocky platform, safely insulated from the edge of the precipice by a stone wall.

The drama and danger felt by 18th- and 19th- century tourists perched on this small platform of rock, with nothing to stop them falling hundreds of feet down to the river below, has surely been lost. This sublime experience was hard-earned: tourists had to climb 650 feet (200m) from the base of Coldwell Rocks and the route through the trees was so uncertain that a guide was needed. Robert Bloomfield describes how his party ascended the rock:

Some airy height he climes amain,
And finds the silver eel again.
No fears we form'd, no labours counted,
Yet SYMMON'S YAT must be surmounted!
A tower of rock, that seems to cry
'Go round about me neighbour WYE'.
On went the boat, and up the steep
Her straggling crew began to creep,
To gain the ridge, enjoy the view,
Where the fresh gales of summer blew.
The gleaming WYE, that circles round
Her four mile course, again is found;
And crouching to the conqueror's pride,
Bathes his huge cliffs on either side;
Seen at one glance, when from his brow
The eye surveys twin gulfs below.

Plate 28. Susan Peterken The view from the Rock
Pastel 2005
I visited Yat Rock late on a winter's afternoon and the strong shadow cast by the hill on the left seemed to add a new dimension to the familiar view. I wanted to explore the ambiguity between reducing the shapes to a flat pattern and maintaining a feeling of depth and space. I chose purple for the shadow shape and the other colours developed from that (Wye Tour Exhibition)

Louisa Twamley certainly felt the effort of climbing up to the Rock was worthwhile:

In due time we gained the platform of rock crowning the narrow ridge, and I was well rewarded for my toils and tumbles, by the grand view spread around; with the Wye

Plate 29. John Preston Neale
The Wye at Symond's Yat Oil
Date unknown
This view upriver, shows Symonds
Yat Rock on the right, with the
Coldwell Rocks, now the peregrine
nesting site, curving round the
bend beyond. The wooded nature
of the gorge is well illustrated
here. John Neale was well
known for his architectural pen
drawings but this painting shows
his mastery of oils, dramatic
composition and his subtle
treatment of the tree canopy
(Llyfrgell Genedlaethol Cymru/
National Library of Wales)

Plate 30. W H Bartlett New Weir from Symond's Yat rock Watercolour c.1840
Looking downriver towards Monmouth, this picture shows the Longstone as one of the pinnacles on the left with the
Great Doward on the right. The weir is very conspicuous, demonstrating that it formed a considerable obstacle to river
traffic (Llyfrgell Genedlaethol Cymru/National Library of Wales)

winding about below, ... Numbers of mules laden with coal pass over this high ridge, from the forest of Dean, and descend on the south side, where they are ferried over the Wye, and carry their burdens up to the kilns on the Great Doward, which are wholly supplied in this manner.

The mules and their packs are clearly shown in W.H. Bartlett's watercolour (Plate 30). Curiously, the mules had changed into cattle when the painting was turned into a lithograph.

Analysis rather than enjoyment was what the Revd T.D. Fosbroke had in mind:

> From hence is a superb bird's-eye-view of the adjacent objects, and a far-extending prospect in what may be called from Claude's Pictures, the painter's map style. The near view is Salvator Rosa, the distant that of the master first named. The summit itself is a romantic green floor, walled in, without any formality, by copse-wood, and is approached by a winding, rocky road between high banks, under arches of hazel and underwood.

Baedeker's guidebook compared the view to one on the continent: 'The tourist may leave the boat to navigate this bend, while he ascends Symond's Yat (660ft), the hill at the neck of the loop, commanding an exquisite view of rocks, and woods, and meadows, not unlike the view from the Marienburg at Alf, on the Moselle.' There was indeed a remarkable similarity between the two views. The loop of the river is actually 3.5 miles (5.6 km) long, but writers usually quote four or five miles, and Henry Skrine was impressed enough in 1798 to go further: 'Looked down in astonishment on the river forming a prodigious circle of seven miles round this grand promontory.'

The view north and east from Yat Rock cannot have changed much. On a recent January visit, I looked down on the reach flowing under Coldwell Rocks and swinging north: pastures still extend along the far bank, the slopes of Coppet Hill were glowing tawny-brown with dead bracken, and Huntsham Hill is still covered with trees, albeit embellished with an L-shaped conifer plantation. In contrast, the westward view across the south-flowing loop has changed considerably, for the slopes of the Doward are now covered with a scatter of large houses, interspersed with trees. Louisa Anne Twamley noted:

> The Great Doward is galleried and quarried from head to foot, and the smoke rising from the numerous lime-kilns scattered about, half-hiding the cottages which are perched high and low amid the cliffs and precipices, renders the scene one of great wildness and grandeur.

Mr and Mrs Hall described the sights and sounds associated with the industry:

> Now and then, a boat, with oars or sail, or a laden barge, passes up or down, the boatman's song ascending; or you hear the workman's tool ringing through the air as he forces the limestone from the mass, to burn in lime kilns, picturesquely scattered on the hillside.

A.G. Bradley decided that the best vista from Yat Rock was from the path down to New Weir:

> From hence he will look right down the gorge where the now large river flashes away southwards in a succession of sparkling rapids and surging salmon pools, between lofty precipitous hills, wooded from their summit virtually to the water's edge, and like the rest buttressed with jagged and castellated crags of limestone rock.

Plate 31. Gordon Trow September at Symonds Yat *Oil 2005*
The subject interested me because of the September afternoon light on the
sparkling water and of course the autumn colouring
on the wooded background (Wye Tour Exhibition)

This view, or one from a similar vantage point, is shown by William Bartlett in his watercolour of about 1840 (Plate 30), but trees now obscure it, as we discovered when we walked down a long diagonal track, with occasional gleams of the river below through the winter trees. However, the Long Stone, the largest of the remaining pinnacles, still reared up against the sky on our left like a dark misshapen church tower. Much the same view can be seen from a newly-opened overlook, reached by a short path behind the Forestry Commission's café. From here I could look down onto New Weir, where a few canoes were braving the rapids close to a wooded island. The channel on the far side, which is where the lock used to be, is now almost as wide as the main river, but an early 20th-century photograph shows it to have been completely silted up.

New Weir was an important industrial centre immediately west of Yat Rock, set against a backdrop of precipitous woods and limestone towers. The name has disappeared from maps and guidebooks to be replaced by Symonds Yat East and West, both straggles of hotels, shops and houses, but still connected by a rope ferry across the river from The Saracen's Head. Gordon Trow's oil painting (Plate 31) and Susanna Birley's watercolour (Plate 32) show two very contrasting interpretations of boats and buildings on the river. When William Gilpin approached by boat he was impressed:

> From these rocks, we soon approached the New-Weir; which may be called the second grand scene on the Wye. The river is wider, than usual, in this part; and takes a sweep round a towering promontory of rock; which forms the side-screen on the left; and is the grand feature of the view. It is ... a woody hill, from which large projections, in two or three places, burst out; rudely hung with twisting branches, and shaggy furniture; which, like mane round the lion's head, give a more savage air to these wild exhibitions of nature ... Its lower skirts are adorned with a hamlet; in the midst of which, volumes of thick smoke, thrown up at intervals, from an iron-forge ... add double grandeur to the scene ... But what particularly marks this view, is a circumstance on the water. The whole river, at this place, makes a precipitate fall; of no great height indeed; but enough to merit the title of cascade ... all was agitation and uproar; and every steep, and every rock stared with wildness, and terror.

There had been an iron forge at New Weir since 1684 and most of the Wye tourists were impressed by the combination of the smoke and the sounds of the hammers and the water rushing

Plate 32. Susanna Birley Wye rapids – Symonds Yat *Watercolour 2005* This particular viewpoint was impossible to sketch. I had to hang right out over the river in order to take a photograph! I wanted to show how the weir, which was in place in the 18th century has now worn away *(Wye Tour Exhibition)*

33. Michael 'Angelo' Rooker New Weir *Oil 1780s*
The iron works were still in operation when this picture was painted and the associated buildings can be seen in the middle distance. On the far bank, pack horses and a team of bow hauliers are depicted, while a trow waits in the lock (Nelson Museum Monmouth)

Plate 34. Doug Eaton The Wye at New Weir *Oil 2005*
I wanted to achieve a fairly dramatic picture with the river as the focal point, using the extreme tones and simple construction to do so (Wye Tour Exhibition)

over the weir, as Thomas Whateley described in 1770, quoted in chapter 3. By the end of the 18th century, there were two hammers, three furnaces, one chafery, one rolling mill and at least three water wheels, but by 1836, Thomas Roscoe noted:

> Now, however, all is tranquil, save the noise of the rapid current over the river where the Weir was erected – the works are pulled down and the population gone.

At one time, there were several locks on the Lower Wye, but, according to Charles Heath: 'Being considered, some years ago, rather a disadvantage than a benefit ... the river [was] divested of the impediments, except New-wear, which ... is now the only lock of the river Wye.' Michael 'Angelo' Rooker's large oil painting, recently acquired by Monmouth Museum, (Plate 33) shows a considerable drop in water-level below the weir. There was usually some difficulty in getting the boats out of the lock, as Heath describes:

> No sooner is the signal made for assistance, than young and old, boys and girls, fly to the rope, and, with a zeal the most hearty, soon deliver the vessel from the otherwise stationary situation, to the active current of the river.

The weir and flash lock were removed in 1814, which improved both the navigation and the salmon fishing. Doug Eaton's dramatic low angle view of the river shows the island by the rapid and the widening lock channel (Plate 34).

New Weir to Monmouth

From Symonds Yat to Monmouth the Wye threads its way through a magnificent gorge, but few accounts say much about it: perhaps tourists were still excited by the memory of New Weir or tired towards the end of their first day. Mr and Mrs Hall certainly glossed over this stretch: 'The scenery of this neighbourhood, although it has much beauty, has much sameness – rocks and trees overhanging water.'

On a bright warm January day, George and I set out to walk to Monmouth from the old station at Symonds Yat, now a large car park bordered until recently by the remains of the railway picket fence above the river. Our path along the old railway track has recently been resurfaced as a cycle track, though we saw no cyclists this time. The thick woodland on both sides was broken by rock outcrops, picked out by dark yew and ivy, which contrasted with the pale winter twigs of beech, oak, ash and lime, and the purple haze of buds and catkins on the alders lining the banks. Ahead, the river bends sharply to the right, so that the steep wooded slopes of the Highmeadow Woods looming straight ahead, appear to block its passage completely. Biblins Bridge appeared suddenly round the bend. Built in 1957 as a suspension bridge to carry a footpath, then rebuilt forty years later with long approach ramps instead of steps, it sways and bounces alarmingly as we cross. On the far side we made a small detour upriver to inspect the Dropping Well, which Mr and Mrs Hall described as:

> A singular formation of rocks, scattered without order, the result, probably, of some terrible earth-shaking ages ago. The water has a petrifying influence, resembling that of certain wells in Yorkshire and Derbyshire, and it has given a remarkable character to the hill sides and the huge masses of conglomerate stones which abound on the flat land that skirts the river.

We continued our walk on the right bank, through the Forestry Commission camp site, empty now, but very busy in the summer, a scene that the Wye tourists could not have imagined. As we turned the next bend, the first of the Doward Rocks emerged from dense woodland ahead of us, looking much more encroached on by vegetation than the bare rocks in the engraving after Edward Dayes (Plate 4). When Robert Bloomfield floated past the trees must have been stripped of their bark before being felled, for he noted the 'dark brown saplings flay'd alive'. These rocks are known now as the Seven Sisters, but Thomas Roscoe's colourful description suggests that only three had names:

> Lofty rocks now rise on both sides, robed in infinite varieties of wood and shrub of every imaginable tint, showing the pale grey of the limestone contrasted richly by the bright red, green, yellow and brown of the Autumn foliage. Many portions of the craggy cliffs have the appearance of ruined castles and towers. Three remarkable ones are named the three sisters, Ann, Mary and Elizabeth, right venerable personages.

Twamley invoked supernatural forces to explain the scene:

> Towers, turrets, buttresses and bastions rise behind and above one another, and the changes they perpetually assume, as the boat varies the point of view, are as beautiful, as they are strange and novel. I felt half inclined to turn round and see if Merlin, or Michael Scott, or some wizard body were not working a mighty magic spell for my mystification.

Fosbroke, normally sedate and analytical, was nearly as fanciful in trying to describe the effect of all the cliffs from Coldwell to the Little Doward:

> Castles and towns, amphitheatres and fortifications – battlements and obelisks, mock the wanderer, who fancies himself transported into the ruins of a city of some extinct race ... This extraordinary formation reaches for nearly eight miles to within about three of Monmouth.

The path continued under the Sisters, trees hiding the crags above. Soon, however, a continuous rock wall ran along the base of the hill, with numerous hillocks, the spoil heaps from quarrying. As we approached the grounds of Wyastone Leys we began to hear the distant drone of traffic on the A40. A magnificent line of planted poplars, lumpy with mistletoe, stood opposite a fair-sized island covered with willow scrub, and on the opposite bank three sinister-looking cormorants perched in the stubby branches of a dead alder, framed by the hill known as Fiddler's Elbow. As we emerged onto the meadows, the shapely cupolas of Wyastone Leys appeared ahead above the trees. Built in 1795 and enlarged in 1861, the house has recently been the headquarters of the Nimbus recording company, with a purpose-built concert hall and, further on, industrial buildings hidden incongruously amongst the trees. The former wealth of the estate can still be appreciated in the 100-foot glass-house, but the iron observation tower on the Little Doward above, which later Wye tourists would have seen, has long gone: for fear of lightning it was never completed and then in 1920 it was demolished. Below the unending reverberation of traffic on the A40's split-level carriageways, we looked back to the Little Doward, where larches were planted in the shape of a crown to commemorate the Queen's coronation, and in maturity these are still distinct against the darker surrounding conifers. The hill was certainly barer 200 years ago, as the large conglomerate boulders described then are no longer visible. One measured by Heath was 27 feet long, 7 feet broad and 6 feet thick.

Our walk continued through pasture beside the river to the arches of Monmouth's Wye Bridge. This long, straight reach is alive with rowing skiffs of various sizes in summer. As we approached the town, a line of Lombardy poplar trees echo the church spire, and early 20th-century houses straggle up the road to Hereford, where the Haberdashers' Girls' school stands out above the skyline. On the opposite bank, a large water treatment works stand above the river, glass panels in the roof glittering in the sun, then a line of (non) mobile houses and neat gardens. We skirted the Rowing Club building, and walked through a tunnel, guarded by flood gates, under the main road and into the town.

The author of the *Penny Magazine* article lyrically described his approach to Monmouth:

> The sun was setting when we came in sight of the bridge and town of Monmouth, and then the Wye lay before us like a broad path of burnished gold ... The interior of picturesque towns is not always the most comfortable. Monmouth, however, has a broad and handsome street, a capacious market-place, and seems clean and neat throughout ... As for the castle, it is gone – the last of its tottering walls fell down suddenly some years ago ... Against one dislocated bit of a wall a shed had been erected for the stabling of cart-horses and asses.

Chapter 6
A journey down the Wye – Monmouth to Chepstow

Most tourists reached Monmouth by the end of their first day and many stayed more than one night in order to visit other attractions before continuing to Chepstow. There was plenty to see around Monmouth. Mr and Mrs Hall, for example, provided a map of twenty targets, including Llanthony Abbey, Raglan Castle, Caerleon and the Forest of Dean. Continuing down the Wye, some tourists rode through Trellech directly to Tintern, but the majority kept to the boats.

The Kymin

The Kymin is a conspicuous hill overlooking Monmouth, formed where the Brownstone scarp is capped by the Quartz Conglomerate outcrop. It was regarded as one of the two 'lions' close to Monmouth, and unsurprisingly even some of the tourists who stayed only one night here found time to toil up the winding path from the town before resuming their voyage down the Wye. As Louisa Anne Twamley explained:

> [It] is a lofty eminence on the Gloucestershire side of the Wye, crowned with a fine wood, where walks have been laid out, and a pavilion erected, in order that visitors may enjoy themselves after the natural manner, in going to see the prospect from without, but paying chief attention to that within; dinners and pic-nics being frequent here.

Tourists were rewarded with a view that many considered impossible to describe, including William Coxe, who then nevertheless proceeded with a description:

Plate 35. John Arthur Evans The Kymin *Oil Late 19th century*
A fine example of late Victorian recreation. The Round House is partly obscured by trees and the Naval Temple
still has its canopy, whilst Monmouth features in the extensive view beyond. Evans lived in a cottage on the Kymin, so
probably saw this view every day when he took his dog for a walk (Nelson Museum Monmouth)

Plate 36. Hazel Pickering The Kymin
Mixed media 2005
I have painted the Kymin many times from all angles and I love the contrast of the round shape against the angular shapes. The white colour of the tower reflects the many colours of the sky and surrounding vegetation, although I didn't want to give too much importance to the vegetation, hence the predominance of blue, whilst the pink add a bit of fairy tale quality. I also wanted to exaggerate the perspective of the structure to give a feeling of the building floating above the hill. I'm not sure what Nelson would have felt about this but maybe navy men also hope for castles in the air! (Wye Tour Exhibition)

The pavilion is ... provided with five windows commanding different views over Monmouthshire, Glocestershire [*sic*], and Herefordshire backed by the distant counties of Worcester, Salop, Radnor, Brecon, Glamorgan and Somerset. I shall not attempt to describe the unbounded expanse of country which presents itself around and beneath, and embraces a circumference of nearly three hundred miles. The eye ... is attracted with the pleasing position of Monmouth, here seen to singular advantage, admires the elegant bend and silvery current of the Monnow ... and the junction of the two rivers, which form an assemblage of beautiful objects.

The Round House, as it is now known, was built in 1793-4 by wealthy Monmouth men as a summer house, and was used to host meetings, dining parties and a picnic club. Tourists were charged sixpence to enter and given instructions on how to look in the correct picturesque way at each of the five views through its windows. Then as now the tower was clearly visible from the Wye, though John Arthur Evans' oil painting shows that it was partly masked by trees in the early 20th century (Plate 35). The Round House itself has a fairytale atmosphere, brought out in Hazel Pickering's mixed media picture (Plate 36). It stirred Robert Bloomfield to write a few descriptive lines after waking up from his night on a houseboat, though he evidently confused it with the nearby Naval Temple:

> Mark the bold Kymin's sunny brow
> That gleaming o'er our fogs below,
> Lifted amain with giant power
> E'en to the clouds his Naval Tower;
> Proclaiming to the morning sky
> Valour and fame and victory.

This Naval Temple was the only memorial to the navy in Britain when it was built in 1801 to celebrate Nelson's victory at the Battle of the Nile. It also commemorates 16 admirals and other important naval battles. When it was restored in 1882 a sloping canopy was added – seen in the painting by Evans (Plate 35) – but it was later removed. David Young's acrylic painting (Plate 37) shows how much it obscured the memorial's inherent grace. Admiral Nelson took part in the Wye Tour in 1802, and, sent off by crowds of cheering people lining the banks of the river at Ross, he expressed surprise 'at being known on such a little gut

37. David Young The naval temple, Monmouth *Acrylic 2003*
I wanted a subject associated with the site of an art society painting day and did a small pastel sketch. The chief problem was the quantity of green foliage which I approached by varying the greens and stylising the brush strokes
(Wye Tour Exhibition)

38. Susan Peterken View from the Kymin *Charcoal 2005*
I have painted this complex view a few times in pastel and oil without much success, so I decided to reduce the complexity by removing colour and concentrating on tone. I wanted to capture the exhilarating feeling of standing on this high point, sweeping my eyes from left to right, but also looking down onto Monmouth then up and away to the Black Mountains on the horizon (Wye Tour Exhibition)

of a river'. As his boat came into view at Monmouth, four-pounder guns boomed out from the Kymin. He returned a month later and had a 'handsome breakfast' in the Round House, toured the Naval Temple, and thought the view one of the finest in the country.

In 1902 the Kymin became one of the National Trust's earliest acquisitions. Today the Round House is opened regularly for visitors, though not for diners, and the main view over Monmouth is kept open, but the walks through Beaulieu Grove are sadly overgrown. Two hundred years ago these walks led to six seats with views, which were maintained by tying back the branches on either side. William Coxe again:

> At one of these seats placed on a ledge of impending rocks, I looked down on a hanging wood, clothing the sided of the declivity, and sloping gradually to the Wy ... and beyond the luxuriant and undulating swells of Monmouthshire, terminated by the Great and Little Skyrrid, the Black mountains and the Sugar Loaf, in all the variety of sublime and contrasted forms.

I have painted the view looking westwards from the Kymin on at least three occasions, and each time my easel and painting have been blown over by the wind whipping up the face of the hill. Even up here the sound of the speeding traffic is always present, and one can appreciate the brutal split between the town and its river caused by the dual carriageway of the A40. The other great change since the 18th and 19th centuries is the considerable growth in housing around Monmouth, particularly around Wyesham immediately below, and more recently at the western end of the town, all of which can be seen in my charcoal drawing (Plate 38). The watercolour of about 1836 by David Cox overlooking Monmouth (Plate 39), drawn from a hill further west, shows a much smaller settlement.

Monmouth to Brockweir

Tourists who were not delayed by a climb to the Kymin often embarked very early on the second stage of their journey, partly to avoid unfavourable tides at Tintern and Chepstow. They started near the Wye Bridge, constructed in 1615 but widened in 1879, leaving the original arches below the new ones. Below Monmouth they glided uneventfully past meadows that William Gilpin described as particularly beautiful, with sheep on the higher slopes and cattle on the lower ground.

Similar views can still be seen from the Wye Valley Walk, which follows the left bank of the river to Redbrook. On a slightly gloomy February day, we squelched along the muddy path round the edge of the Haberdashers' Boys' School sports field. We made a diversion to the riverbank over swampy ground with scattered willow trees which enabled us to approach the confluence with the Monnow, behind which the A40 traffic dives into a tunnel under the wooded Gibraltar Hill. At this point the Wye curves south and passes under the rusty girders of the Troy bridge, which carried the Ross and

39. David Cox Snr & Jnr Monmouth from above Mitchel Troy *Watercolour* c.*1836*
David Cox has noted on the back of this watercolour, that this was Thomas Gray's favourite view of Monmouth –
'Monmouth, a town I never heard mentioned, … is the delight of my eyes, and the very seat of pleasure.' Taken from
Mitcheltroy Common, the Wye bridge is seen in the centre, with the Kymin on the right (Nelson Museum Monmouth)

Monmouth railway over to Troy station, and from here we could see the twenty stone arches of the viaduct that carried the Wye Valley railway to the same station. This bridge has gone, but the arches approaching from Wyesham remain, and they towered above us, magnificently heavy with ivy, making us realise how much atmosphere was lost by ivy removal from Tintern Abbey and Goodrich Castle. Across the river, Troy House, rebuilt in the 1670s by the first Duke of Beaufort, at a spot described by John Byng as 'very damp', appeared in the distance, partly screened by trees.

Thereafter, as one approaches Redbrook, the valley narrows and the woods crowd close to the river bank. Mr and Mrs Hall recorded that: 'Soon we reach a very different scene, affording all the advantages of contrast; for, rising above a mass of thick foliage, is the dense column of smoke that tells the whereabouts of a manufactory.' This manufactory, the tinplate works, is shown complete with smoke in Plate 7, with a Wye Tour boat in the foreground.

Approaching Redbrook by road from Monmouth today, the first sign of the village is the conspicuous line of white council houses winding round the slopes of Highbury Hill, overlooking a narrow side valley, down which a small brook flows along an ancient meander of the Wye. The lower tinplate works closed as late as 1961, the last factory in Britain making tinplate by hand, and the oldest steam-driven rolling plant in the world. Now the valley is filled with 'executive' houses, the land between the road and the river has become a Millennium Green and a football pitch has replaced the railway sidings, where iron bars were offloaded for the tinplate works. The railway bridge still strides diagonally across the river, with a footbridge tacked onto its side that links the Boat Inn at Penallt to its customers in Redbrook. The inclined bridge which once carried the tramway linking the ironworks of Upper and Lower Redbrook, still straddles the road to Newland.

At Bigsweir, a few miles below Redbrook, the valley opens out into the amphitheatre that is the ancient meander of the Wye below St Briavels. William Coxe described the scene:

> The banks are less steep, expand into gentle undulations, are skirted by narrow meadows, and admit occasional views of the distant country; among which the church and castle of St Briavals [*sic*], crowning the summit of an eminence in the forest of Dean, are pleasing objects.

Here the road crosses over to Wales by what was once a toll bridge. Erected in 1828 to carry the new road down the valley, its 50m span of four ribs of cast iron cost £5,982, according to Clarke's guide-book. Its design was praised by the *Penny Magazine* and it is still frequently photographed:

> At Big's Weir, where the current is very rapid, the river eddies over fragments of rock, which leave only a narrow open space for the passage of boats. Near to this place a new and very graceful bridge, called Big's-weir Bridge, spans the river with a single arch.

A mile below Bigsweir on the Welsh side is Llandogo, a village that attracted Samuel Ireland (Plate 8) and delighted Mr and Mrs Hall:

> Here we find evidence of active trade; for there are boats moored at small quays on either side the river. It is to its exceeding beauty of situation that Landogo owes its fame. The church … stands in a dell at the foot of a mountainous glen, in every crevice of which there are white cottages; each cottage having its 'bit of land' laid out as a garden, where flowers and vegetables are pleasantly intermixed.

On the English side the next settlement beyond Bigsweir is Brockweir, which stands only a mile or so above Tintern. The Wye tourists passed endless meadows on both banks, rising on the English side into the Hudnalls, a wooded common that was still being vigorously cut by the people of Llandogo (as described by Heath) and settled by commoners. After 1800, tourists would have seen the scatter of squatter houses clearly, but today many are hidden in tall woodland of lime, beech and oak. Brockweir, which lies at the practical upper limit of most tides, was an important port possessing sixteen pubs, largely inhabited by bargemen and regarded by some as lawless. Here boats were built and cargo was transferred from upriver trows to sea-going vessels. In 1906, its ferry was replaced by a visually intrusive girder bridge, which today brings traffic across the river at the level of the bedrooms of houses on the quay.

Tintern

Tintern Abbey was the highlight of the tourists' second day. This great Cistercian monastery was founded in 1131 on the banks of the Wye at the southern end of Tintern village and from there it managed substantial estates on both sides of the river. After it was closed in 1536, much of the stone-work was used for building elsewhere, but enough of the abbey's church survived to become an early tourist attraction. The monks used the power in the Angiddy, which descends steeply into Tintern from the Trellech Plateau, to drive mills and iron works, and these continued to operate and develop well into the 19th century. Thus, when the first Wye tourists swept round the bend in the river and took in their first sight of the abbey, they encountered not the quiet ambience and manicured lawns that greet modern tourists, but a village reverberating to the sound of industry and abbey ruins surrounded by hovels. Unsurprisingly, their reactions ranged from ecstasy through disappointment to disgust.

Most tourists arrived at the abbey by boat, but a few approached by other means, and this must have influenced their first impressions. William Coxe, for example, following his antiquarian interests, disembarked above Tintern and walked through the village:

> As we advanced the village, we passed some picturesque ruins hanging over the edge of the water, which are supposed to have formed part of the abbot's villa, and other buildings occupied by the monks; some of these remains are converted into dwellings and cottages, others are interspersed among the iron foundries and habitations.

John Byng descended on horseback down the Angiddy Valley and recorded a fine description of the industrial and wooded context of the abbey:

> I descended into immense woods, with a rippling stream on my right hand, heard but not seen ... here and there a cottage appear'd with scarcely ground sufficient for their small garden and apple trees. To this succeeded the incessant thump of furnace hammers; which might appall (in the night) a stouter heart than Sancho's, by their 'dreadful note of preparation'; and terrify'd poor Jock most exceedingly. Here I approach'd a noble foundery of cannon; and now, continued by, and often crossing this rapid stream, which turns a variety of mills, soon arrived at the village of Abbey-Tintern.

The early tourists found a ruin that was already popular enough to be titivated. Around 1750 the Duke of Beaufort cleared the interior and made a lawn, but kept the piles of broken masonry lying in picturesque confusion and left the ivy and other wild plants to add 'nature's ornament to the decoration of art'. The ivy survived into the 20th century, and the hovels and the industrial buildings were gradually adapted and replaced in the course of the 19th and 20th centuries by the tourist facilities one finds today.

Visitors were encouraged to experience the abbey to the full, according to Thomas Roscoe:

> By means of steps, rails, and planks, all travellers, even elderly ladies, may safely traverse the walls of Tintern from summit to floor, a circumstance greatly extolled by many wanderers in search of the picturesque, but to me, a material detraction from enjoyment; such pretty arrangements and contrivances are quite out of taste with the solemn grandeur of this glorious relic.

The tourists came to see a spectacular ruin in a picturesque setting. The associated industry did not necessarily detract, but provided a spectacle and a valuable counterpoint. Some, like William Coxe, were antiquarians and all came with individual predilections and prejudices. Many reacted with unqualified pleasure and approval. Thus, in their contrasting styles, Robert Bloomfield, the poet, decided that ecstasy was the required response:

> Tintern, thy name shall hence sustain
> A thousand raptures in my brain:
> Joys, full of soul, all strength, all eye,
> That cannot fade, that cannot die.

And Mr and Mrs Hall (1861) enjoyed the abbey from all angles:

> From the water, from the heights, from the road – no matter on which side approached, or from what position beheld – the abbey excites a feeling of deep and intense veneration, or solemn and impressive awe ... the perfect harmony of all its parts, and the simple, yet sublime, character of the whole, give it high place among the glorious bequests of far-off ages.

Thomas Roscoe was so entranced by the ruin that he thought it superior to the abbey when it was first built:

> Roofed only by the vault of heaven – paved only with the grass of earth, Tinterne is, probably, now more impressive and truly beautiful, than when 'with storied windows richly dight' for nature has claimed her share in it adornment, and what painter of glass, or weaver of tapestry, may be matched with hers?

The Halls, in contrast, were inspired by thinking of its original use:

> It was no hard task for Fancy ... to hear the mingled music of a thousand voices rolling round sculptured pillars, ascending to the fretted roof; to follow, with the eye and ear, the tramp of sandaled monks – nay, to watch them as they passed by, their white robes gleaming in the mellowed light, solemnly pacing round and about the ruin, restored to its state of primal glory and beauty.

Such tourists must have been greatly uplifted by their visit, and perhaps this was how the majority of the visitors who left no record felt, but a surprisingly large minority responded equivocally at best. Their criticisms and disappointments took several forms and were not consistent amongst themselves. Many complained that their views were spoiled by the hovels or cottages round the base of the abbey and were appalled or intrigued by the hosts of beggars that swarmed round the boats as they alighted. Gilpin, as befitted a clergyman, was more concerned about their condition than most:

> One poor woman we followed, who had engaged to shew us the monk's library. She could scarce crawl; shuffling along her palsied limbs, and meagre, contracted body, by the help of two sticks. She led us, through an old gate, into a place overspread with nettles, and briars; and pointing to the remnant of a shattered cloister, told us, that was the place. It was her own mansion. All indeed she meant to tell us, was the story of her own wretchedness.

Some tourists found that their expectations had been raised too high. Joseph Farington declared:

> At half past Eleven oClock we got to the little village of Tintern, and had a very good breakfast, and saw the Abbey. The external appearance of it was not equal to my expectations, the Scene collectedly is too crowded.

Fortunately, many, including Gilpin, thought that the inside of the abbey was far superior to the outside view: 'But when we enter it, we see it in most perfection: at least, if we consider it as an independent object, unconnected with landscape.' And Roscoe commented: 'Yet the lack of enthusiasm we feel on the outside, seems to serve only as a greater enhancement of the glory within.' Sadly, even this did not impress Farington:

> The interior was also less striking than my imagination had formed it from description and views. The South window has most Ivy upon [it], a drawing by Thos Hearne is the best I have seen of it.

Perhaps the greatest disagreements were about the balance between natural processes and obtrusive management. Many visitors preferred their ruins to be in a state of decay, crumbling masonry covered in mature ivy. This gave them a sense of nature reclaiming the ground and induced a feeling of melancholy in contemplating the vulnerability of man's efforts in building the abbey to the ravages of time. Thus, Gilpin commented on the detail that 'Nature has now made it her own. Time has ... blunted the sharp edges of the chisel; and broken the regularity of opposing parts.' However, he contradicts this in the passage most often quoted from the Wye Tour:

> No part of the ruins of Tintern is seen from the river, except the abbey-church ... Tho the parts are beautiful, the whole is ill-shaped ... a number of gabel-ends hurt the eye with their regularity; and disgust it by the vulgarity of their shape. A mallet judiciously used (but who durst use it?) might be of service in fracturing some of them; particularly those of the cross isles, which are not only disagreeable in themselves, but confound the perspective. But were the building ever so beautiful, incompassed as it is with shabby houses, it could make no appearance from the river.

Some took exception to the custodians' efforts to tidy the ruins. For example, in 1775, Francis Grose, an antiquarian, obviously felt that ruins should be left in their 'natural' state to achieve the right atmosphere:

> Here, at one cast of the eye, the whole is comprehended – nothing is left for the spectator to guess or explore; and this defect is increased by the ill-placed neatness of the poor people who show the building, and by whose absurd labour the ground is covered over by turf as even and trim as a Bowling-green, which gives the building more the air of an artificial Ruin in a Garden than that of an ancient decayed Abbey.

On the other hand, nearly a hundred years later, the Halls thoroughly approved of the management:

> Everything is cared for that ought to be preserved: the debris is never left in unseemly places; the carpet of the nave is the purest and healthiest sward; the ivy is sufficiently free, yet kept within 'decent bounds'; and there is no longer any danger of those vandal thefts that robbed the church and all its appendages to mend by-ways and build styles.

However, it was the ivy that most brought out the differences in opinion. Aged growth, climbing to the gable tops and descending in wreaths of dark foliage, was mentioned in many descriptions and featured prominently in paintings. William Coxe, who had to cross the river and walk downstream to find an unobstructed angle, seemed neutral:

> The grand east window, wholly covered with shrubs and half mantled with ivy, rises like the portal of a majestic edifice embowered in wood. Through this opening and along the vista of the church, the clusters of ivy, which twine round the pillars or hang suspended from the arches, resemble tufts of trees.

Thomas Roscoe appreciated other plants and flowers as well, without worrying about a melancholy atmosphere:

Plate 40. John 'Warwick' Smith Tintern Abbey by moonlight *Oil 1789 John 'Warwick' Smith, a student of Gilpin's father and brother, was well-known for his richly lit watercolours, and this oil painting also makes good use of moonlight to give a romantic atmosphere. The abbey is given prominence in the picture by being shown very large in relation to the size of the wooded background hills (Llyfrgell Genedlaethol Cymru/National Library of Wales)*

... the rich heavy folds of Nature's most graceful drapery, luxuriant ivy, which adorns the lofty aisles and transepts of this majestic edifice, and scarcely suffers us to regret that it is a ruin. Small ferns and flowers of many hues spring from wall and buttress, and the presiding genius of such spots, the fragrant and beautiful wall flower wanders over arch and window, decking them with its fair garb of green and gold, and crowning the decaying pile with a halo.

John 'Warwick' Smith took another view, for he completely omitted the ivy from his 1789 *Abbey by Moonlight* (Plate 40): perhaps he felt it spoilt the lines of the building. At about the same time, John Byng approved of the ivy, but had outrageous suggestions for embellishing the building: 'It is well over grown by ivy, and properly inhabited by Choughs and Daws; but I wish his grace wou'd adorn it with evergreens, cypresses &c and make the doors in gothic character.'

By 1880 it was difficult to find new words to describe the place. H. Shutz Wilson, writing in *Picturesque Europe* somehow managed to see the construction of the abbey as a natural process:

The place looks, not as if it had been built up slowly by mason hands, but as if it had grown naturally, as a flower grows. The subtle essence of its witchery transcends definition. Truly, Tintern is a poem in stone!

Artistic responses have been as varied as written opinions. Turner contrasted the soaring lines of the building with the tangled disorder of mature ivy, and Samuel Grimm's late 18th century pen and wash pictures of the interior (Plate 41) shows ivy on nearly every column, whilst the wooded slope through the window indicates the abbey's setting. By excluding the ivy, John 'Warwick' Smith anticipated modern paintings, in which Christine Hunt (Plate 42) could emphasize the clean lines of the building and the bold shadows without the distraction of ivy; Dick Ray (Plate 43) could use the diagonal shadow across the wall of the cross aisle which echoes the moon's shadow in Smith's painting; and Maldwyn Charles (Plate 44) could represent the effects of light on ancient stone walls.

Today, the hovels and their beggars have long

Plate 41. Samuel Grimm Tintern Abbey *Pen and wash 1781*
Published just before Gilpin's book, this picture was included in Henry Wyndham's A Tour through Monmouthshire and Wales. The pen and wash drawing shows a precise delineation of the ivy covered arches, without any of the drama of Turner's painting, but it does give a subtle indication of the light falling through the arches onto the floor of the abbey (Llyfrgell Genedlaethol Cymru/ National Library of Wales)

Plate 42. Christine Hunt Autumn lights *Oil 2005* I wanted to capture not only the magnitude of this magnificent ruin, but also the amazing colours of Autumn, particularly spectacular along this stretch of the Wye. As I stood in the middle of this towering structure the brilliant sun shining through the skeleton of the Abbey casting golden rays and mysterious shadows all around me, the glimpse of the trees in their Autumn splendour looking as if on fire, viewed through the vast windows, tumbling down to the river, the colours reflected back as they hit the surface of the water (Wye Tour Exhibition)

Plate 43. Dick Ray Tintern Abbey *Oil 2005* I began with a pen and wash sketch, focusing on technical accuracy. Back home I produced an oil on board version attempting to achieve dramatic evening light effect with a very limited palette. I also wanted to portray the abbey in its setting close to a tidal river. I decided that the muddy river bank did nothing for the picture, so I cut it off. This accounts for the unusual dimensions! (Wye Tour Exhibition)

Plate 44. Maldwyn Charles Texture, light and translucent shadow, Tintern *Watercolour 2005*
I was drawn to Tintern through my knowledge of one of the Turner paintings of the site. Indeed, after my first visit I found out, rather eerily as it turned out, that Turner had also done some other works at Tintern. I say 'eerily' because I discovered from my first set of sketches, notes and photographs that the views I had chosen were made from the exact viewpoints that Turner had used all those years ago. This realization did raise the hairs on the back of my neck for a while, and if nothing else, it gave me an insight into Turner's methods. The work uses modern media to turn the traditional process of watercolour on its head, changing it from an additive process (the addition of transparent wash over wash) to a subtractive one based on the technique of 'lifting out'. The view and composition I chose was very much deliberate and I like to think of the picture more in musical terms, with the main notes being those of the angular symmetry produced by the light and shade which is then played against the deeper underlying tone of the architecture's strict symmetry. In the centre of the composition, in the lighter wall area, the weathered stone and plaster seemed to form for me the shape of a white dove, [with] its counterpart the small bird perched near the high window. One bird exists in the natural world and is free, the other, which is the very symbol of freedom and peace is imprisoned within its own image (Wye Tour Exhibition)

since gone and have been replaced by vast car parks – an unimaginable sight 200 years ago. By 1861 the Halls noted: 'There is nothing like misery, nor much that looks like poverty, to be found now in the village and neighbourhood of Tinterne'. Few visitors now enjoy their first sight of the abbey from a boat, though a similar view is available from the far end of the wireworks bridge, which was built in 1875, to join the works to the Wye Valley railway. The walls of the abbey rise cleanly behind neat modern houses with dark conifers planted conspicuously in their gardens, perhaps a tidy substitute for the ivy. The inhabitants of Tintern still hope to extract money from tourists, and now provide cafes, pubs and hotels as well as a changing population of gift shops, craft shops, antique shops and art galleries.

Plate 45. Hazel Pickering Tintern in repair *Mixed media 2005*
*Tintern is a building trying hard to retain its dignity, whilst covered
in scaffolding, green protective netting and men with buckets and hammers!
I was interested in the hard angular patterns of the scaffolding against the worn
stone construction. I did the drawing in charcoal to achieve a basic simplicity
and added watercolour washes and some collaged items, showing a ground plan
and detail of a painting in a brochure, to remind viewers of the way things
could be as against how it is seen in its present state*
(Wye Tour Exhibition)

Nevertheless, the abbey still transcends its immediate surroundings and can look quite astonishing when the afternoon sun lights the ruins against a background of dark cloud. I have lived not far from Tintern for fourteen years and drive past it regularly. Every time I come round the bend and catch a glimpse of the abbey with the hills behind, I feel a moment of surprise and awe, and it is even more breathtaking when floodlit at night. In all these years I have hardly ever seen the building without the shell of scaffolding on some part of its ageing body, as captured by Hazel Pickering (Plate 45).

Devil's Pulpit to Wyndcliff and Lancaut

Tintern people could walk through an arch near the 17th-century Anchor Inn and take the foot ferry across the river to the Abbey Road or Monks Path and follow this north to Brockweir. Tourists in contrast would leave the ferry to climb up the hill to the Devil's Pulpit, a pillar of carboniferous limestone jutting out from the Plumber's Cliff – as the boatmen called it – some 180m above the river, where they gained a breathtaking view over Tintern. From here the Devil was said to preach to the monks below, tempting them with promises of wealth and fame if they would leave the abbey. At this point the Pulpit coincides with the highest point of this stretch of Offa's Dyke, the bank built in the late 8th century by Offa, King of Mercia to mark the western edge of his kingdom. Long considered to be the symbolic boundary between England and Wales, the Dyke covers 80 miles (129km) of the border, with some sections of the bank still standing 25 feet (8m) above the bottom of the ditch. The ferry operated at least until 1905, but modern visitors now use the wire-works bridge.

The Devil's Pulpit was hardly popular during the earlier part of the Wye Tour, perhaps because its high viewpoint was deemed unpicturesque, but William Bartlett must have reached it in the 1840s (Plate 6). Jim Meenaghan also shows the Pulpit in the foreground (Plate 46), but he enlarged the abbey so that it becomes the focal point of the picture. His smoke rising from the woods behind harks back to earlier Wye Tour descriptions. The cover picture by David Prentice in watercolour and reed pen shows the abbey in a wider setting, but still as the focal point.

Louisa Twamley knew about the viewpoint, but may have saved herself the climb by relating what the boatmen told her:

Plate 46. Jim Meenaghan Tintern Abbey from the Devil's Pulpit
Acrylic 2005
It started out as a nice view, then as the painting developed all sorts of metaphors popped into my head and guided the finished work.
There's the water of life in the river, the smoke indicating fire and cleansing, the darkness around the Devil's Pulpit, and central to all, the Abbey, warmed and lit by the sun. For better effect, I increased the size of the Abbey and 'moved' it slightly (Wye Tour Exhibition)

An ancient intrenchment runs along the hills opposite Tintern; and one point, on the summit of a fine cliff, and commanding an extensive prospect, is called the Devil's Pulpit, but of this name I could gain no explanation, except the well-attested penchant of the uneducated, to ascribe any singular place, building or event to supernatural, and particularly to diabolic patronage or agency.

The Halls on the other hand certainly toiled up:

> On the same ridge of hill as it diverges southward, and at a similar altitude, there is a peculiar and romantic eminence standing out from the surrounding wood, called 'the Devil's Pulpit'. ... Another steep ascent, striking off to the right hand, by a winding path ... The rock was, until successive rains and frosts had pulverised the rude ascending staircase, very much in form like a pulpit, jutting out from underneath overhanging branches of dark yew-trees.

A few yews remain nearby, but the staircase has gone, leaving modern walkers with a considerable scramble to get up on to the rock, allowing a brief moment of sublime danger.

Tourists continued their voyage still glowing from the atmosphere of the abbey, as William Coxe described:

> The impression of pleasing melancholy, which I received from contemplating the venerable ruins, were increased by the deep solitude and romantic grandeur of the woods and rocks overhanging the river, and heightened by the gloom, of a clouded atmosphere.

However he, like many others, disliked the increasingly muddy river banks and the lack of reflections:

> From Tintern the Wy assumes the character of a tide river; the water is no longer transparent, and except at high tide the banks are covered with slime; to enjoy therefore the full beauty of this part of the navigation, the traveller should seize the moment in which it begins to ebb, when the height and fullness of the river, aided by the picturesque scenery, compensates for the discoloured appearance of the stream.

Modern tourists cannot follow the Wye banks below Tintern, even where farmland comes down to the banks, and can hardly see it from the road. However, from the road to Chepstow, they cannot avoid noticing the enormous pale craters of the Tintern quarries amongst the woods opposite, especially now that many roadside trees have been felled. The quarries dwarf the natural outcrop of Banygor Rocks, which lie round the next bend and which must have seemed impressive to the original tourists. Coxe could describe them from the river:

> The long line of Banagor crags forms a perpendicular rampart on the left bank, wholly bare except where a few shrubs spring from the crevices or fringe their summits; on the opposite side, the river is skirted by narrow slips of rich pasture rising into wooded acclivities, on which towers the Wynd cliff, a perpendicular mass of rock, overhung with thickets.

The Wyndcliff was and remains, in Gilpin's words, 'one of those grand eminences which overlooks the Wye', and was described by Fosbroke as '... not simply grand, but dreadfully sublime; and that not by mere naked cliffs ... but cloathed precipices of savage grandeur ... What a cathedral is among churches, the Wynd Cliff is among prospects'. Gilpin left his boat and climbed it:

> We landed with some difficulty on an ouzy beach. One of our bargemen, who knew the place, served as a guide; and under his conduct we climbed the steep by an easy, regular zig-zag; and gained the top.

Tourists with more time available floated on to Chepstow and returned next day to the Wyndcliff, and this gave them an opportunity to see Piercefield as well. Before it was cut off by the new main road from Tintern to Chepstow, the Wyndcliff was the destination and literal high point of the Piercefield Walks. Known as Eagle's Nest from Victorian times, when a grotto was built there, it became more accessible in 1828-9 when the Duke of Beaufort built 365 steps up the cliff face and added Moss Cottage at the base. This rustic building must have intrigued the tourists: thatched with heather, the walls with moss, it was embellished with a verandah supported by tree trunks and gothic windows set with coloured glass. Inside was a table made from a slice cut from a walnut tree that once grew in Chepstow Castle. In the late 19th and early 20th centuries a four-horse coach called the Eclis, operating from Chepstow to Tintern, stopped at Moss Cottage for an hour to allow tourists to climb up the Wyndcliff before it continued to Tintern, where passengers had two hours to walk round the ruins.

The viewing arrangements, as recorded by the Halls, were designed to exclude the riff-raff:

> Each visitor is requested to pay sixpence, and no more … The fee is designed to effect what it does effect – a barrier to prevent the intrusions of mere idlers from the town, who would disturb the tranquility of the scene … the carriage stops at 'the Moss House', a rustic cottage, prettily built.

They decided to make the climb up to the Wyndcliff:

> … in the cool shadows of evening … for it is a labour when the sun is up, and half its beauty will be lost in the glare of mid-day … You climb up a steep for a mile or more, by a narrow zigzag footway, made through underwood at the foot of forest trees … You may pause occasionally to obtain views of delicious bits; and to aid you, judicious openings have been made in many places.

Plate 47. Hazel Pickering Morning mist *Acrylic 2005*
I travelled up to Eagles Nest [Wyndcliff] on Christmas Eve 2005, and after climbing up to the viewing post found, disappointingly, only thick mist and nothing to see. After waiting around for an hour or so and just about to give up and go home – the sun suddenly burnt through the mist at just the point of the confluence of the Wye and Severn with a blinding flash. I managed to produce something near to the simple form I was looking for, the focus almost entirely on this blinding streak of light where the two rivers meet (Wye Tour Exhibition)

Plate 48. J.M.W. Turner Junction of the Severn and the Wye
Sepia mezzotint, drawn etched and engraved by Turner 1811
Based on a much earlier sketch, this was almost the last of Turner's Claudean compositions.
Dark trees in the foreground frame a well-lit middle and background, balanced by a classically reclining figure.
Turner's viewpoint was in Piercefield Park, not far from the 'Alcove', now overgrown with trees.
The mezzotint technique allows for a dramatic range of tones with subtle gradations
(Chepstow Museum)

Fosbroke, however, thought that early morning was the best time to visit: 'Like Snowdon, it ought to be visited at sunrise, or seen through a sunrise-glass, called a *Claude*, which affords a sunrise view at mid-day, without the obscuration of the morning mist.' I have gazed at the view at various times of day, photographed it and painted it, but have always felt that the light would have been better either earlier or later. Perhaps one day I will get up early enough to experience it at sunrise! Hazel Pickering was lucky to catch a few minutes of sun shining through mist on the water of the Wye and Severn, and this became the subject of her acrylic painting (Plate 47): this picture was awarded first prize in the Wye Tour exhibition. Turner also featured the confluence of the rivers, but from a lower viewpoint near Piercefield House, which allows the castle to become an important element in the composition (Plate 48).

Like Fosbroke, I consider the view from the Wyndcliff to be unique. It deserves to be far better known than it is today. On a clear day one could evidently see parts of Monmouthshire, Glamorganshire, Breconshire, the Beacons in Powys, Gloucestershire, Avon, Wiltshire, some of

Herefordshire and Worcestershire, including the Malverns, and Devon, but it is not the extent which makes the view so unusual, but the nature of the fore- and middle grounds. Fosbroke described it well:

> Although it may find a counterpart in tropic climes, it is, in regard to England, probably unique. The spectator stands upon the edge of a precipice, the depth of which is awful to contemplate, with the river winding at his feet. The right screen is Piercefield ridge, richly wooded; the left screen is a belt of rock, over which, northward, appears the Severn ... The first foreground appears to the eye like a view from the clouds to the earth, and the rich contrast of green meadows to wild forest scenery, – the farm of Lancaut, clasped in the arms of the winding river, backed by hanging wood and rock.

Thomas Roscoe was equally enthusiastic:

> In the valley, the eye follows for several miles the course of the Wye, ... which then forces its foaming way to the right, along a huge wall of rock, nearly as high as the point where you stand, and at length, beyond Chepstow Castle, which looks like a ruined city, empties itself into the Bristol Channel ... three miles broad, thronged with white sails ... Inexhaustible in details, of boundless extent, and yet marked by such grand and prominent features, that confusion and monotony, the usual defects of a very wide prospect, are completely avoided.

Despite all the praise, not everyone was impressed. Francis Kilvert must have visited at low tide:

Plate 49. George Eyre Brooks Wyndcliff *Lithograph by T.M. Baynes* c.*1840*
A caption under the print reads: "View from the Wynd Cliff embracing the Banygor Crags – Lancaut cliffs
– Peninsula farm – The twelve Apostle Rocks and Piercewood – Piercefield House and Park – The Bishop's Palace
above the town of Chepstow – The Magnificent Estuary of the Severn – Kingroad at the entrance of the Avon, or
Bristol River; and in the distance the counties of Gloucester, Wilts, and Somerset (Chepstow Museum)

Any view would be spoilt by the filthy ditch which they call the Wye in the foreground, a ditch full of muddy water at the best of times ... but now a scene of ugly foreshore and waste of hideous mud banks with a sluggish brown stream winding low in the bottom.

Two lithographs show this view at high tide, with the muddy banks covered. Brook's picture (Plate 49) takes in a wider field of view than Greenwood's one (Plate 2), and appears to be from a standpoint 250m further east, judging by careful alignments of the estuary with the Lancaut peninsula on a map. Both pictures show the fields of Lancaut 'clasped in the arms of the winding river'. These fields also feature in David Prentice's watercolour and pen painting (Plate 50), which includes a dark foreground tree to give the picture depth in the Claudean manner. John Harris painted a similar section of the view (Plate 51), but in a more abstract way, with the Severn Bridge drawing the eye up the painting.

Some visitors to the Wyndcliff sought not rapturous contemplation, but high excitement. As Arthur Young described as far back as 1768:

... the surprising echo, on firing a pistol or gun from it. The explosion is repeated five times very distinctly from rock to rock, often seven; and if the calmness of the weather happens to be remarkably favourable, nine times. The echo is curious.

Plate 50. David Prentice Confluence of the Wye and Severn *Watercolour and reed pen 2005*
Working on the banks of the Wye was a relaxing process of instinctive engagement with the realities of the river. An awareness of the long tradition of earlier artists' work on the river was very instructive (Wye Tour Exhibition)

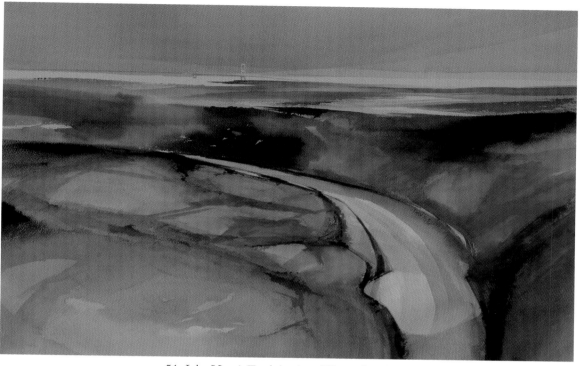

51. John Harris Eagle's view *Watercolour 2005*

From Eagle's Nest [Wyndcliff] I was struck by the abstract shapes of the landscape, the downward view to the river then up to the horizontal lines of the Severn with the bridge in the distance. After several attempts I think I achieved a balance which was quite a difficult exercise (Wye Tour Exhibition)

Many tourists came armed with a pistol to test the echo for themselves.

A little further downriver on the Gloucestershire bank, Louisa Twamley found yet another view-point on the top of the Lancaut cliffs:

> There were the stunted oak, the light and graceful birch, that 'Lady of the woods', the mountain ash ... the sober yew, making still duskier the dim ravines where it loves to dwell ... Opposite to our rocky couch ... spread the whole domain of Piercefield – woods, lawns and cliffs. On our right towered the lofty Windcliff; in the deep hollow at our feet lay the tiny church of Llancaut, embosomed in trees; and beside it rolled the WYE, deep below us, chafing against our citadel of rocks ...

Today, if one takes one's life in one's hands, one can peer over Wintour's Leap from behind the crash barrier on the Tidenham road and see much the same view.

Piercefield to Chepstow Castle

Piercefield is considered to be one of the most important early designed picturesque landscapes in Britain. In the 1750s when Valentine Morris inherited the estate from his father, he laid out the park in the style of Capability Brown. In deliberate contrast, he hired at vast expense Richard Owen

Cambridge, a Gloucestershire gentleman-poet, to design a series of walks through woodland high above the meanders of the Wye. Known as the Piercefield Walks, spurs from the main path along the edge of the cliffs led to ten or more 'stations' affording views to the river below, all carefully composed on picturesque principles.

Tourists intent on experiencing the whole Wye Tour in two days would leave their boats to enjoy the Piercefield Walks, while others with more time preferred to walk back from Chepstow the following day. William Coxe suggested:

> To view these delightful scenes, in full perfection, the traveller ought to visit the place at high tide, when the river is full; he should pass through the village of St Arvans, to the upper part of the grounds, and descend from Lover's Leap to the alcove, by which he will enjoy the whole scenery in proper succession, and to the greatest advantage.

It was already a tourist attraction when William Gilpin gave his approval:

> Mr Morris's improvements at Persfield ... are generally thought as much worthy a traveller's notice, as any thing on the banks of the Wye ... Little indeed, was left for improvement, but to open walks and views, through the woods, to the various objects around them. All this the ingenious proprietor hath done with great judgment, and hath shewn his rocks, his woods, and his precipices under various forms, and to great advantage ... The winding of the precipice is the magical secret, by which all these inchanting scenes are produced.

Gilpin, foist with his own strict set of picturesque rules, must have been in two minds about the place, for he continued:

> We cannot however call these views picturesque. They are either presented from too high a point; or they have little to mark them as characteristic; or they do not fall into such composition, as would appear to advantage on canvas.

Stebbing Shaw, in contrast, thought the views too good for mere canvas:

> Opposite the cave are bow railings with a seat, which if we may compare the works of nature with those of art, may be a front box of one of the compleatest theatres in the universe ... here wants no painted canvas to express its scenery, nature's sweet landscape is quite enough.

The three miles of walks today are decidedly dilapidated, though a plan exists to restore them. Starting out, like the townspeople of Chepstow and the more relaxed Wye tourists, from the Chepstow end (from the Leisure Centre car park), we soon passed close to Turner's standpoint for the sketch that later became the mezzotint (Plate 48), but it was totally overgrown. A little further on we came to the first station, known as the 'Alcove', a stone seat on a promontory, where the original railings can still be seen collapsed down the slope below a newer fence. The view back to Chepstow is much obscured by trees now, but we could still look down on the river and along to the castle, strung out along the top of the cliffs like a ruined citadel, with a crowded car park at its base, once occupied by a large horse pool. The church is to the left, with the towers of the Severn Bridge rising gracefully above it, slightly marred by a giant pylon carrying cables across the Severn. Joseph Farington walked back to this viewpoint to make a drawing:

> The chapel of the castle here becomes a principal feature in the Landscape of a good form and beautiful colour. I began a drawing and was so fortunate as to have the Sun breaking out giving effect and distinction to the parts and all the splendour of light and shade to the whole.

Half a mile further on, we came to the 'Platform', a flat, stone-faced mound hidden in a thicket of yew, beech and lime trees, now a viewpoint without a view, but which once afforded clear sight of the river. After a few zig-zags, the main path cuts across the peninsula and passes through a small iron age fort, within which is the remains of the 'Grotto', a brick half-dome, originally lined with minerals, iron cinders and rock crystals. The whole area is now covered in cherry laurels, but beyond them, there is still a view, at least in winter, down to the river and across to Lancaut, the Wyndcliff and upriver to distant houses on the slopes above Brockweir.

Near Piercefield House, by a large cedar and close to where the footpath from the park joins the main path, tourists reached the 'Double View', where they could look left down onto the Wye and right over the park to the Severn. We could still see enough of the view to imagine what it must have been like before the ash wood-land grew up. A diversion along the path to the front of the house brought us to the sad ruin, deteriorating rapidly as trees grow up from the drawing room and through the roof. Penny Robson's watercolour (Plate 52) shows one of the pavilions engulfed by vegetation, and Susanna Birley's

52. Penny Robson The Pavilion *Watercolour 2002*
A sense of nostalgia led me to paint Piercefield many times – childhood memories of exploring through the undergrowth to discover new and secret places inspired this painting (Wye Tour Exhibition)

Plate 53. Susanna Birley Piercefield House *Watercolour 2005*
I thought that an interesting way to emphasize the dereliction of Piercefield
House was to zoom in on the façade and illustrate the state of ruined
walls and undergrowth visible inside. This also made a satisfying geometric
composition (Wye Tour Exhibition)

painting features the window openings framing patterns of shrubs and creepers within (Plate 53). Rumours of a possible rebuilding occasionally spread, but it would be a daunting prospect, for the roof is long gone, a sole pillar is left of the imposing portico, lintels are giving way, though surprisingly some of the chimneys are still intact. This is not the house that the early Wye tourists would have seen. Valentine Morris left Piercefield a bankrupt in 1772, then in 1785 the estate was bought by George Smith, who engaged John Soane to build a new house. However, Smith, too, became bankrupt, and in 1793 before the roof was completed he sold the house to Mark Wood, who finished and extended the house at a cost of at least £30,000. All this was not enough to impress Joseph Farington, who thought the house was 'a specimen of very bad taste in Architecture', but even so, it was famous for its sumptuous interior, including the mirrored panels in the entrance hall, which reflected the view. Ralph Lucas's watercolour of about 1840 (Plate 54) shows the house and the park, complete with a fashionable ha-ha, and strangely includes a tree, which seems to cut the picture in two. In 1802, Nathaniel Wells, the offspring of an English gentleman and a black slave, bought Piercefield for £95,000. He was an admirable squire, but, being, in Farington's words, 'a Creole of very deep colour', he was viewed with great curiosity by Wye tourists. The house suffered from dry rot from the outset and, understandably perhaps, it was abandoned in 1923.

The much-admired view of Chepstow from the park is now partly hidden by trees, but in the hazy February sun we could just make out the confluence of the Wye with the Severn, the curves contrasting with the verticals of the Severn Bridge towers, the intruding pylon, one tall redwood and a Lombardy poplar. My pastel painting shows a similar view, and was drawn on a clearer day from a point some way in front of the House (Plate 55).

Plate 54. Ralph Lucas Piercefield House and Park *Watercolour c.1840*
Piercefield House, complete with carriage approaching the portico, is shown in its setting within the Park,
which was laid out in the style of Capability Brown, with clumps of trees framing the view
to the Severn and the estuary of the Wye (Chepstow Museum)

Plate 55. Susan Peterken Towards the Severn *Pastel 2005*
When standing in front of Piercefield House, my eye is inevitably drawn to the powerful elegance of the Severn Bridge,
which links the background plane to the middle ground, and places the picture in modern times. The lines introduced in
the foreground help to give a feeling of swooping down hill to the dark band of trees. The land beyond the Severn was
a dim greyish-purple on the day I visited, and the other colours flowed from that (Wye Tour Exhibition)

Returning to the main path, we soon came to the remains of the 'Druid's Temple', originally a circle of standing stones in a small amphitheatre. One pointed stone remains upright by the path and three other stones lie nearby. About half a mile from the house, we came down to the most dramatic station, the 'Giant's Cave'. In front is a small platform, with a view down through the bare branches onto the river curving under Piercefield Cliffs, the fields of Lancaut and the cliffs beyond. Cut through a limestone buttress, the cavern narrows to a tunnel before exiting to the north side. When it was first created, a stone giant perched above the entrance to the cave, holding a boulder above his head, but in 1806, Charles Heath commented that it was already in a poor state and minus its arms.

After backtracking briefly, we took the path zig-zagging up along the edge of the park by the north end of the race track. Heading north, we came after half a mile to 'Lovers' Leap', a viewpoint above a precipice. Valentine Morris once fell here but was saved when he landed in a tree. John Byng recorded that: 'The Lovers' Leap is well rail'd; so that none but the very desponding would take it; I have never heard that it was attempted; the first leap would cure the most heart-felt pangs.'

The original railings still remain, the palings still with their rusty, spear-pointed tips. We looked straight down several hundred feet to the Martridge brook, and across to the Wyndcliff. The river, glimpsed between young ash and whitebeam trees, curved away northwards under Banygor Rocks and then beneath the great scars of Tintern Quarry, which is still eating into the hillside. The 'Temple', a turret with viewing platform near here, was demolished about 1790.

The other path beyond the Giant's Cave led down to the 'Cold Bath', where the Martridge stream had been redirected into a rectangular, brick-lined depression. Today, this is overgrown with laurels, but the huge ornamental plane trees still stand over it, and a few of the tiles lining the pool have survived along with a corner fireplace. After this the original path doubled back down to the river bank and eventually climbed up to the house via steps cut out of the rocks. Much of this was already overgrown when John Byng arrived in the 1780s: 'The walks are ill-kept, some of them almost impassable, viz the zig-zag walk to the water, and that to the cold-bath.'

Not all the Wye tourists appreciated the artifice of the walks. Thomas Roscoe declared:

> Certainly a very pretty specimen of landscape-gardening; but so much puerility of design is mixed with the grand and simple beauty of nature ... Grottos fabricated where grottos could not naturally exist, with dilapidated giants in stone over their entrance, and inscriptions not of the highest order of composition, are very well calculated to make the unlearned stare, and as sure to make the judicious grieve.

Tourists who proceeded by boat to Chepstow sometimes faced difficulties. Gilpin was forced to walk because the tide was too low to 'carry' his boat. William Coxe, however, following his own advice to visit at high tide, had enough water:

> At the further extremity of this peninsula, the river again turns and stretches in a long reach, between the white and towering cliffs of Lancaut, and the rich acclivities of the Piercefield Woods. In the midst of these grand and picturesque scenes the embattled turrets of Chepstow Castle burst upon our sight; and as we glided under the perpendicular crag, we looked up with astonishment to the massive walls impending over the edge of the precipice, and appearing like a continuation of the rock itself.

Chepstow

The approach to Chepstow by river is dominated by the castle walls rising directly from the cliff above the Wye, with the bridge linking Monmouthshire with Gloucestershire beyond. This dramatic perspective was recorded in Paul Sandby's aquatint of 1775, which also shows a Wye tour boat close in under the cliffs (Plate 56). Most tourists were as enthusiastic as Louisa Anne Twamley:

> Built on the summit of a lofty cliff, which is perpendicular on the river side, its walls seem a continuation of the rock, from which towers and battlements rise up in varied and picturesque groups. What was grim and threatening in its day of power and pride, is now softened into beauty by time and decay.

But Sir Richard Colt Hoare was not satisfied:

> I could wish the bank before it on the left were covered with wood, as it appears in part only over a narrow neck of land not in a very advantageous point of view; whereas it would break on the sight most nobly and surprize every beholder if it could possibly be hidden till the boat turns the angle.

Plate 56. Paul Sandby Chepstow Castle *Aquatint 1775*
This, one of the first aquatints published in Britain, helped to popularize the Wye eight years before Gilpin's book appeared in print. The dramatic composition, with its masterly control of tones and effects of light, emphasizes the way that the castle appears to grow out of the rocky bluff when seen from the water. Note the figures struggling through the mud on the bank (Chepstow Museum)

The town itself impressed the tourists. The most effusive was Henry Wyndham:

> The beauties indeed are so uncommonly excellent, that the most exact critic in landscape would scarcely wish to alter a position in the assemblage of woods, cliffs, ruins and water, which form the various prospects around Chepstow.

The article in the *Penny Magazine* described the town, like Monmouth, as picturesque:

> [It] is built on a hill gradually ascending from the river, and it is as cheerful and animated (not without something of an old-fashioned ancient air) within as it is externally picturesque.

All tourists would have become aware of the great rise and fall of the tide, especially those who had to clamber up steep mud banks at low tide. William Coxe, with his customary precision, attempted to measure the depth of the river at high tide:

Plate 57. Annabel Clements Chepstow Castle revisited *Oil 2005*
I have always loved the dramatic situation of Chepstow Castle. I wanted to recreate a Turneresque image, using oil paints loosely as in watercolour, with modern use of colour in the water and hills, contrasting with more traditional earth colours (Wye Tour Exhibition)

The perpendicular height, from the bottom of the channel to the surface of the water was 47 feet 3 inches ... an average 50 or 60 feet, and on some extraordinary occasions not less than 70.

The old 13th-century bridge, seen in Paul Sandby's aquatint, was damaged – and seven passengers were drowned – when a pleasure boat fouled another boat's mooring rope, which was itself tied to the bridge, so in 1816 it was replaced by a cast iron bridge with five graduated arches, described in the *Penny Magazine* as: 'not "elegant, light, and airy," as the guide-books style it, but massive and grand'. Later tourists could glimpse a new view of the castle, as Mr and Mrs Hall recorded: '[It] has a fine effect from the railway, as the train passes over the bridge.' Brunel's unique asymmetrical bridge, built in 1852 and later considerably modified, had track girders suspended on diagonal chains from two arched wrought iron tubes supported at each end by masonry towers.

The great castle was, however, the principal attraction and had drawn in visitors since the 1750s. Many artists chose to paint it from the opposite bank. Annabel Clements included the old bridge with a fairytale castle behind in her modern interpretation of Turner's 1793 watercolour (Plate 57). Philippe de Loutherbourg's watercolour sketch, completed about 1787, was taken from directly opposite the castle (Plate 11), and Colin Simmond's impressionist oil painting looks obliquely across the river (Plate 58). Anthony Sully found a pool which reflected the castle and surrounding trees for his

58. Colin Simmonds Chepstow Castle, silvery tones *Oil 2005*
I responded to an expanse of shimmering river with the cliff and castle continuing a similar tonality above. My intention was to create a sense of space as you look towards the castle, using oil paint applied in a variety of ways with a palette knife and brushes in a range of silvery tones (Wye Tour Exhibition)

Plate 59. Anthony Sully View from Elmdale *Acrylic 2005*
I was surprised to discover this lake which lies beside the River Wye, and found it presented me with the best reflection of Chepstow Castle (Wye Tour Exhibition)

118

acrylic painting (Plate 59). Joseph Farington selected a nearer viewpoint for one of his sketches – he drew the south side of the Great Tower, looking across a ravine from what is now a large car park (Plate 10). This corresponds with the entry in his diary for September 19th: 'I passed the remainder of the day in making another drawing of the Chapel of the Castle where it is the principal feature of a wood scene.'

The Great Tower of the castle, one of the most important medieval building in Wales, was initiated by William fitz Osbern, Earl of Hereford and Lord of Striguil, soon after the Norman Conquest. In 1189, William Marshal acquired the castle by marriage and spent vast sums on new work, including the most sophisticated gatehouse of its date in the whole of Europe. Two round towers guarded the gate passageway, which had two portcullises, and a barbican wall protecting the approach. During the Civil War in 1645 and again in 1648, Chepstow Castle, a Royalist base, was besieged by the Parliamentarians. Mr and Mrs Hall recounted a well-known story of the second siege:

> But the garrison ... even then refused to surrender, under promise of quarter, hoping to escape
> by means of a boat ... A soldier of the parliamentary army, however, swam across the river, with
> a knife between his teeth, cut the cable of the boat, and brought it away.

Following the Restoration, Charles II used the castle as a fort, barracks and prison, the most famous inmate being Henry Marten, one of the signatories to the death warrant of Charles I. Marten spent just 12 years (in relative comfort) in what was known as Marten's Tower, not the 27 years recorded by Joseph Farington, nor the 30 years by the poet Southey, nor even the 20 years that Mr and Mrs Hall noted:

> The portion ... that attracts most attention, and is carefully examined by all visitors, is the KEEP,
> which contains the PRISON of Henry Marten. Southey's memorable lines, written when Southey
> was a republican, have been quoted by all tourists.

After completing their river trip, Wye tourists usually spent the night in the town then returned to the castle on the following day. They walked down Bridge Street and skirted the Castle Pool, now filled in and transformed into the car park. As Louisa Anne Twamley noted:

> We advanced to the tower-guarded gateway, where the ancient gates still remain. They consist
> of thick oaken planks, covered with iron plates laid upon a strong lattice, and fastened by iron
> bolts.

The original gates, dated to the end of the 12th century, replaced by replicas in 1964, are now displayed in the Earl's Chamber. They are the first known example of certain carpentry techniques in the whole of Britain and Northern France, and are beautifully illustrated in an engraving from 1880 (Plate 60).

Once through the wicket gate, early visitors were met by the ancient guide, a Mrs Williams, who was famous for living to the age of 90 and whose mother, grandmother and great grandmother had all lived to be over 100. They were confronted by a farmyard, the Duke of Beaufort having leased out the castle, gardens and a small orchard in front of the main gate. The tenants treated the first court as a smallholding and lived in the castle's buildings, where they inserted new windows that horrified Louisa Twamley. The ancient walls 'looked indignant at a poor little dimity curtain, that was giving itself great airs at an open casement'. The towers and apartments were used for industry – Charles Heath recorded a stable, dog-kennel, a malt house and a glass house, or factory – and at other times tenants established sail- and nail-factories and a wholesale wine cellar. Most early tourists only visited the Great Tower, known as the chapel, and even that was difficult to approach through the surrounding nettles and brambles. Later visitors could see more of the castle, including the 'Dungeon', described by Twamley as:

> A damp and gloomy subterranean vault, with a groined roof ... On peering through the opening, the Wye is seen at a great depth below, rolling heavily along, and the head grows dizzy with gazing from the murky dungeon down the terrific precipice.

In fact, this 'Dungeon' was the wine cellar, where wine barrels and other provisions had been hauled up from a boat moored below.

The castle continued to decay. In 1803 J.T. Barber noted:

> Owing to the neglect of the roof the upper stories of the building were swimming with water, and perishing very fast. It is hoped that the Duke of Beaufort's agents have looked to their charge, and adopted proper means to prevent entire loss of a useful habitation, and an interesting remnant of antiquity.

By 1821 Charles Heath, in the 7th edition of his guidebook, reported enthusiastically that the castle had been cleared of rubbish and brambles and a rampart walk had been opened. In the 1840s the castle interior was embellished with lawns and spreading walnut trees. These improvements were no doubt influenced by the increasing numbers of tourists, brought in by the new steam packet boats from Bristol. One such visitor is shown in the frontispiece: in 1880 he sat sketching the view down on to the river; today he would have a camera.

Plate 60. Artist unknown A peep through the Gateway, Chepstow Castle *Wood engraving* c.*1880 The original gates, dating to the end of the 12th century, show one of the earliest examples of lattice bracing, with a wicket gate inserted later. The bridge over the Wye shows clearly through the doorway (Picturesque Europe)*

Chapter 7
Changing attitudes to landscape

In 1801, when the first census was taken and the Wye Tour was still gaining in popularity, the population of Britain stood at eight million. 200 years later it has reached over sixty million. This remarkable increase is only one facet of the social, political, economic, cultural, educational, environmental and artistic changes that have influenced our perception and valuation of wild landscapes in general, the Wye Valley in particular, and how we portray them visually.

Travel at home and abroad

Wye tourists, who only passed fleetingly through the valley, and residents, who knew it more intimately, understandably differed in their attitude to the Wye Valley landscape. Tourists frequently commented on the similarity between different stretches of the river, whereas Charles Heath, who lived in Monmouth, described the variety within and between each section. Gilpin was obviously bored with the second part of his first day:

> Below the *New-Weir* are other rocky views of the same kind, though less beautiful. But description flags in running over such a monotony of terms. *High, low, steep, woody, rocky*, and a few others, are all the colours of language we have to describe scenes; in which there are infinite gradations; and, amidst some general sameness, infinite peculiarities.

Fosbroke, who lived in the area, criticised Gilpin who, he thought, 'hurries over a fine scene of continual change and inimitable groupings', but Mr and Mrs Hall, perhaps influenced by Gilpin's words, said:

> ... that when the voyage has been made between Ross and Monmouth, the eye and mind have wearied of the perpetual succession of rock, wood and water, seldom but little varied.

This implies that you need to live in a landscape or visit it regularly if you are to appreciate it fully, a point that Gilpin made in his introduction:

> To criticize the face of a country correctly, you should see it oftener than once; and in various seasons. Different circumstances make such changes in the same landscape, as give it wholly a new aspect.

Even in the 19th century, visitors from overseas were amazed at how little the British valued their own landscapes. The article in the *Penny Magazine* quotes a book called *Tour of a German Prince*:

> Never ... was I more convinced than here, that a prophet has no honour in his own country. How else would so many Englishmen travel thousands of miles to fall into ecstacies at beauties of a very inferior order to these!

Likewise, Leith Ritchie in the introduction to his guide book of 1841 felt that we needed to travel abroad in order to appreciate our own landscapes:

> Foreigners have often expressed their surprise that the English should travel so far in search of picturesque scenery, when they have abundance at home: ... We do not travel for the mere scenery. We do not leave the Wye unexplored, and go abroad in search of some other river of its own identical character. What we gaze at in strange lands is not wood, and water, and rock, but all these seen through a new medium – accompanied by adjuncts which array universal nature herself in a foreign costume ... The proof of this is our keener perception of the beauties of English scenery after returning from abroad ... An untravelled Englishman is ignorant of his own country. He must cross the seas before he can become acquainted with home. He must admire the romance of the Rhine – the sublimity of the (mountain) Rhone – the beauty of the Seine and the Loire – before he can tell what is the rank of the Wye, in picturesque character, among the rivers of Europe.

Russell quotes part of the preface of *Great Britain Illustrated*, published by Charles Tilt in 1830, which expresses a similar view:

> This Volume is presented to the Public under a conviction that a Series of Views, taken from our native country, will be at least as favourably received as if the talents of the eminent Artists engaged in their production had been employed in portraying the beauties of a foreign land ... [the English] neglect comparatively their own beautiful and interesting Island, many parts of which ... are equal if not superior to any scenery to be found abroad.

We still seem to think that fresh landscapes are better than our own. The cost of foreign travel is now so low, and, barring fogs, strikes, and congestion at Heathrow, so easy, that thousands of us have holiday homes abroad and think nothing of travelling many times a year to Continental Europe. However, with increasing global warming possibly limiting air travel in future, and Mediterranean countries becoming too hot for comfort in summer, more of us may decide to holiday at home and rediscover, or discover for the first time, British landscapes.

Bypassing the Wye Valley

The Lower Wye Valley today is less popular in relative terms than many of the other old picturesque areas, most of which have become either National Parks (Lake District, Snowdonia, Peak District and, eventually, Loch Lomond) or world-famous for their industrial archaeology (Severn Gorge, New Lanark). Tourism developed during the 19th and 20th centuries into a rush to the edges, either the seaside or the remoter parts of Britain, such as Cornwall and Pembrokeshire. There was increasing interest in gaining access to wild places, such as Dartmoor and the North York Moors, and this reinforced interest in Snowdonia, the Lake District and the western Highlands. Rambling, hill walking and boating became popular, and these activities required easy access from cities, rugged country (which popularized scarp landscapes, such as the Cotswolds and Chilterns), tame water (Thames, Broads) and estuaries and harbours. The rising interest in natural history and ecology attracted people to 'natural' areas. Latterly, of course, vast numbers of tourists have gone abroad.

Against this background, the Lower Wye is not outstanding. It is not remote, wild or natural enough, not sufficiently close to conurbations, nor is it blessed with an outstanding industrial or historical heritage, except for Tintern Abbey. Modern boating is difficult: the river is not tame and the estuary is dangerous.

The Lower Wye may also have suffered because it provided the best fit with picturesque ideas – not just because of Gilpin's book, but also because it was the only area where the scenery was viewed mainly from a boat as a moving stage-set of side-screens, limited distant views and foreground detail. With the decline in popularity of the picturesque, the Wye was bound to become less popular, and, lying on the borders of England and Wales, had no single local authority to promote it.

Conservation of Wye Tour sites

In 1971 the outstanding quality of the Wye Valley landscape was recognised by designation as an Area of Outstanding Natural Beauty (AONB), with the object, as far as possible, of maintaining the character of the landscape. Quite what was meant by 'natural' has not been precisely defined. The present landscape is more densely inhabited than ever before, traffic noise is almost unavoidable, and the shape of the valley has been modified by the removal of vast quantities of limestone, not just the Lancaut quarry, which is removing one of the interlocking spurs, and the Tintern quarry, which has left a great scar on the valley side, but also earlier works, such as the Pen Moel quarry above Chepstow and the removal of all but one of the rock towers at New Weir. Nevertheless, the term 'natural landscape' does have some meaning, for the old industries have gone, felling and charcoal burning no longer break up the woods, the density of large trees is higher than at any time in the last millennium, many of the valley-side fields are now rough with scrub and bracken, and even the weirs have gone from the river. The picturesque tourists would hardly have known how to react, either to the changes on the ground, or to our attitudes. After all, they rather liked to contrast the 'natural' scenery with industrial activity; they used the charcoal-burners' smoke to emphasise perspective in their paintings; and they would have regretted the deterioration of their Walks and the obliteration by trees of their favourite views.

Recognising these changes and acknowledging the role of the Picturesque Movement in developing present-day attitudes to landscape, local and national organisations have joined with the AONB office to develop a plan for restoring the old viewpoints and reinstating the Walks. Under the neatly double-edged title 'Overlooking the Wye', a bid was prepared for support from the Heritage Lottery Fund, and at the time of writing the first stage has been successful. Detailed reports on the industrial heritage and the viewpoints have been prepared by specialists. The latter identified over 50 sites and supported the claim that the Lower Wye Valley, with its Wye Tour, was the birthplace of British tourism and that the attitudes shaped in the valley influenced how we perceive and evaluate landscape today.

If it is fully funded, the bid will enable many of the sites made famous by the Wye Tour to be made more accessible, cleared of obstruction, and brought to a wider audience through leaflets and display boards. Work should start in 2008 and last for three years. Many sites will be enhanced, including several described in this book. Riverside improvements will include The Prospect at Ross, Goodrich Castle, the quaysides at Lydbrook, Monmouth, Llandogo and Brockweir, and the docks at Chepstow. Viewpoints at Symonds Yat Rock, the Kymin, Devil's Pulpit, and Upper Wyndcliff will be improved, with renovation of the 365 steps. Industrial sites will be enhanced at the New Weir forge, the tin plate works at Lydbrook, and the lower wireworks at Tintern. At Piercefield the plans are to open up more of the walks and the viewpoints, stabilise structures and provide interpretation.

Wilderness and tourism

The Picturesque Movement lives on – we still use the word picturesque, mainly in relation to landscapes, but the meaning has become much less specific and changed to pretty, quaint or maybe dramatic – a view worthy of a picture postcard. Picturesque theory tried to explain our response to landscapes, but they could only be appreciated by those who were educated in the history of poetry and painting. The need to analyse a scene before deciding on their reaction stifled an immediate emotional response and suppressed imagination. Today we respond in a more direct way to nature, but our habit of searching out, responding to and recording natural landscapes and ruins started in the 18th century, when there was a change in attitudes, from admiring peaceful pastoral landscapes to appreciating wilderness and mountains. This change in attitude has become more pronounced, as increasing intensification of agriculture has diminished the visual qualities of farmland. In a world of rapidly increasing change, we feel the need to connect with a wild landscape that does not appear to have changed, and has apparently endured for centuries despite our depredations. Before the Industrial Revolution, most of the population lived in the countryside, but now 90% of us live in towns and cities, and we flock to the National Parks and heritage sites in ever increasing numbers. Despite a relative downturn in the popularity of the Wye Valley, the absolute number of visitors has increased significantly in the last forty years. There were an estimated 4 million visitors to the Forest of Dean and Wye Valley in 2006, according to tourist board figures, and the Wye Valley AONB estimated 2.5 million visits to the Wye Valley alone. Astonishingly, Don Gifford, in an essay called *The touch of landscape*, also quoted 4 million for the estimated number of visitors to the world-famous Grand Canyon as late as 1993.

Just as the Wye tourists were isolated in their boats from the realities of the landscapes they floated past, modern tourists also pass through an area enclosed in glass and steel yet feel they have 'done' it. But, as Gifford says, speed gives a different relationship to the parts of a landscape, between a blurred foreground, a fleeting glimpse of the middle ground and a relatively stable background. We need to get out of our cars and walk, canoe, cycle, get tired and muddy, before we can begin to find the spirit of a place. But, with increasing visitor numbers, quiet enjoyment of landscape and wild-life is at risk. Gifford reported in 1993 that Imax theatres were appearing at the entrances to some American National Parks, with vast screens that gave the viewers the feeling that they were right in the landscape. The justification was that 80% of visitors to National Parks do not have the opportu-nity to take part in white water rafting, hiking in canyons or camping in the wilderness anyway, and visitor pressure on the parks was also alleviated. In the absence of real boat trips, here is a marketing opportunity for an Imax theatre in the Wye Valley showing a virtual Wye Tour!

Proliferation of images

As well as Imax theatres, throughout the 20th century we have been bombarded with landscape images, not just photographs in newspapers, magazines, calendars, travel brochures, picture post-cards, advertisements and websites, but also moving images on TV and in the cinema. In the mid-18th century, the lower and middle classes saw very few images: maybe an engraving of a Dutch or Italian landscape on the parlour wall, or, towards the end of the century, engravings and aquatints of British landscapes in books and folios. The upper classes were better endowed: they had access to foreign landscape paintings and drawings collected on their Grand Tours, and they commissioned topographical artists to produce pictures of their estates. Few of these pictures were ever seen by the public. In fact, there were no exhibitions of paintings for sale by living artists until 1760, no public collections of pictures before 1814, and no exhibitions outside major cities until the 1820s.

When landscape images were rare, each one would have been precious and indelibly impressed on the memory. Many would have been associated with quotations from favourite poets. Throughout the 19th century, however, demand for topographical, picturesque and romantic prints increased. As picturesque tourism developed, more and more travellers felt the need to write diaries and produce their own sketches of the places they visited, mostly as keepsakes but also to impress their friends with their drawing skills and their sense of adventure.

With the invention of photography everything changed. Landscape photography became familiar in the 1860s and by 1900 picture postcards were popular and readily available. With the development of small cheap portable cameras in the 1890s, personal photography was simplified. Anyone could wield a Box Brownie and produce some sort of image, and millions of albums were filled with small, blurred, fading snapshots. Now digital photography has brought down the marginal cost of a picture to zero and even more images are clogging our computers. Moreover, we produce travel blogs about our journeys and encourage our friends to look at them.

The act of photographing a landscape has several similarities with drawing or painting, and indeed, many artists use photographs to help them compose a picture. Viewfinders frame an image and concentrate our attention on one part of the landscape. We must think about composition and decide on a focal point. With one rotation of a lens, we contract from a wide-angle 17th-century prospect picture to zoom in to a picturesque concentration on details in the foreground. Interestingly, the Claude glasses used by the Wye tourists performed much the same function and, by reducing landscapes to a series of planes, produced a tonal map and helped artists compose their picture. Both Claude glasses and modern viewfinders isolate us from the physical landscape by reducing it to a set of visual images. Indeed, some tourists become so involved in trying to capture the best photograph or the best sketch that they forget to enjoy the view.

Changes in artistic style

Images made by artists on the Wye Tour cannot be confused with those entered into our exhibition in 2006. The style of the pictures has changed and the images selected here enable us to see how the artistic and technical developments of the last 200 years have influenced the changes. My comparison may be biased, since the images from the Wye Tour are necessarily represented by a high proportion of drawings and sketches, whereas all the modern works are finished paintings.

The first thing to strike me is the explosion of colour in the modern paintings compared with the earlier watercolours and oils. The use of colour has become much more exciting in the last 200 years, partly as a result of improvements in pigments, but mainly as a result of breaking away from artistic 'rules'. Early watercolours are just tinted drawings, for example Philippe de Loutherbourg's Chepstow Castle and Samuel Grimm's Tintern Abbey, though later watercolours, such as those by William Bartlett and David Cox, have more colour (Plates 11, 30, 39 and 41). Modern pictures which show a free and non-representational use of colour include Hazel Pickering's Wyndcliff and Coldwell Rocks, and my Symonds Yat Rock pastel (Plates 25, 28 and 47).

Tones also are used in a stronger way today to give drama to a painting, as can be seen in Anthony Sully's pictures of Lydbrook and Chepstow Castle, Hazel Pickering's and David Prentice's Wyndcliff, Doug Eaton's New Weir, Jennifer Catterall's Goodrich Castle, David Young's Kymin and John Harris's Goodrich Castle and Coldwell Rocks (Plates 14, 16, 21, 23, 34, 47, 50 and 59). Turner used mezzotint, which is particularly good for depicting light and shade, in his *Junction of the Severn and Wye* and Sandby's Chepstow Castle is another example of an earlier picture which used tone dramatically (Plates 48 and 56).

Some of the modern artists have concentrated on the effect of light on local colour, perhaps reflecting the influence of the Impressionists. Good examples are Colin Simmonds's Chepstow Castle, Doug Eaton's New Weir, Hazel Pickering's Wyndcliff, and the paintings of Tintern Abbey by Christine Hunt, Dick Ray and Maldwyn Charles (Plates 34, 42, 43, 44, 47 and 58). Light is also important in some of the 18th- and 19th-century pictures, notably John 'Warwick' Smith's Tintern Abbey and Paul Sandby's Chepstow Castle (Plates 40 and 56), but here the light has been portrayed by tones rather than colour. Reflections, another aspect of light, are important in some pictures, indeed David Prentice's Lydbrook picture could be said to be mainly about reflection. Other examples are Doug Eaton's New Weir picture, Anthony Sully's Chepstow Castle and my pastel of Coldwell Rocks (Plates 22, 24, 34 and 59).

On the whole, the Wye Tour artists are very concerned with detail and texture, with a tendency, as in most topographical art, to show the same level of detail all over the picture, the exceptions being three 19th-century vignettes, which fade out at the edges (Frontispiece, Plates 6 and 7). The best examples of modern paintings which concentrate on detail are Penny Robson's Pavilion at Piercefield, and Jim Meenaghan's view from the Devil's Pulpit (Plates 46 and 52). In contrast, some of the 21st-century pictures have large areas of flat colour and more sense of large-scale pattern, which reflects the influence of the Abstract Movement. Composition, colour, pattern and tone become as important as the subject and the ambiguity between an illusion of depth versus flat pattern may be explored. Examples are Hazel Pickering's Coldwell Rocks and her view from the Wyndcliff, John Harris's Wyndcliff, Susanna Birley's window pattern at Piercefield and my pictures of the view from Symonds Yat Rock and Coldwell Rocks. Lindsay Steele's mixed media picture of the View from Symonds Yat Rock uses flat areas of texture to convey the composition (Plates 24, 25, 27, 28, 47, 51 and 53).

A striking fact is that very few of the pictures, old or new, could be called classically pictur-esque. Modern images with picturesque elements, include Stephen Curtis's Claudean composition of Ruardean church, Ann Baxter-Wright's dead trees at Goodrich Castle, David Prentice's view from the Wyndcliff with a dark foreground tree, John Harris's Coldwell Rocks and Doug Eaton's New Weir pictures, with their low viewpoints and dark sidescreens (Plates 15, 18, 23, 34 and 50). The inclusion of people in pictures is common in the later picturesque period, but rarer in the modern landscape paintings, the only example in the book where people are prominent being Anthony Sully's couple at Lydbrook (Plate 21). I rarely include people, because I like the feeling of timelessness that an 'empty' landscape conveys, or the feeling that the landscape endures whether we are there or not. Amongst the earlier artists, William Bartlett, John Evans, Samuel Ireland, George Eyre Brooks and C.J. Greenwood at Wyndcliff, Michael 'Angelo' Rooker at New Weir, David Cox and Turner included people (Plates 2, 8, 30, 33, 35, 39, 48 and 49), and it is interesting to see how much the clothes on the figures date the paintings.

As well as ruins, old paintings often included contemporary structures, such as industrial build-ings, whereas modern paintings usually exclude motorways and pylons and emphasise instead the historic structures. The old pictures showing contemporary objects are those that included Wye Tour boats and trows (Plates 4, 7, 8, 9, 12, 33 and 56), the industry at Redbrook (Plate 7) and the Round House and Naval Temple on the Kymin (Plate 35). Despite suggestions to artists that they might choose to show changes in the landscape since the 18th century, very few did so, though Anthony Sully included a modern bench at Lydbrook, Hazel Pickering showed scaffolding at Tintern Abbey, Susanna Birley included modern houses and boats at New Weir, and the Severn Bridge is shown in both John Harris's view from the Wyndcliff and my own picture from Piercefield (Plates 21, 32, 45, 51 and 55). Several of the new pictures have a nostalgic air or deliberately look back to the past, notably Gordon Trow's autumnal glow at New Weir, Annabel Clements re-interpretation of a Turner painting, Audrey Hart's depiction of industrial Lydbrook, and Penny Robson's mouldering pavilion at Piercefield House (Plates 20, 31, 52 and 57).

Changes in perceptions and attitude also emerge. A few of the 18th- and 19th-century pictures exaggerate heights and shapes to add drama, but even so, through modern eyes, most seem to be less exciting than the landscapes themselves. The main atmosphere conveyed by the older pictures is one of dispassionate serenity, whereas the written descriptions emphasize the awful sublimity and the sense of standing on the edge of a precipice. In contrast, some of the modern pictures seem more exciting than the landscapes they depict, emphasising pattern, tones, light, emotions and colours in a way unimaginable 200 years ago. Inevitably, the influence of 20th-century developments in art, particularly Impressionism, Post Impressionism and the Abstract Movement, can be seen in most of the pictures from the exhibition.

Equally important is the influence of photography, which has liberated artists from the need to record a landscape accurately in the topographical tradition, and allowed them to express their emotional reactions to places. This expressionism can be seen in colour, shapes and brush marks, particularly in Hazel Pickering's view from the Wyndcliff and Round House on the Kymin, Jennifer Catterall's moody use of colour at Goodrich Castle, Annabel Clement's Chepstow Castle, John Harris's pictures of Goodrich Castle, Coldwell Rocks and the Wyndcliff, Ann Baxter-Wright's ghostly trees at Goodrich, and Stephen Curtis's Ruardean church (Plates 14, 15, 16, 18, 23, 36, 47, 51, 47 and 57).

Seeing through artists' eyes

Art critics repeatedly tell us that painting is *dead*. Evidently 'landscape art' now consists of ephemeral installations in the countryside, or careful arrangements of stones on gallery floors. However, the contemporary pictures in this book show that painting at a regional level is alive, that many artists still find excitement in British landscapes, and that they discover a great variety of ways to express their reactions. Most of us, who have seen so many images of spectacular landscapes in other parts of the world, have perhaps lost the sense of awe that earlier tourists experienced, and the quotes and paintings selected here go some way to demonstrate that. Nevertheless, I hope this book will help world-weary travellers to take a fresh look at landscapes at home and give them a greater visual appreciation of what they see. To return to Gilpin's words quoted in Chapter 1, visitors can have a new purpose in examining 'the face of a country', but they do not need to be confined by picturesque rules. They can view Wye Valley landscapes through the eyes of some of the artists in this book, seeing shapes, patterns, lines, colours, tones and light, as well as hills, trees, rocks, ruins and the river.

Bibliography
Where I have not read the original, the source or main source is given

Allen, Brian et al. (2007). *Paul Mellon's Legacy. A Passion for British Art.* Yale Center for British Art. Royal Academy of Arts.

Andrews, Malcolm (1989). *The Search for the Picturesque. Landscape Aesthetics and Tourism in Britain, 1760 – 1800.* Stanford University Press.

Anon. (1920s). *Hereford. The centre for the Wye Valley. Official Guide.* City Council and Chamber of Commerce.

Anon. (1936). *Monmouth. The Touring Guide for the Far-Famed Wye Valley. Official Guide.* Monmouth Chamber of Trade.

Anon. (*c.*1936). *Ross. The Gateway to the Wye Valley.* Ross on Wye Chamber of Commerce.

Anon. (1835). *The Penny Magazine*, Monthly Supplement July 31 – August 31. In www.igreens. org.uk/wye_in_1835.htm

Anon. www.ross-on-wye.com/index.php?menu=ross_&page=ross_410-The_Wye_Tour

Austen, Jane (1798). *Northanger Abbey.*

Austen, Jane (1813). *Pride and Prejudice.*

Austen, Jane (1814). *Mansfield Park.*

Baedeker (1905). *Great Britain Guide book.* In www.urban75.org/photos/wales/tour.html

Ballantyne, Andrew (1994). *Turbulence and Repression: re-reading The Landscape.* In Daniels and Watkins.

Barber, J.T. (1803). A *tour through South Wales and Monmouthshire etc.* In Turner and Johnson.

Barbier, C.P. (1963). *William Gilpin: His Drawings, Teaching and Theory of the Picturesque.* Clarendon Press. In Andrews.

Bazarov, Konstantin (1981). *Landscape Painting.* Octopus.

Bentley-Taylor, David (2001). *Wordsworth in the Wye Valley.* Logaston Press.

Blandford, Chris, Associates (1996). *The Wye Valley Landscape.* Countryside Commission.

Bloomfield, Robert (1811). *The Banks of the Wye. A Poem. In Four Books.* Venor, Hood and Sharpe. In Kissack (1978), Andrews and in www.Miall--tintern.Bloomfield.htm

Bradley, A.G. (1910). *The Wye.* Black.

Brayley, E.W., ed. (1805). *The Works of the late Edward Dayes.* Mrs Dayes. In Munro.

Burke, Edmund (1756). *A Philosophical Enquiry into the origin of our Ideas of the Sublime and the Beautiful.* In Andrews and Rosenthal.

Byng, John (1781 & 1787). *The Torrington Diaries.* Ed. C. Bruyn Andrews (1934-8) [2nd ed. Eyre & Spottiswoode 1954]. In Kissack (1978) and Andrews.

Carpenter, Patrick and Graham, William (1971). *Art and Ideas.* Mills and Boon.

Chitty, Peter (2004). *Pastor and polymath. Rev William Gilpin.* Boldre Enterprises.

Clarke, Edward (1791). *A Tour through the South of England, Wales and parts of Ireland in 1791.* In Russell.

Clarke, J.H., ed. (*c.* 1875). *Tours from Ross and Monmouth.* Clarke Usk.

Clarke, Kenneth (1949). *Landscape into Art.* John Murray.

Coates, S.D. (1992). *Water powered Industries of The Lower Wye Valley.* Monmouth Borough Museums Service.

Collins, Wilkie (1859-60). *The Woman in White.*

Coombes, William (1809). *The Tour of Dr Syntax in search of the Picturesque.* In Russell and Andrews.

Cooper, Gordon (1951). *A fortnight in the Wye Valley.* Percival Marshall.

Cox, David (1813). *Treatise on Landscape Painting and Effect.* In Grigson.

Coxe, William (1801). *An Historical Tour in Monmouthshire Vol. I.* Cadell and Davies. Reprint 1995, Merton Priory Press.

Crawford, Donald (1993). *Comparing natural and artistic beauty.* In Kemal and Gaskell.

Daniels, Stephen and Watkins, Charles, eds. (1994). *The Picturesque Landscape.* University of Nottingham.

Davies, Sneyd (1742). *A Voyage to Tintern Abbey.* In www.PoetryRomanticTheSisterArts–BritishGardening,Painting,&Poetry1700-1832.htm

Dayes, Edward (*c*.1804). *From a note on Joseph Farington c.1804.* In Grigson.

Dreghorn, William (1968). *Geology explained in the Forest of Dean and the Wye Valley.* David and Charles.

Farington, Joseph (1803). *The Wye Tour of Joseph Farington.* In Newby.

Fosbroke, T.D. (1818). *The Wye Tour, or Gilpin on the Wye, with historical and archaeological additions.* Ross.

Gainsborough, Thomas (*c*.1764). *Letter to Lord Hardwicke.* In Grigson.

Gibbings, Robert (1942). *Coming down the Wye.* Dent, London.

Gifford, Don (1993). *The touch of landscape.* In Kemal and Gaskell.

Gilpin, William (1768). *An Essay upon Prints; containing some remarks about Picturesque Beauty.*

Gilpin, William (1782). *Observations on the River Wye, and Several parts of South Wales, etc. relative chiefly to Picturesque Beauty; Made in the Summer of the Year 1770.* [2nd ed. 1789]. Blamire.

Gilpin, William (1792). *Three essays:- on Picturesque Beauty:- on Picturesque Travel:- and on sketching landscape: to which is added a Poem, on Landscape Painting.* In Andrews.

Goffe, Michael (2003). *Camping on the Wye.* Logaston Press.

Green, Colin (1991). *Severn Traders.* Black Dwarf.

Grigson, Geoffrey (1975). *Britain Observed.* Phaidon.

Grose, Francis (1775). [*Journey to South Wales, 1775*] British Library Add MS 173988. In Andrews.

Hall, Mr and Mrs S.C. (1861). *The book of South Wales, the Wye and the Coast.* Reprint, 1979, Charlotte James.

Handley, B.M. and Dingwall, R. (1998). *The Wye Valley railway and the Coleford branch.* Oakwood Press.

Hardy, Thomas (1878). *The return of the native.*

Hartley, Beryl (1994). *Naturalism and sketching: Robert Price at Foxley and on tour.* In Daniels and Watkins.

Heath, Charles (1799). *The Excursion down the Wye from Ross to Monmouth.* [1808 edition, Heath].

Helme, Andrew (1989). *Monmouth and the River Wye in old photographs.* Alan Sutton.

Hogarth, William (1753). *The Analysis of Beauty.* [Ronald Paulson ed., 1997, Yale University Press].

Hughes, Pat and Hurley, Heather (1999). *The Story of Ross.* Logaston Press.

Humphries, Peter (1995). *On the trail of Turner in North and South Wales.* Cadw.

Hussey, Christopher (1927). *The Picturesque: studies in a Point of View.* In Andrews.

Ireland, Samuel (1797). *Picturesque Views on the River Wye.* In Jeremiah and Andrews.

Jenkins, Stanley (2002). *The Ross, Monmouth and Pontypool Road Line.* Oakwood Press.

Jeremiah, Josephine (2004). *The River Wye. A pictorial history.* Phillimore.

Kemal, Salim and Gaskell, Ivan, eds. (1993). *Landscape, natural beauty and the arts.* Cambridge University Press.

Kissack, Keith (1978). *The River Wye.* Terence Dalton.

Kissack, Keith (1975). *Monmouth The making of a County Town.* Phillimore.

Kissack, Keith (2003). *Monmouth and its buildings.* Logaston Press.

Knight, Richard Payne (1794). *The Landscape, a didactic poem.* In Daniels and Watkins.

Lochran, Katherine (2004). *Turner Whistler Monet.* Tate Publishing.

Mason, Edmund (1987). *The Wye Valley.* Robert Hale.

Mason, William, ed. (1775). *The poems of Mr Gray to which are prefixed Memoirs of his Life and Writings.* In Andrews.

Meyer, Laure (1992). *Masters of English Landscape.* Terrail.

Morgan, Virginia and Vine, Bridget, eds. (2002). *A history of Walford and Bishopswood.* Logaston Press.

Morris, Martin H. (1980). *The Book of Ross on Wye.* Barracuda Books.

Munro, Jane (1994). *British Landscape Watercolours 1750 – 1850.* Fitzwilliam Museum.

Newby, E. (1998). *The diary of Joseph Farington.* Yale University Press.

Newdigate, Robert (*c.*1754). *Account of Wye Tour.* Warwick RO CR 136/48. In Whitehead.

Nicholls, H.G. (1858). *Forest of Dean. An historical and descriptive account.* John Murray.

Peterken, George (2008). *The Wye Valley.* New Naturalist 105, Harper Collins.

Phelps, Humphrey (1982). *The Forest of Dean.* Alan Sutton.

Price, Uvedale (1794). *Essays on the Picturesque.* In Andrews and Daniels and Watkins.

Rainsbury, Anne (1989). *Chepstow and The River Wye in old photographs.* Alan Sutton.

Rainsbury, Anne (2006). *Chepstow Castle as a Picturesque Ruin.* In Turner and Johnson.

Ritchie, Leith (1841). *The Wye and its Associations A Picturesque Ramble.* Longman, Orme, Brown, Green and Longmans.

Rogers, Samuel (1791). In P.W. Clayden (1887), *The early life of Samuel Rogers.* In Andrews.

Roscoe, Thomas (1836). *Wanderings in South Wales, including the river Wye.* Tilt and Simpkin.

Rosenthal, Michael (1982). *British Landscape Painting.* Phaidon Press.

Rosenthal, Michael (1983). *Constable the painter and his Landscape.* Yale University Press.

Rowlands, M.J. (1994). *Monnow Bridge and Gate.* Alan Sutton.

Russell, Ronald (1979). *Guide to British topographical prints.* David and Charles.

Schama, Simon (1995). *Landscape and Memory.* Harper Collins.

Shaw, Stebbing (1789). *A tour to the West of England in 1788.* In Andrews.

Skrine, Henry (1798). *The successive tours throughout the whole of Wales.* London.

Wilson, H. Shutz (1880). In *Picturesque Europe Vol. 1 The British Isles.* Cassell Letter and Galpin.

Stratford, J.A. (1896). *The Wye Tour.* In Hughes and Hurley.

Thomas, Keith (1983). *Man and the Natural World.* Allen Lane.

Thompson, M.W. (1793-1810). *The Journeys of Sir Richard Colte Hoare through Wales.* In Andrews.

Turner, Rick and Johnson, Andy, eds. (2006). *Chepstow Castle. Its history & Buildings.* Logaston Press.

Twamley, Louisa Anne (1839). *An Autumn Ramble on the Wye.* The Annual of British Landscape Scenery. Charles Tilt.

Valentine, L. (1894). *Picturesque England. Its landmarks and historic haunts as described in Lay and Legend, song and story.* Frederick Warne. In www.mspong.org/picturesque/valley_wye.html

Wall, Tom (1994). *The Verdant Landscape: The Practice and Theory of Richard Payne Knight at Downton Vale.* In Daniels and Watkins.

Walters, Bryan (1992). *The Archaeology and History of Ancient Dean and the Wye Valley.* Thornhill Press.

West, Thomas (1778). *Guide to the Lakes.* In Andrews.

Whateley, Thomas (1770). *Observations on Modern Gardening.* In Andrews.

Whitehead, David (2005). 'The Wye Tour and its Place in the Picturesque Movement'. *The Picturesque Journal* No 52.

Whittle, Elisabeth (1992). *The Historic Gardens of Wales.* Cadw HMSO.

Wilenski, R.H. (1933). *English Painting.* Faber and Faber.

Williams, Isaac (1926). *Welsh Topographical Prints.* Catalogue, National Museum of Wales. In Andrews and Russell.

Wilton, Andrew (1979). *The Life and Work of J.M.W. Turner.* Academy Editions. In Humphries.

Wilton, Andrew (1984). *Turner in Wales.* Catalogue, Mostyn Art Gallery, Llandudno. In Humphries.

Wyndham, Henry P (1775). *A Gentleman's Tour through Monmouthshire and Wales, in the months of June and July, 1774.* In Turner and Johnson.

Young, Arthur (1768). *A Six week tour through the Southern Counties of England and Wales.* In Andrews.

Index

Numbers marked in bold denote illustrations

COURSE

COMPANION

OCR GCE ENGLISH LANGUAGE & LITERATURE

OCR
RECOGNISING ACHIEVEMENT

OXFORD
UNIVERSITY PRESS

Official Publisher Partnership

Great Clarendon Street, Oxford OX2 6DP
Oxford University Press is a department of the
University of Oxford.
It furthers the University's objective of excellence in
research, scholarship, and education by publishing
worldwide in
Oxford New York
Auckland Cape Town Dar es Salaam Hong Kong
Karachi Kuala Lumpur Madrid Melbourne Mexico
City Nairobi New Delhi Shanghai Taipei Toronto
With offices in
Argentina Austria Brazil Chile Czech
Republic France Greece Guatemala Hungary Italy
Japan South Korea Poland Portugal Singapore
Switzerland Thailand Turkey Ukraine Vietnam
Oxford is a registered trade mark of Oxford University
Press in the UK and in certain other countries
Text © Steven Croft and Robert Myers 2009
The moral rights of the authors have been asserted
Database right Oxford University Press (maker)
First published 2009

British Library Cataloguing in Publication Data
Data available
ISBN 978 019 8387589
10 9 8 7 6 5 4 3 2 1
Printed in Great Britain by Bell and Bain Ltd., Glasgow

Paper used in the production of this book is a natural,
recyclable product made from wood grown in sustain-
able forests. The manufacturing process conforms
to the environmental regulations of the country of
origin.

Acknowledgements

We are grateful to the following for permission to reproduce and adapt
extracts from their copyright material:

Steven Croft and Robert Myers: *Exploring Language and Literature*
(Oxford University Press © 2008)

Steven Croft and Helen Cross: *Exploring Literature* (Oxford University
Press © 2008)

We are also grateful for permission to reprint the following copyright
extracts:

BBC: Extract from BBC Tees (formerly BBC Radio Cleveland) transcript
from live football commentary by Ray Simpson and Kevin Smith,
reprinted by permission of the BBC. **BBC**: Extract from BBC Television
transcript of an extract from interview between Michael Parkinson and
Billy Connolly, *Parkinson*, BBC Television, December 1999, reprinted
by permission of Michael Parkinson, Tickety-boo Ltd for Billy Connolly,
and the BBC. **Gail Anderson-Dargatz**: extract from *The Cure for Death
by Lightning* (Virago, 1997), copyright © Gail Anderson-Dargatz 1997,
reprinted by permission of the publisher, Little, Brown Book Group.
Joanna Briscoe: extract from *Skin* (Phoenix, 1997), copyright © Joanna
Briscoe 1997, reprinted by permission of Curtis Brown Group Ltd, London
on behalf of Joanna Briscoe. **Winston Churchill**: extract from 'Their finest
hour', speech given on 18 June 1940, reprinted by permission of Curtis
Brown Group Ltd, London on behalf of the Estate of Winston Churchill.
Andrew Clarke: 'Helicopter hit by waterspout', *The Guardian*, 7.8.2003,
copyright © Guardian News and Media Ltd 2003, reprinted by permission
of Guardian News and Media Ltd. **Russell T Davies**: extract from 'Smith
and Jones' Episode 1 of *Doctor Who* Series 3, reprinted by permission
of the BBC and The Agency (London) Ltd on behalf of the author. **Jane
Gardam**: extract from 'Stone Trees' from *The Pangs of Love* (Hamish
Hamilton, 1983), reprinted by permission of David Higham Associates
Ltd. **David Hare**: extracts from *Murmuring Judges* (Faber, 1991), reprinted
by permission of the publisher, Faber & Faber Ltd. **Susan Hill**: extract
from 'In the Conservatory' from *A Bit of Singing and Dancing* (Long
Barn Books), copyright © Susan Hill 1973, reprinted by permission of
Sheil Land Associates Ltd. **Barry Hines**: extract from *The Heart of It*
(Michael Joseph, 1994), copyright © Barry Hines 1994, reprinted by
permission of Penguin Books Ltd. **John Irving**: extract from *A Prayer
for Owen Meany* (Bloomsbury, 1989, 1994), reprinted by permission of
the publisher. **Sebastian Junger**: extract from *The Perfect Storm* (Fourth
Estate, 1997), copyright © Sebastian Junger 1997, reprinted by permission
of HarperCollins Publishers Ltd. **Geraldine McCaughrean**: extract from
The Kite Rider (OUP, 2006), copyright © Geraldine McCaughrean 2006,
reprinted by permission of Oxford University Press. **Anita Shreve**:
extract from *Eden Close* (Abacus, 1994), copyright © Anita Shreve 1990,
reprinted by permission of the publisher, Little, Brown Book Group.
Tom Stoppard: extracts from *Rosencrantz and Guildenstern are Dead*
(Faber, 1973), reprinted by permission of the publisher, Faber & Faber
Ltd. **Alice Walker**: extract from *The Color Purple* (Weidenfeld & Nicolson,
2007), reprinted by permission of David Higham Associates Ltd. **Marcia
Williams**: extract from 'Julius Caesar ' in *Mr William Shakespeare's Plays*
(Walker Books, 2000), copyright © Marcia Williams 1998, reprinted by
permission of Walker Books Ltd, London SE11 5HJ.

Although we have made every effort to trace and contact all copyright
holders before publication this has not been possible in all cases. If
notified, the publisher will rectify any errors or omissions at the earliest
opportunity.

Contents

Introduction

Important note: The OCR GCE specification for English Language and Literature is the document on which assessment is based; it specifies the content and skills to be covered in delivering a course of study. At all times therefore, the information below should be read in conjunction with the specification. If clarification on a particular point is needed then reference should be made in the first instance to the specification.

The new OCR GCE in English Language and Literature consists of four units: two at AS Level and two more at A2. This introduction will guide you through the specification for each unit, and also introduce you to the Assessment Objectives relevant in each case.

AS Unit F671: Speaking Voices

Unit F671 is the examined unit of the English Language and Literature AS Level, and carries **60%** of the marks at this level. The exam will consist of a **written paper lasting two hours**, which carries a total of **60 marks.** It is a closed text examination, which means that you will not be able to bring your copy of the prose texts in with you.

The unit is divided into two sections:

- Section A: The construction of voice in prose fiction and in transcripts of real speech
- Section B: The creation of meaning in texts of different types and the relationships between them

Section A

You will study one of three prose fiction texts for this section. The set texts are:*

- *Surfacing* by Margaret Atwood
- *The Curious Incident of the Dog in the Night-Time* by Mark Haddon
- *Hawksmoor* by Peter Ackroyd

*The set texts for this specification will change from June 2012: please consult the specification for information after this date.

In the exam, you will answer **one** question based on a passage from your chosen novel, comparing it to a passage of speech transcript. You will need to show knowledge of your text, as well as analytical skills and critical understanding.

Section B

For this section of the exam, you will study one of three prescribed novels, all of which are notable for the distinctive features of the narrative voice. The texts are:*

- *The Great Gatsby* by F. Scott Fitzgerald
- *Wide Sargasso Sea* by Jean Rhys
- *A Room with a View* by E. M. Forster

*The set texts for this specification will change from June 2012: please consult the specification for information after this date.

You will answer **one** essay-style question on your chosen novel. The question will focus on a particular subject or theme and also present you with one or two unseen non-fiction extracts on the same theme. Some of these extracts may be multimodal, which is a form of text that combines different modes of communication, such as speech, writing, sound, video or images, to create meaning. In your answer, you should consider how the theme in the question is presented in your chosen text and compare and contrast the non-fiction extract/s with your text.

Assessment Objectives

In this unit, your examiner will mark your work on the basis of three Assessment Objectives: AO1, AO2 and AO3.

AO1: Select and apply <u>relevant concepts and approaches</u> from integrated linguistic and literary study, using <u>appropriate terminology</u> and <u>accurate, coherent written expression</u>.

This means that:

- you will need to understand different approaches to literary and linguistic study: literary concepts (such as narrative structure, viewpoint, narrative voice and tone) and insights gained through applying linguistic frameworks (including features of spoken language, grammar, lexis, syntax and register)
- you should be able to recognize and understand technical vocabulary and use this terminology appropriately in your writing
- you should write coherently, ensuring that your spelling, punctuation and grammar are of a high standard and that you are able to develop your ideas in some detail.

AO2: Demonstrate <u>detailed critical understanding</u> in <u>analysing</u> the ways in which <u>structure, form and language</u> shape meanings in a range of spoken and written texts.

This means that you will be required to read the text closely, identifying the choices made by each speaker or writer in terms of form, structure and language and analyse how these language choices affect the way meaning is created.

AO3: Use integrated approaches to explore <u>relationships between texts</u>, analysing and evaluating the significance of <u>contextual factors</u> in the production and reception of texts.

To fulfil this Assessment Objective, you will need to explore the relationships between texts as well as the contexts in which they were produced and in what they are received. This means you should:

- develop your understanding of prose fiction as a genre
- learn about different types of text: spoken, written and multimodal
- consider the circumstances in which the texts were written and in which circumstances they have been and continue to be received.

AO3 is the dominant (most important) Assessment Objective in Unit F671.

AS Unit F672: Changing Texts

Unit F672 carries the remaining **40%** of the marks at English Language and Literature AS Level, and is a coursework unit. You must submit a coursework folder of a maximum of **3000 words**, which will be assessed out of a total of **40 marks**.

To complete the tasks for your coursework folder, you will need to study **one** written text from any genre, which has a related multimodal text.

You will need to complete **two tasks**:

- Task 1: Analytical study **(20 marks)**
- Task 2: Multimodal text and commentary **(20 marks)**

Task 1: Analytical Study

For this task, you will produce a study of your chosen literary text and related multimodal text. The study should be **1000–1500 words** in length. It should include exploration of the scope of the original text for multimodal transformation, and the factors that have shaped the multimodal text.

Task 2: Multimodal Text and Commentary

For this task, you will produce your own re-creative text **(1000–1500 words)** based on an original literary text. Your re-creative text must be multimodal, which means that is must include more than one mode (such as: speaking, writing, language, image, sound) and can use a medium other than printed text. It can be a complete text or it can be presented as a section of a much larger work.

You will also need to write a critical commentary and include this in your folder. The commentary should explain your chosen approach to producing the multimodal text and the links between the original passage and your own work.

Assessment Objectives

The two different tasks in this unit will assess you on two different sets of Assessment Objectives. For Task 1, your work will be marked on the basis of AO1, AO2 and AO3. For Task 2, your essay will be marked on the basis of AO1 and AO4. The four Assessment objectives are equally important in your assessment.

AO1: Select and apply <u>relevant concepts and approaches</u> from integrated linguistic and literary study, using <u>appropriate terminology</u> and <u>accurate, coherent written expression</u>.

For Tasks 1 and 2, this means that:

- you will need to understand different approaches to literary and linguistic study: literary concepts (such as narrative structure, viewpoint, narrative voice and tone) and insights gained through applying linguistic frameworks (including features of spoken language, grammar, lexis, syntax and register)
- you should be able to recognize and understand technical vocabulary and use this terminology appropriately in your writing
- you should reflect on what is achieved in transforming a text
- you should write coherently, ensuring that your spelling, punctuation and grammar are of a high standard and that you are able to develop your ideas in some detail.

AO2: Demonstrate <u>detailed critical understanding</u> in <u>analysing</u> the ways in which <u>structure, form and language</u> shape meanings in a range of spoken and written texts.

This means that you will be required to read the text closely, identifying the choices made by the writer of the original text and of the multimodal adaptation in terms of form, structure and language, and analyse how these language choices affect the way meaning is created.

AO3: Use integrated approaches to explore <u>relationships between texts</u>, analysing and evaluating the significance of <u>contextual factors</u> in the production and reception of texts.

To fulfil this Assessment Objective, you will need to explore the relationships between the two texts as well as the contexts in which they were produced and in which they are received. This means you should:

- learn about different types of text: spoken, written and multimodal
- consider the contextual factors that influence the creation and reception of a multimodal text.

AO4: Demonstrate <u>expertise and creativity</u> in using language appropriately for a variety of <u>purposes and audiences</u>, drawing on insights from linguistic and literary studies.

This means that you will demonstrate your creativity and knowledge of writing for a particular audience and purpose in your response to Task 2, using the insights you have gained from your literary and linguistic study.

A2 Unit F673: Dramatic Voices

Unit F673 is the examined unit of the English Language and Literature A2 Level, and carries **30%** of your total marks at GCE. The exam will consist of a **written paper lasting two hours**, with a total of **60 marks** available. It is a closed text examination, which means that you will not be able to bring your copy of the drama texts in with you.

In this unit you will study two drama texts, which will be linked by theme, approach or setting. One will have been written before 1800 and the other will be a modern text. The texts are*:

- *Doctor Faustus* by Christopher Marlowe and *The Crucible* by Arthur Miller
- *Hamlet* by William Shakespeare and *Rosencrantz and Guildenstern Are Dead* by Tom Stoppard
- *The Duchess of Malfi* by John Webster and *Top Girls* by Caryl Churchill

*The set plays for this specification will change from June 2013. Please consult the specification for information after this date.

The unit is divided into two sections:

- Section A: Analytical comparison of an extract from a pair of set texts
- Section B: An essay based on one set text, exploring a proposition that raises an issue central to the integrated study of language and literature

Section A

In this section of the exam, you will answer **one** question based on extracts from **both** of your chosen set texts. You will be asked to write a comparative analysis of how a specific theme is presented in the **two** extracts, and in the two plays as a whole.

Section B

For this section, you will be asked to answer **one** essay question based on **one** of your set texts. You will be given a critical proposition that will focus on a particular issue; this might be a quotation from one of the plays. You will then be asked to explore this issue in your essay. You should limit your exploration to one of the texts that you have studied.

Assessment Objectives

In this unit, your examiner will mark your work on the basis of three Assessment Objectives: AO1, AO2 and AO3.

AO1: Select and apply <u>relevant concepts and approaches</u> from integrated linguistic and literary study, using <u>appropriate terminology</u> and <u>accurate, coherent written expression</u>.

This means that:

- you will need to understand literary concepts such as the linguistic and literary features of Elizabethan and Jacobean drama
- you should be able to use the associated terminology, for example, tragedy and blank verse
- you should write coherently, ensuring that your spelling, punctuation and grammar are of a high standard and that you are able to develop your ideas in some detail.

AO2: Demonstrate <u>detailed critical understanding</u> in <u>analysing</u> the ways in which <u>structure, form and language</u> shape meanings in a range of spoken and written texts.

This means that you will be required to read each play closely, identifying the dramatic technique of the writer including choices of form, structure and language, and analyse how these choices affect the way meaning is created.

AO3: Use integrated approaches to explore <u>relationships between texts</u>, analysing and evaluating the significance of <u>contextual factors</u> in the production and reception of texts.

To fulfil this Assessment Objective, you will need to explore the relationships between the two plays as well as the contexts in which they were written and performed. This means you should:

- develop your understanding of drama as a genre
- learn about literary tradition and the features of culture and society at the time the plays were written
- consider how similar factors of culture and society have shaped the way the plays have been received in the past and are received today.

A2 Unit F674: Connections across Texts

Unit F674 is a coursework unit, and carries the remaining **20%** of your total GCE English Language and Literature marks. You must submit a coursework folder of a maximum of **3000 words**, which will be assessed out of a total of **40 marks**.

In order to complete your coursework folder, you will need to focus on **one** text from any genre. This text should fall outside the literary canon, but must be one that could be considered influential or culturally significant. Your study should also include **two** other supporting texts for comparison and contrast. Of the total three texts, one must be a spoken language text and one must be a non-literary text.

You will need to complete **two tasks**:

- Task 1: Analytical study **(20 marks)**
- Task 2: Creative writing and commentary **(20 marks)**

Task 1: Analytical Study

For this task, you will produce a study of **1500 words**, exploring relationships between your key text and your chosen supporting texts. You will need to compare and contrast the texts, and apply relevant techniques of literary and linguistic analysis. You should also consider the context in which the texts were created and any relevant connections with the rest of your AS and A2 study.

Task 2: Creative Writing and Commentary

For this task, you will produce a piece of creative writing (**1500 words maximum**) arising out of your study in Section A of A2 Unit F673 (it does not, however, have to be based on any one of the chosen texts). It could be a complete text, but it could also be presented as a section of a much larger work.

You will also need to write a critical commentary and include this in your folder. The commentary should explain the approach taken by commenting on the stages of production, demonstrating how your combined understanding of linguistic and literary factors have helped to shape your text. You should indentify links between the analytical study and your own writing, and you should also evaluate your writing in comparison to the original texts studied.

Assessment Objectives

The two tasks in this unit will assess you on two different sets of Assessment Objectives. For Task 1, your work will be marked on the basis of AO1, AO2 and AO3. For Task 2, your essay will be marked on the basis of AO1 and AO4. The four Assessment Objectives are equally important in your assessment.

AO1: Select and apply <u>relevant concepts and approaches</u> from integrated linguistic and literary study, using <u>appropriate terminology</u> and <u>accurate, coherent written expression</u>.

For Tasks 1 and 2, this means that:

- you will need to consider relevant approaches to literary and linguistic study; for example, register, voice, lexis, semantics, syntax, grammar
- you should be able to recognize and understand technical vocabulary and use this terminology appropriately in your writing
- you should write coherently, ensuring that your spelling, punctuation and grammar are of a high standard and that you are able to develop your ideas in some detail.

AO2: Demonstrate <u>detailed critical understanding</u> in <u>analysing</u> the ways in which <u>structure, form and language</u> shape meanings in a range of spoken and written texts.

This means that you will be required to read the text closely, identifying the choices made by the writers of both the original text and of the multimodal adaptation, in terms of form, structure and language, and analyse how these language choices affect the way meaning is created.

AO3: Use integrated approaches to explore <u>relationships between texts</u>, analysing and evaluating the significance of <u>contextual factors</u> in the production and reception of texts.

To fulfil this Assessment Objective, you will need to explore the relationships between the texts as well as the contexts in which they were produced and in which they are received.

AO4: Demonstrate <u>expertise and creativity</u> in using language appropriately for a variety of <u>purposes and audiences</u>, drawing on insights from linguistic and literary studies.

This means that you will demonstrate your creativity and knowledge of writing for a particular audience and purpose in your response to Task 2, using the insights you have gained from your literary and linguistic study.

Your Course Companion

This book will support you in developing a number of the skills you will need to tackle the above specification successfully. Chapter 1 discusses how to analyse texts, Chapter 2 introduces you to the analysis of prose, while Chapter 3 examines creative and re-creative production for AS and A2 coursework. Chapter 4 deals with the analysis of drama and Chapter 5 looks at preparing for assessment. Finally, the Glossary on page 115 may offer useful support for your ongoing studies.

You will also find a CD-ROM at the back of this book, which contains a bank of support materials for use alongside the Course Companion. The CD-ROM contains a range of activity sheets and example extracts to help you practise some of the skills covered in this book.

1 Approaching texts

Introducing analysis

This course is exactly what its name implies: it is the study of both English Language and Literature, and the specification has been designed with the total integration of these two aspects of the subject in mind. Consequently, you will be asked to study a range of writing representing a variety of genres, including the main literary types of prose, poetry and drama, from both literary and linguistic viewpoints. In addition to this, you will also be expected to study a selection of non-literary texts.

You will furthermore be required to study features of speech and be expected to analyse transcripts of spontaneous speech and the representation of speech in multimodal texts. You will compare how meaning is created across different types of texts and explore how these texts relate.

Aims of the course

This course aims to cultivate a deeper understanding of both English Language and English Literature than that gained at GCSE level, by examining **texts** from both literary and linguistic viewpoints.

> **Text**
>
> A text is simply a piece of writing or a piece of speech. The linguist, Michael Halliday famously outlined the possible range of texts as being 'prose or verse, dialogue or monologue, it may be anything from a single proverb to a whole play, from a momentary cry for help to an all-day discussion on a committee'.

By examining a variety of texts in this way, you should be able to see whether a literary, linguistic or integrated analytical approach helps you to understand a text more fully. You will to do this by applying differing analytical **frameworks**.

> **Framework**
>
> A framework is a critical skeleton around which you can build the body of your analysis. Different frameworks may be more suited to different texts and it will be up to you to learn which one best serves your analysis.

Frameworks can be made up of a variety of critical 'bones', and this book will help you learn the most effective ways of constructing your own frameworks for analysis, when to apply them and how to review their effectiveness.

However, it is also necessary for you to be able to apply the detail of the frameworks to different texts; to do this, you need to be aware of the different 'bones' that join together to make different frameworks. You will have learned some of these 'bones' at GCSE level (alliteration, imagery and metaphor, for instance), but there will be many more that you need to become familiar with so as to increase the breadth and effectiveness of your analytical interpretations and responses. The most notable difference from your GCSE studies is that you will need to become familiar with linguistic terms; all aspects of the course require you to understand this terminology.

The advantage of engaging in combined literary and linguistic study is that you can use terms from both disciplines to inform your analyses. You will learn which terms and which frameworks help you to deconstruct texts most effectively.

There are other points that must be taken into account before we begin the study of the content relevant to each part of the course. There are certain underlying principles that you need to be aware of when you are engaged in AS and A2 study. You will need to study a minimum of four set texts across the course. In addition to this, you will study one substantial written text that can be from any genre. This text must have a related multimodal text. You will also study a non-literary text, which can be taken from any genre and could be considered influential or culturally significant.

Together with these you will be expected to engage independently and creatively with a range of other spoken, written and multimodal texts. At AS Level you are required to study two prose fiction set texts, and one substantial written text of your choice from any genre that has given rise to a related multimodal text. At A2 Level, you will study two set drama texts: one modern and one written pre-1800. You will also study another substantial text of your choice, which should fall outside the literary canon. This text will be used for comparison with two other texts. Of the total three texts, one must be a spoken language text and one must be a non-literary text.

This text will guide you through these sections, which will require you, at all times, to consider the **purpose**, **audience** and **context** of each piece of writing you study, as well as taking other points into consideration, such as comparison, textual adaptation and authorial attitudes.

Textual analysis

Because textual analysis is a skill that you need to learn from the outset, it is useful to spend a little time building an initial framework for analysis, which you can then apply throughout this book, adapting it and refining it as you see fit. Textual analysis lies at the heart of this subject, and the application of it (through whichever framework or method you choose) will enable you to become a more confident, informed and skilful critic of English language and literature.

All texts, whether written or spoken, have a **purpose**, **audience** and **context**; these terms are all dealt with in much greater detail in the rest of the book. Essentially, the terms refer to what a text does, who it is written for and where it appears. When you are engaging in textual analysis, it is always a good idea to start with these three areas, as they will help you to find a route into the text. When you have identified these, you can continue by examining the text at a variety of levels, moving from individual words through phrases, sentence structures and other grammatical and syntactical issues, to how the text is put together, and finally on to what it looks like as a whole.

Use the flow chart below to help you use one method of deconstructing a text you are studying; once you have become accustomed to the methodology, you can adapt it for your purposes.

One method of textual analysis

What? Who? Where?		
1 What is the text trying to do?	➤	Purpose
2 Who is it trying to communicate these ideas to?	➤	Audience
3 Where will the text appear?	➤	Context
4 What does it look like?	➤	Form
↓		
How?		
5 Use of specific words or terms from a certain area	➤	Semantic field/ Field-specific lexis
6 Use of certain types of words and word classes	➤	Grammar
7 Use of other constructions in phrases and sentences	➤	Syntax
8 Use of sound features and style devices	➤	Phonology and stylistic features
9 How the text fits together	➤	Cohesion
10 What the text looks like and how it is laid out	➤	Graphology
↓		
Effect?	**Evaluation of ...**	
11 Does the text do what it sets out to do?	➤	Purpose
12 Does it hit its target readership?	➤	Audience
13 Does the place where it appears help the text?	➤	Context
14 Does its layout help?	➤	Form

Of course, analysing a text in such a way does not construct an argument for you. A simple and effective way to do this is simply to chain your points together by using a three-point critical structure. For each point you would:

1   identify the point you want to discuss

2   give an example from the text

3   comment on how it works within the text in terms of purpose and audience.

This is a tried and tested method that helps you to focus on each example that you choose to discuss. You may have been taught a variation of this at GCSE level (one such version is PEE: point – evidence – explanation). Use the version you have been taught if it is easier for you and has worked in the past.

Activity

Read the following texts; they are all short examples of the different types of written genre you may come across during the course. Choose one of them and then follow the task outlined below to write your first piece of short textual analysis.

1 Identify examples and ideas that you could use in a textual analysis.

2 Tabulate your findings: this will give you a series of points that you can use as the basis for your response.

3 Using the flow chart on page 3, organize your findings into relevant sections.

4 Write out your textual analysis of the piece you have chosen.

Prose non-fiction

Helicopter hit by waterspout

A helicopter carrying oil workers from a North Sea oil rig suffered serious damage to its tail rotor after being pitched about by a giant waterspout off the Shetland Islands, accident investigators have reported. The Super Puma helicopter, with 18 people on board, was flying at 500ft in February last year when it encountered a vortex of air, the result of a miniature tornado, which caused seawater to shoot into the clouds.

An official report by accident investigators revealed that the pilot had left the engine on autopilot. When it reached the spout the helicopter 'violently pitched, rolled and yawed'.

The change in direction was so fast that all five of the tail rotors touched the tail pylon, leaving a 15 cm gash which was later discovered by engineers.

An on-board flight recorder showed the helicopter had rolled 9.5 degrees to the right then 34 degrees to the left within two seconds, with the nose pitching sharply down.

The incident was far more severe than the helicopter was required to withstand for certification. The 51-year-old captain was quickly able to regain control and made an announcement to reassure shaken passengers on the helicopter's public address system.

A spokesman for Bristow Helicopters, which owns the aircraft, said: 'Waterspouts aren't that unusual around the coast, but actually flying into one is. In this case there was nothing the pilots could do to avoid it.'

Guardian, Thursday 7 August 2003

The Perfect Storm

A soft fall rain slips down through the trees and the smell of ocean is so strong that it can almost be licked off the air. Trucks rumble along Rogers Street and men in t-shirts stained with fish blood shout to each other from the decks of boats. Beneath them the ocean swells up against the black pilings and sucks back down to the barnacles. Beer cans and old pieces of styrofoam rise and fall and pools of spilled diesel fuel undulate like huge iridescent jellyfish. The boats rock and creak against their ropes and seagulls complain and hunker down and complain some more. Across Rogers Street and around the back of the Crow's Nest Inn, through the door and up the cement stairs, down the carpeted hallway and into one of the doors on the left, stretched out on a double bed in room #27 with a sheet pulled over him, Bobby Shatford lies asleep.

He's got one black eye. There are beer cans and food wrappers scattered around the room and a duffel bag on the floor with t-shirts and flannel shirts and blue jeans spilling out.

Sebastian Junger

Prose fiction

The Cure for Death by Lightning

When it came looking for me I was in the hollow stump by Turtle Creek at the spot where the deep pool was hidden by low hanging bushes, where the fishing was the very best and only my brother and I figured we knew of it. Now, in spring, the stump blossomed purple and yellow violets so profusely that it became something holy and worth pondering. Come fall, the stump was flagrantly, shamefully red in a coat of dying leaves from the surrounding trees. This was my stump, where I stored my few illicit treasures: the lipstick my mother smuggled home for me in a bag of rice; the scrap of red velvet that Bertha Moses tucked in my pocket as she left the house on the day of my fifteenth birthday; the violet perfume I received as my gift at the Christmas pageant the year before; and the bottle of clear nail polish my father threw into the manure pile after he caught me using it behind the house, the bottle I had salvaged, washed, and spirited away.

I was in there, hiding, my knees up to my nose, listening to the sound of it rushing, crashing through the bush, coming for me. A cobweb stretched over my face, an ant roamed over the valleys in my skirt, spiders invaded my hair, and an itch started on my nose and traveled to my arm, but I stayed still.

Gail Anderson-Dargatz

The Kite Rider

Below him, the Mongols sacking Yangcun, who feared nothing but the gods and lightning, took to their heels and fled. They did not stop running until they reached the supply wagons. Then they dragged their yurts off the luggage wagons and rolled themselves in the folds of the hide, shutting out the noise, shutting out the light, shutting out all but the terror which was so great that they were not even ashamed to show it. Their gods were angry, and while the storm raged, there was nothing to be done but to hide as completely as possible from the eyes of heaven.

The storm, born a thousand miles away at sea, took no sides between Mongol and Chinese. It picked nails out of the ancestral temple and demolished it, flag by mirror by birdcage. Like insects fleeing a termite hill, people spilled from the base and scattered in all directions. Such a storm might have been sent by their ancestors, to save them from the Mongols, but if so, why were the lightning bolts striking the town and why was the rain filling the river, minute by minute, to bursting point?

Haoyou also saw the river fill: like a snake swallowing a rat, its whole brown shape bulged. Its surface was rough as a grater, with the intensity of the rain.

Geraldine McCaughrean

Drama

The Tempest

Act 1 Scene 2

Miranda: If by your art, my dearest father, you have
Put the wild waters in this roar, allay them.
The sky, it seems, would pour down stinking pitch,
But that the sea, mounting to th' welkin's cheek,
Dashes the fire out. O, I have suffered
With those that I saw suffer: a brave vessel –
Who had, no doubt, some noble creature in her –
Dash'd all to pieces! O, the cry did knock
Against my very heart – poor souls, they perish'd.
Had I been any god of power, I would
Have sunk the sea within the earth or ere
It should the good ship so have swallow'd, and
The fraughting souls within her.

Prospero:　　　Be collected.
No more amazement. Tell your piteous heart
There's no harm done.
Miranda:　　　O, woe the day!
Prospero:　　　No harm.
I have done nothing but in care of thee,
Of thee, my dear one, thee, my daughter, who
Art ignorant of what thou art; nought knowing
Of whence I am, nor that I am more better
Than Prospero, master of a full poor cell,
And thy no greater father.

William Shakespeare

Doctor Who

Martha: [*On the phone to* Tish *but distracted by* Julia. *At* Julia, *who's staring beyond* Martha; *at the window*] … What?

Julia: … the rain.

Martha: It's only rain.

[*quiet*]

Tish: [*Out of vision; voice on the telephone*] Martha. Have you seen the rain?

Martha: Why's everyone fussing about rain?
[*Said, turning round to the window. Martha stops dead.*]

[*Camera: the window. The rain on the glass is running up.*]

Julia: … it's going up.

Tish: [*Out of vision; voice on phone.*] The rain is going up.
[Martha & Julia *walk forward, gobsmacked …*]

[*Camera: reverse from the opposite side of the window, tracking in on Martha & Julia, water running up the glass ...*]

[*Cut to city street, Tish still on the phone the – rain normal about her – but she's just gaping, and other people are beginning to stop and stare ...*]

[*Camera: the hospital in the distance, ominous grey clouds circling right overhead, rain flying upwards, hugging close to the building: an unnatural sight.*]

[*Camera: Tish's point of view, bolts of lightning all around the hospital – and again, they're going up, ground to sky –*]

[*Cut to the staff kitchen –*]
[*Camera: flashes of lightning, close to the window, and then –*]
[*Camera: slam! - the window fills with solid bright white light –*]
[*Martha & Julia throw their hands up, blinded –*]

[*And all hell breaks loose! Like an earthquake – with the window staying a bright, constant white, the whole room shakes violently – with a 'whumph!', Martha & Julia thrown left! –'whumph!' – right! – 'whumph!' – left again – !*]

[*The cupboards fly open, stuff flying out, then being flung in the opposite direction, like a ship at sea in a storm –*]

[*Martha & Julia drop to the floor, Camera down with them. Then ... it stops.*]
[*Calm. Silence. Hushed:*]

Martha: What the hell was that ..?

Russell T. Davies

2 Analysing prose

Approaching Prose

A substantial proportion of your Language and Literature GCE will be taken up with the study of prose. For your AS Level, you will study two set prose fiction texts. In your exam you will approach one text by comparing it to transcripts of speech and the other in relation to unseen extracts of prose non-fiction that will be offered to you in the exam. For your AS Level coursework, you may also study a prose text. This may be selected from any genre and you will analyse it in relation to a multimodal text, which may include prose elements too, as well as other forms of media such as sound, images or video.

The study of prose continues to be important as you progress to A2 for which you will be required to complete a coursework folder that will involve focusing on some form of prose, whether it is transcripts of speech, non-fiction prose or other forms of non-literary texts. You may deal with other genres of text for this unit too.

This section will begin by considering some of the basic linguistic characteristics of prose, before moving on to consider particular forms of prose such as literary prose fiction.

Syntax

Syntax simply means sentence structure. Basically, the term 'sentence' can be applied to any group of words that makes complete sense, and the usual visual markers of the sentence are a capital letter at the beginning and a full stop at the end. In spoken language a meaningful utterance may not seem, at first consideration, to be a sentence, but could be easily understood. In fact, if you look at a transcript of spontaneous speech you will find few complete sentences in the grammatical sense, although meaning may be communicated perfectly effectively. For example, in response to the question 'What are you doing?' the answer could be 'Going out'. This is perfectly acceptable. The context enables us to supply the missing parts, and so it is unnecessary to say 'I am going out'. In many ways the rules for written and spoken language are different. In grammatical terms, a complete sentence must have two things:

a a **subject** – the person or thing the sentence is about

b a **predicate** – describing what the subject is doing.

In some sentences the predicate may consist of a verb only, as in 'James runs'. Or there may be an additional element known as the **adjunct**. This could be an adverb (or modifier) as in 'James runs quickly' or a noun phrase, 'James runs to the house'. All subjects will include a noun or pronoun – 'James' or 'he' – or they can be lengthened by **determiners** (such as: *a*, *the* and *that*) or adjectives (modifiers).

Sentences can be divided into three basic kinds:

1 **Simple** sentences have one main clause (one subject and one verb).
2 **Compound** sentences have two (or more) main clauses, i.e. two subjects and two verbs that are linked by co-ordinating words or **conjunctions** (*and*, *but*, *or*, *nor*, *either*, *neither*).

3 **Complex** sentences, like compound sentences, consist of two or more clauses, but these are linked together by **subordination** using words such as *because*, *when*, *although*. This kind of sentence is the most complicated and in prose usually signals a fairly sophisticated style.

In analysing a writer's stylistic technique, however, it is of no use simply to be able to recognize whether he or she uses simple, compound or complex sentences. The real questions are 'What purpose do the sentences serve?' and 'What effect do they have on the piece of writing concerned?'

In answer to this first question, a sentence may perform various **functions**.

For example:

- **Declarative** sentences state things (make statements, if you prefer).
- **Interrogative** sentences ask questions.
- **Imperative** sentences issue commands.
- **Exclamatory** sentences always end with an exclamation mark and contain exclamations.

When analysing prose it is important to be able to say something about the syntax, but it is not sufficient to simply say things like 'this piece uses long sentences' or 'a lot of hard sentences are used here'. You need to be able to recognize why the writer has chosen to use particular sentence structures, and what effect they have on the tone, mood and impact of the writing overall.

Here are some general pointers:

- **Declarative** sentences could be used to create a sense of drama.
- **Interrogative** sentences may produce a questioning, probing effect.
- **Imperative** sentences could be used to create an attacking, critical or off-hand effect.
- **Exclamatory** sentences could heighten drama, express shock or surprise, or communicate anger.
- Short, **simple** sentences could be used to give the sense of action speeding up, or a sense of breathlessness.
- Longer, **compound** sentences could produce a slowing effect on the narrative.
- **Complex** sentences might create a contemplative, philosophical mood.

Remember that these are just some examples of the effects different sentence types can create. In reality, each type of sentence can create a variety of effects, so to determine exactly what effects the syntax has on a piece of prose you must assess it within the context of the individual piece you are examining.

Literal and non-literal language

A piece of writing has potentially two different sorts of meaning:

a a literal meaning

b a non-literal or implied meaning.

Literal meaning is a meaning that is fixed for a particular word or group of words. Many groups of words, also have a non-literal meaning or an implied meaning.

Literary devices that are used to create particular effects through non-literal meaning are known collectively as **figurative language**, and include **metaphors**, **similes** and **symbolism**.

Rhetorical techniques

Writers can also make use of rhetoric in their writing, to persuade readers and shape their responses in various ways. You should take account of the use of rhetorical devices when studying a particular writer's stylistic techniques. Here are some of the features you should watch out for:

- repetition, of sounds, words and sentence structures
- juxtaposition
- listing
- parallelism
- hyperbole
- the rhetorical question.

Cohesion

Structure is given to prose by cohesion. In most texts there is some kind of connection, in terms of ideas expressed or actions described, which holds the piece of writing together. The sentences normally link together in a structured way to convey the meaning of a piece of writing to the reader. This structure is called **cohesion** or **coherence**.

Writers can create coherence in their texts in different ways in order to produce particular effects. Understanding how a writer creates coherence can help you to understand more fully the effects created through the writing.

Normally some of the 'connectedness' of a text comes from the topic or subject matter of the piece of writing. This prompts a key question: 'How do you know what a text is about?' In some cases the answer to this may be obvious – you understand what a text is about because of the knowledge you already possess about the topic it deals with, and the words used relate to that topic.

The term **lexis** refers to the type of language used in a text. If we note in the lexis of a piece that words like *surgery*, *doctor*, *nurse*, *scalpel*, *stretcher* and *ward* are used, it is likely that the piece is in some way connected to a hospital or medical situation. These are **collocations** of words – clusters of words that may occur in texts of a similar kind. Words that are generally less common, such as specialist or technical terms, tend to suggest more specialized contexts. Collocations are sometimes referred to as **semantic fields**, that is groups of words that each reflect a particular subject matter.

Besides subject matter and vocabulary, there are other forms of connections between sentences. They can indicate relations of sequence, such as **causality** (one thing leads to another), **exemplification** (giving an example), **implication** (suggesting something) and so on.

Sometimes particular words signal connections between sentences and therefore cohesion in a text. Such markers can be of various kinds.

- Words and phrases co-refer in that they refer to people, situations or things already mentioned. **Pronouns** such as *he, she, they* and *it* refer back to people or things already introduced.

- Words like *the* and *this* refer back to earlier mentions of things.
- Verbs that have already been used are repeated in condensed, or substitute, forms, e.g. *She thought she might be late. If so* [be late] *she would have to get a taxi.*
- Connective words and phrases primarily signal directions, for example:

consequence: *therefore, because of this*
ordering: *firstly, finally*
continuation: *furthermore, then*
simultaneity: *meanwhile, in the meantime*
concession: *admittedly, yet*
opposition: *nevertheless, in spite of this*

Taken together, these various elements create what is often known as the texture of a text – presenting it as a unified and connected whole rather than as a random selection of sentences.

Analysing prose fiction

This section will focus on the ways in which writers use language in fiction texts and the effects that they create. For the course of your study of Language and Literature, the study of prose fiction texts will be closely linked to detailed language analysis and also a consideration of what relationships exist between fiction and other forms of writing such as non-fiction and multimodal texts.

In your AS Level written exam, you will be expected to compare the prose fiction text that you have studied to a range of unseen extracts of non-fiction prose. In looking at the language of prose fiction, both linguistic and literary issues will be examined, and you will need to prepare yourself by examining literary issues through the language of the texts you study, noting how writers use language to achieve and enhance literary effects and address issues.

In AS Unit F671 you will need to show:

- a critical awareness of prose fiction as a literary form in relation to other text types
- an understanding of ways in which voices in narrative fiction and natural speech are represented
- an understanding of and ability to use appropriate technical vocabulary
- an understanding of how form, structure and language are significant in creating meaning
- an awareness of contextual factors that influence the production and reception of texts.

The nature of prose fiction

Many of the prose fiction texts that you are likely to come across in this specification are of the kind we refer to as narrative prose – narrative in the sense that they all 'tell a story' in one way or another, usually in the form of a novel or short story. Narrative prose consists primarily of the telling of a sequence of connected events, by some kind of narrator. Although narrative prose fiction can be difficult to place in specific categories, most prose fiction has certain features in common.

Here are some of the key features you might have listed:

- there is usually a narrator of some kind and therefore the story is told from a particular **point of view**
- narrative prose is usually **structured** so it has a beginning, a middle and some kind of ending
- it usually has a point – it is told for a **purpose** – to explore an idea, or theme, or simply to tell an entertaining story
- it usually contains **characters** that are presented in certain ways by the writer.

Although every novel or short story is different and each writer makes decisions about the **purpose** and **style** of his or her prose, most narrative prose has one function in common. This function is to entertain – although, of course, the vast majority of authors do much more than this. Narrative prose can raise a reader's awareness of a particular theme, or issue, or group of ideas, and thus prose may educate and inform as well as entertain.

Features of narrative prose

Theories of narrative usually identify two main levels of narrative. These are:

1 The basic events or actions of the narrative, given in the chronological order in which they are supposed to have happened. In basic terms, this level is often referred to as the **story** or the **plot**.
2 The techniques and devices used to tell the story. These are often called the **narrative techniques**.

The recognition of a distinction between the story itself and the way in which it is told is important because it acknowledges that the same story can be told in different ways depending on the **point of view** of the teller.

Point of view

The point of view is of central importance to narrative prose because the reader needs to know who is telling the story. The term can be used literally to describe the visual perspective from which the story is presented. It can also be used to indicate the ideological framework from which the story is told, or the bias contained in the text. This is what we are commenting on when, for example, we say that a text presents a 'female perspective', or that the story is told from 'the point of view of the ordinary worker'.

A third way in which the term can be used is to describe basic types of narration – in other words, the relationship between the narrator of the story and the reader. At a simple level, there is a distinction between the two basic and most common types of narration: **first-person narration** and **third-person narration**.

First-person narration

In a first-person narrative, the 'I' narrator tells of the events that he or she experiences. This kind of narration is found in a range of novels and short stories covering a wide variety of styles and periods; for example, Mary Shelley's *Frankenstein* (1818), Charlotte Brontë's *Jane Eyre* (1847), Alice Sebold's *The Lovely Bones* (2002), Valerie Martin's *Property* (2003) and Khaled Hosseini's *The Kite Runner* (2003). Several features of first-person narrative are worth bearing in mind:

- First-person narrative allows the reader directly into the mind of the narrator.
- Sometimes the events of the novel can be viewed retrospectively, so the narrator's view of things can change as he or she matures.
- events are sometimes related second-hand, as occurs in F. Scott Fitzgerald's, *The Great Gatsby*, which can make the authority of the narrator's view of events seem questionable.
- sometimes there is more than one narrator; Emily Brontë uses multiple narrators to tell her story in *Wuthering Heights* and each presents the story from his or her own viewpoint, which can be biased or questionable. Sometimes these are referred to as unreliable narrators.
- This form of narration often gives only one person's view of the story and can therefore present a biased account of events. By its nature it seems more subjective than third-person narration.

Third-person narration

In a third-person narrative the narrator is often omniscient, which means he or she 'sees all' and 'knows all' that is going on. There is no 'I' figure and so the story is related directly to the reader. There are two types of **omniscient narrator** – the **intrusive** and the **unintrusive**. The intrusive narrator enters into the novel by explicitly commenting on events and characters. Authors such as Thomas Hardy, E. M. Forster and George Eliot do this frequently and, to some extent, Anita Shreve does this in *Eden Close*. On the other hand, the unintrusive narrator tells the story from a distance without the reader being aware that the narrator is making judgements or voicing opinions.

Third-person narration can also work in other ways. For example, the narrative point of view can be either **internal** or **external**. Third-person narration can simply describe events, characters, and so on as they are observed from the outside, but it can also describe them from the inside. Such a narrator can seem able to see into the minds of the characters and tell us about how they think and feel; hence the term 'omniscient' narrators.

Another distinction that can be made in third-person narration is between **restricted** and **unrestricted** narration. In some novels the narrator apparently has no restrictions on the knowledge he or she possesses concerning the characters and events. On the other hand, some writers deliberately give their narrators restricted knowledge. Such limitations are often signalled by phrases such as *it seemed*, *appeared* or *looked as if*.

Sometimes this restricting of the narration reflects the fact that the narrative identifies closely with a single character, while at the same time remaining in the third person. It is important to recognize this as it shows that sometimes third-person narration is not necessarily objective, and it can operate from more subjective and restricted viewpoints.

Other forms of narrative you might come across in your studies do not fit easily into the categeries of either first- or third-person narration. For example, interior monologues can be used to reflect and develop the thoughts in a character's head. You may well be familiar with this form of writing through such works as Alan Bennett's *Talking Heads* and *Talking Heads 2*, but other writers frequently use this approach too, sometimes as a part of a larger narrative. Many nineteenth-century novelists use passages of interior monologue to allow the reader to see how a character's thoughts are developing.

Another form of narrative you might come across is **stream of consciousness** writing, in which thoughts are written as if they have been spilled out of the character's mind on to the page. One of the features of this kind of writing is that it appears unstructured, unpunctuated and chaotic. However, it is important to remember that the writer has deliberately structured it in this way to reflect the complex outpourings of the human mind. Perhaps the best-known writers to experiment with this style of writing are James Joyce and Virginia Woolf.

Narrative voice

Closely associated with the idea of narrative viewpoint is the idea of narrative voice. Different narrators and different narrative techniques change a story, affecting not just how we are told something but what we are told and how we respond to it. The feelings and attitudes of the narrator can be detected through the tone of voice adopted, thus providing the writer with another way of shaping the responses of the reader.

Authorial intentions

In your examination of narrative prose it is important that you are able to identify what the writer is trying to achieve at various points in the narrative. Authorial intention can take various forms, but here are some possible kinds:

- creating characters
- describing or presenting a scene
- creating a particular mood or atmosphere
- experimenting with language.

Creating characters

We have already looked at ways in which writers can use first- or third-person narrative to reveal character. In both these types of narrative, other linguistic and stylistic techniques also have a part to play in the creation of the overall effect.

The most obvious way a character can be created is through physical description. In analysing such description, it is important to establish from the outset whose view is being given, the writer's, another character's, or the narrator's, in order to make some assessment of its reliability.

Describing or presenting a scene

Scene setting is obviously very important if the writer wants to convince the reader of the fictional world created. Physical details of time and place can help to enable the reader to visualize the background against which the action takes place. Although separate from atmosphere, the setting could be closely linked to the atmosphere and mood the writer wishes to create.

Creating a particular mood or atmosphere

The creation of different atmospheres can be very important to the overall impact of a novel. If readers are to be convinced of the fictional world created it is important that the writer successfully arouses the reader's emotions. By creating, various atmospheres and moods the writer can persuade the reader to feel things in certain ways, perhaps evoking a sympathy for one of the characters or anger at a particular situation, for example.

Experimenting with language

Writers often experiment with non-standard language in order to intensify particular aspects of the fictional world that they have created. By using variations of language for different characters, the writer can make them seem more realistic and individual and can place them more specifically in a time or place. Often this is a technique that can be seen in the writer's use of dialogue, reflecting the accents and dialects of characters.

Activity

Read the following extract. How does Walker use language here to achieve her effects? What is the impact of this non-standard use of language?

The Color Purple

Dear God,

Harpo ast his daddy why he beat me. Mr _____ say,

Cause she my wife. Plus, she stubborn. All women good for – he don't finish. He just tuck his chin over the paper like he do. Remind me of Pa.

Harpo ast me, How come you stubborn? He don't ast How come you his wife? Nobody ast that.

I say, Just born that way, I reckon.

He beat me like he beat the children. Cept he don't never hardly beat them. He say, Celie, git the belt. The children be outside the room peeking through the cracks. It all I can do not to cry. I make myself wood. I say to myself, Celie, you a tree. That's how come I know trees fear man.

Alice Walker

Register

The term 'register' is used to describe how language varies to suit the particular audience and purpose. For example, a solicitor might use a form of language containing many legal words and phrases, while a doctor would be more likely to use language dominated by medical words and phrases. You might use formal language when attending a job interview, and an informal register when speaking to your friends.

When you analyse a piece of writing containing spoken language it is important to make sure that you note three key areas related to register:

The mode

Either spoken or written (although there can be subdivision where a speech is written down, for example).

The manner

The particular level of formality of language used by the writer. In basic terms this can be either formal or informal.

The field

The way that the words used are linked to the subject matter being dealt with. For example, a writer dealing with a military theme is likely to use words such as *garrison*, *sergeant*, *unexploded*, *shell*, *artillery*, etc. The field, therefore, is closely related to lexis, and by examining it conclusions can be drawn about the topic or focus of the language being used.

Lexis

Lexis (sometimes called **lexicon**) is the term used to describe the vocabulary of a novel, poem, speech or other form of language use. You may find this feature referred to as **diction** in some books, particularly those dealing with literary criticism.

Lexis deals with the study of words and the way that they relate to one another, and it can take a variety of forms depending on the choices that writers make to achieve their purposes.

When examining the lexis of narrative prose, certain features or kinds of words are worth watching out for. Here is one way to approach the task:

Nouns

Abstract nouns may focus on describing states of mind, concepts or ideas.

Concrete nouns are used more to describe solid events and characters.

Proper nouns are used to refer to specific characters and places.

Verbs

Stative verbs (such as *know*, *believe*) may be used to convey descriptions of states of mind and setting.

Dynamic verbs (such as *go*, *say*) emphasise what is currently happening.

Modifiers

Modifiers, such as adverbs and adjectives, can provide a whole range of added detail, and writers use them a great deal to influence the reader's perceptions. They can add positive or negative connotations and shape readers' responses.

Here is a checklist of other features to look for when examining the word choice of a writer:

- levels of formality (formal or informal)
- technical and non-technical vocabulary
- non-standard vocabulary (colloquialisms, dialect words).

What sorts of vocabulary are being used? Are the words:

- short or long
- simple or complex
- concrete or abstract
- in everyday use or specialist and relating to a particular area
- literal or figurative
- heavily modified or presented with little modification?

Remember, though, that throughout your consideration of lexis you should always bear in mind the time and place in which the narrative is set. The writer's lexical choices will depend very much on the world he or she inhabits and the world he or she creates.

Comparing prose fiction to transcripts of speech

For Section A of AS Unit F671 you will be asked to compare an extract from one of the set prose fiction texts that you have studied to a passage of speech transcript. In order to do this successfully you will need to be able to recognize differences in the ways in which speech is presented in fiction and how it occurs in the real world, whether in the form of spontaneous speech or a speech that has been prepared and practised before its delivery.

This part of the chapter will look more closely at narrative techniques in prose fiction and how this might be compared to the ways in which people communicate using speech.

Speech, dialogue and thought

Narrative prose very often contains speech, through which the characters communicate with the reader or with other characters. If the character is speaking alone, the speech is known as a **monologue**, but if one or more other characters are involved it becomes a **dialogue**. The thoughts of characters are sometimes treated in the same way as speech, as if the character is 'thinking aloud' in order to convey information to the reader.

Writers adopt a number of approaches to convey the speech of their characters through prose. It is worth remembering, though, that these techniques – which present something spoken and heard in the form of writing to be read – are doing something fundamentally artificial with language. Written speech tends to be very much more conventionalized and ordered than speech in real life. The writer's talent, however, lies in convincing the reader of the reality of this artificial dialogue, so that disbelief is suspended.

Direct speech

Direct speech presents the reader with an exact copy of the words spoken. They are enclosed within quotation marks and accompanied by a reporting clause such as *he shouted*, *said*, *called* or *demanded*.

Wuthering Heights

'It is well you are out of my reach,' he exclaimed. 'What fiend possesses you to stare back at me, continually, with those infernal eyes? Down with them! and don't remind me of your existence again. I thought I had cured you of laughing!'

'It was me,' muttered Hareton.

'What did you say?' demanded the master.

Emily Brontë

- -

The use of direct speech gives a prominence and emphasis to the speaker's point of view. It also allows writers to vary spelling, vocabulary, word order and so on in order to give an accurate phonological, lexical and syntactical version to represent a character's accent, dialect or individual manner of speaking.

Indirect speech

Indirect speech presents the material from a slightly different perspective, away from that of the speaker and towards the narrator. For example, if we take the above speech from *Wuthering Heights*, this could be represented in indirect speech in the following way:

He exclaimed that it was well she was out of his reach and asked her what fiend possessed her to stare back at him continually with those infernal eyes. He told her to look down and not to remind him of her existence again and that he thought he had cured her of laughing. Hareton then muttered that it was him.

Activity

Look carefully at the two versions and identify the changes that have taken place.

Check your points against the following:

1   The quotation marks around the speech, which indicate that direct quotation is taking place, have been dropped.
2   A subordinating conjunction – *that* – is used.
3   There is a change from first- and second-person pronouns (*I*, *you*) to third-person (*he*, *she*, *her*).
4   There is a shift in the tense 'backwards' in time (*you are* to *she was*).

Free direct speech

Direct speech has two features which show evidence of the presence of the narrator:

- the quotation marks
- the reporting clause (for example, *she said* or *he said*)

In free direct speech reference to the speaker is not always made. Many writers use this approach when creating speech in their narratives. Here is an example from *Beloved*, where Toni Morrison uses only the occasional supporting clause indicating who is speaking.

Patience, something Denver had never known, overtook her. As long as her mother did not interfere, she was a model of compassion, turning waspish, though, when Sethe tried to help.

'Did she take a spoonful of anything today?' Sethe inquired.

'She shouldn't eat with cholera.'

'You sure that's it? Was just a hunch of Paul D's.'

'I don't know, but she shouldn't eat anyway just yet.'

'I think cholera people puke all the time.'

'That's even more reason, ain't it?'

'Well she shouldn't starve to death either, Denvery.'

'Leave us alone, Ma'am. I'm taking care of her.'

Toni Morrison

Sometimes a writer might use a mixture of direct and free direct speech to create an effect. Dickens adopts this technique in *Bleak House*:

'This won't do, gentlemen!' says the Coroner, with a melancholy shake of the head.

'Don't you think you can receive his evidence, sir?' asks an attentive Juryman.

'Out of the question,' says the Coroner. 'You have heard the boy. "Can't exactly say" won't do, you know. We can't take *that*, in a Court of Justice, gentlemen. It's terrible depravity. Put the boy aside.'

Boy put aside; to the great edification of the audience; – especially of Little Swills, the Comic Vocalist.

Now. Is there any other witness? No other witness.

Very well, gentlemen! Here's a man unknown, proved to have been in the habit of taking opium in large quantities for a year and a half, found dead of too much opium. If you think you have any evidence to lead you to the conclusion that he committed suicide, you will come to that conclusion. If you think it is a case of accidental death, you will find a verdict accordingly.

Verdict accordingly. Accidental death. No doubt. Gentlemen, you are discharged. Good afternoon.

Charles Dickens

> ### Activity
>
> Think about these examples. Why do you think some writers choose to adopt this free direct speech technique? What effect does it have on the narrative?

Here are some possible effects:

- the removal of the distinction between speech and narrative creates the impression that they are inseparable aspects of one unified piece
- Dickens's switch to the free direct form allows him to speed up the usually lengthy concluding processes of the court. This free direct form allows him to focus on the essentials while at the same time retaining the narrative line and the sense of the direct voice.

Occasionally some writers remove the quotation marks entirely. James Joyce, for example, runs speech and narrative together throughout *A Portrait of the Artist as a Young Man*.

Free indirect speech

This is a form of indirect speech in which the main reporting clause (such as *She said that ...*) is missed out, but the tense and pronoun selection are those associated with indirect speech. The effect of this is to merge the approach of both direct and indirect speech.

This form of speech is often used in third-person narratives where the third-person narrator presents the speech (or thoughts) of the characters.

Here, the writer, after a straightforward narrative lead-in, goes into free direct and then free indirect speech mode:

In the Conservatory

She scarcely knew Nancy at all, she had gone to the party in place of her husband, Boris, to whom the invitation was addressed. Boris never went to parties of any kind, but that did not stop the invitations coming. And she had gone with this purpose in mind – to meet someone. For she had decided some weeks beforehand that it ought to be her next experience. I am thirty-two years old, she told herself, eight years married and childless, what else is there for me? I am not unattractive, not unintelligent, yet I have never had any sort of an affair, before marriage or since, there is a whole world about which my friends talk and people write, and about which I know nothing. There are emotions, passions, jealousies and anxieties, which I do not understand. It is time, surely it is time ...

Perhaps, after all, it was not as clear-cut, as fully conscious as that, perhaps there were many doubts and moments of disillusionment. But the decision was in some sort made, and afterwards, she felt herself to be suddenly more vulnerable, more aware, she was receptive to glances and questions and implications. And then, it was only a question of time.

Susan Hill

Activity

Think about how this form varies from the others you have looked at. In what ways do you think it differs from the others? What particular effects do you think could be achieved through its use?

Here are some points for you to think about:

- Free indirect speech blurs the distinction between a character's speech and the narrative voice.
- It offers a way for writers to present words that seem to come both from inside and outside a character at the same time.
- It can give speech the emotional power of coming from the character's perspective while at the same time preserving some narrative distance or detachment from the character.
- It is often used to convey irony because it allows for the introduction of two points of view – the character's and the narrator's – simultaneously.

The presentation of thoughts

In many ways 'thought' can be considered a kind of 'inner speech', and the categories available to a writer in presenting the thoughts of characters are the same as for the presentation of speech. For example:

a He wondered, 'Is the train on time?' (Direct thought)

b Is the train on time? (Free direct thought)

c He wondered if the train was on time. (Indirect thought)

d Was the train on time? (Free indirect thought).

Many narratives use these various methods of telling the reader what is in the minds of characters, and many writers, particularly of the nineteenth and twentieth centuries, have experimented with the use of 'internal speech'. One reason for this is the fact that writers have become more and more concerned with ways of presenting vividly the flow of thought through a character's mind. Taken to its extreme this led to the development of what has become known as **stream of consciousness** writing, in which the character's thoughts are poured out in a constant stream, often without punctuation, just as if they were flowing from the character's mind.

Activity

Read the following passage carefully. It is from Jane Gardam's *Stone Trees* and describes the experiences of a bereaved woman.

1 How does Gardam's use of language here differ from a straightforward description of the scene?

2 What details do you gather from the text that a straightforward description of the scene would not have given you?

3 What details are missed out that a straightforward description would have given you?

4 What effects do you think Gardam wanted to create here?

Stone Trees

The boat crosses. Has crossed. Already. Criss-cross deck. Criss-cross water. Splashy sea and look –! Lovely clouds flying (now that you are dead) and here's the pier. A long, long pier into the sea and gulls shouting and children yelling here and there and here's my ticket and there they stand. All in a row – Tom, Anna, the two children solemn. And smiles now – Tom and Anna. Tom and Anna look too large to be quite true. Too good. Anna who never did anything wrong. Arms stretch too far forward for a simple day.

They stretch because they want. They would not stretch to me if you were obvious and not just dead. Then it would have been, hullo, easy crossing? Good. Wonderful day. Let's get back and down on the beach. Great to see you both.

So now that you are dead –

We paced last week. Three.

Tom. Anna. I.

And other black figures wood-faced outside the crematorium in blazing sun, examining shiny black-edged tickets on blazing bouquets. 'How good of Marjorie – fancy old Marjorie. I didn't even know she –' There was that woman who ran out of the so-called service with handkerchief at her eyes. But who was there except you my darling and I and the Robertsons and the shiny cards and did they do it then? Were they doing it then as we read the flowers? Do they do it at once or stack it up with other coffins and was it still inside waiting as I paced with portly Tom? Christian Tom – Tom we laughed at so often and oh my darling now that you are dead –

Jane Gardam

- -

Overall, we can summarize the presentation of speech in the following points:

- speech presentation is more than a mere technical feature
- different modes present different viewpoints and different relationships with the narrator
- each variation has a different effect, allowing the character to speak as if in his or her 'own words' or filtering them through the perspective of the narrator
- different kinds of interplay between the voice of the narrator and the speech of a character are closely connected to the idea of point of view.

Grammar

In narrative prose, the grammar will reflect the kind of world the writer creates and the viewpoint adopted. Analysing the grammar of a text can be useful in establishing how the text works.

In examining a piece of prose, look out for the following grammatical features:

- **Tense** – most narratives are written in the simple past tense but other tenses are sometimes used to create different effects.
- **Mood** can be reflected through the use of grammar – the declarative mood is the most common, but the use of imperatives and interrogatives can influence the pace and change the focus.
- **Sentence structure** (syntax) can be used to achieve different effects. Simple sentences are often used to give emphasis, while more complex structures can create various effects. Most writers tend to vary their sentence structure to help give the reader variety and therefore sustain interest.

Analysing speech and speech representation

For the purposes of both AS and A2 study, you must also be able to recognize, deconstruct and comment upon spontaneous speech or natural conversation. Your ability to do this, by examining different types of speech and the constituent parts of speech, will enable you to analyse and, ultimately, compare the ways writers choose to represent speech in their works.

Linguistically, there are many differences between speech and writing, and we must take a number of factors into account when studying the differences between the two. These two types of communication are often distinguished by use of the term **mode**.

> **Mode**
>
> The modes are the two methodologies that we choose between when we communicate with each other; that is, we either use the **spoken mode** (speech) or produce the **written mode** (writing).

When a speaker or writer chooses a particular mode, he or she has often made intuitive (if sometimes unconscious) decisions as to why speech or writing should be adopted as a means or mode of communication. Before we look at some of the reasons why we choose a certain mode, let us examine two pieces of language that highlight some of the differences between speech and writing. The following two extracts show that the writers have explicit purposes and audiences in mind, by virtue of the mode they choose and what they do with their language within that mode.

Activity

Look closely at the following two pieces of language. The first extract is from the opening pages of a novel and the second is from a recording of a student speaking. Both pieces have a similar purpose, in that they are introductions to the speaker/ writer.

- What differences can you see between the two pieces?
- For what reasons are these particular modes adopted?
- Who do you think is the target audience for each piece?

For each question, use textual evidence to support your answer.

Skin

I have very pale skin, very red lips. The lips are a fleshy cushion of pink, but I colour them dark scarlet. The skin is naturally pale, that prized magnolia of lovers, the skin of fairy tales and calves, and it is dusted with Shiseido, a white powder. The journalists have always talked about my skin.

Today I'm walking through the Jardin du Luxembourg on my own. It's April, there's a sore yellow light teasing the shadows between the trees, and the young English nannies push babies along the paths and stop at the sandpit.

The shaded section soothes me. I must protect my face from the divings of sunlight because I am using Retin-A, a vitamin A based cream that sheds layers of skin like sheaves of paper. If the sun reaches my face, it will burn. So I use sun block all over, that gives me a greased sheen when I first step out, but which is later absorbed, and will protect me from second degree burning. I am Adele Meier, something of a celebrity, and I must protect my skin.

Joanna Briscoe

Joanne

Key

(.)	micropause
(1.0)	pause in seconds
::	elongation of sound
[*italics*]	non-verbal sounds

My name's Joanne (0.5) I'm eighteen years old (1.0) an' I live in a small village (0.5) called Castleton (0.5) near Whitby (.) on in the middle o'the North Yorkshire Moors (0.5) with m'mum 'n dad (1.0) an' ma brother Simon (0.5) who's twenty-three a:::nd (0.5) erm (0.5) ma sister Emma (1.0) who's (1.0) fourteen (1.0) thirteen (1.0) fourteen (1.5) er (0.5) fourteen (0.5) [*laughs*] also and erm (0.5) I'm at (0.5) studyin' at the moment (1.0) I'm at uni Leeds University (0.5) erm (0.5) which I'm enjoyin' very much (1.0) I've made some really good fr (.) I've bin there since September (0.5) an' I've made some really good friends (.) and (0.5) having a bri::lliant time (0.5) erm (1.0) I'm quite small (3.0) errr (1.0) I like to think I'm quite thin (0.5) but er (0.5) I'm not sure if (0.5) if that's the case at the moment (2.5) um (1.0) I've got long blonde hair (1.0) blue eyes (1.5) a::nd (1.0) big feet (1.0) er:: (1.0) er I've bin home fer a coupla weeks (1.0) an' I went out with ma cousins ter do (.) at a party at a nearby pub (1.0) where we dressed up (0.5) as Reservoir Dogs (1.0) [*quietly laughs*] an' then this mornin' (1.5) I didn't feel too good [*laughs*]

- -

We can best see the main differences between modes through the following distinctions:

1 the differences of **channel** or the way in which each mode is transmitted

2 the different **uses** of each mode, including the kinds of message each sends and the situations or contexts where each is used

3 the differences in **form**; this is the section that will outline the major characteristics of speech and will provide the basis of your understanding of how spontaneous speech operates.

Channel differences

The most obvious differences between speech and writing arise through the way each mode is produced; speech is formed through sound waves, from the mouth and voice box, and is transmitted to the ears. There are also usually other people present when we talk, but not always. Writing, on the other hand, is produced manually and is read, usually by eye, but in the case of blind people by touch.

Writing is often undertaken for other people who are not present at the time of writing. These fairly transparent differences lead to another major distinguishing feature between the two: that is, speech, because it is transmitted orally at a certain point in time, is bound by time, whereas writing is produced for readers who are not present and is as such space bound or spatial. This also results in the fact that the former is essentially temporary (although it can be given permanency through recording) and the latter is more permanent.

When considering channel, it is necessary to consider how the **forms** of each mode supplement the linguistic content, although the specific linguistic forms will be dealt with in much more detail later in the chapter.

In brief, speech includes what are known as **paralinguistic features**, those characteristics that transcend the language. These include:

- intonation, pitch and stress
- volume
- pace and rhythm
- pauses, gaps and silences
- laughter, coughing and other non-verbal sounds
- quality of voice.

On the other hand, the paralinguistic features of writing include:

- paragraphing
- punctuation including the spacing between words
- capitalization.

A sub-set of paralinguistic features is **kinesics**, which can be applied only to speech as it includes all those bodily features that go towards helping us communicate meaning. These include:

- body language, such as use of the hands (pointing) and head (nodding)
- facial expression, including use of the eyes, the mouth (smiling) and the forehead (frowning).

If there is an equivalent of kinesics in writing, it is **graphology**, which would include:

- the design of specific graphemes (individual letters) or the font
- the point size in lettering
- use of colour
- use of white space and margins
- use of illustrations, pictures and other images
- use of columns and layout.

All of the above are, in many ways, incidental differences, but they do help to underpin your understanding of the more concrete differences between speech and writing. Therefore, your understanding of why communicators choose a certain mode, and by implication a certain channel with all its attendant characteristics, should be heightened, especially when in the next section we consider the uses or functions of each mode. Below is a table showing the differences we have considered so far.

Channel characteristics: permanent, dynamic and temporal differences

	Speech	Writing
1	When people speak to each other, they do so in the knowledge that there will be no record of the conversation (except in their minds or memories) and that when the conversation ends it ceases to exist. When they speak they use sounds to communicate.	When people write, they do so to make a record of their thoughts or ideas and they know that their writing will be permanent (as long as the text is kept). When people write, they use handwriting or some mechanical means to represent writing.
E.g.	*a conversation between two sixth-form students on the way to their next lesson*	hand-written (not permanent): *a shopping list* hand-written (permanent): *lecture notes* printed: *a novel or play-script*
2	Speech is most often an interactive process, where there are one or more other persons present. Thus, it can be seen as an active or dynamic process.	Writing is an activity where the audience is distant and very often not known. Thus, writing can be seen as a non-dynamic process.
E.g.	*any face-to-face conversation between two or more people*	audience unknown: *a magazine article* audience known: *a letter to a friend*
3	Speech is bound by time in that it is produced during a certain finite period of time where the participants are present during the interaction. Thus it is temporally bound.	Writing is bound by space as it is produced for readers who are not present at the time of writing; only the writer is usually present at the time of production, although there are exceptions. Thus it is spatially bound.
E.g.	*any verbal interaction that takes place*	space bound: *an essay for a teacher* space bound with participants: *minutes of a meeting*
4	Paralinguistic features and kinesics supplement meaning within speech.	Graphological features supplement the appearance of writing. Conventions of writing aid our understanding of its meaning.
E.g.	*someone telling a dramatic story using intonation and the hands to add to the effect he or she intends*	*the use of capitalization, sentence boundary markers, headlines, columns and photographs in a newspaper article*

Differences in mode usage
Speech

In the previous section on channel characteristics, we discovered that speech has the unique quality of being dynamic and that it is often temporary, in that it is 'lost' as soon as it has been said. However, speech can be made permanent through recording, transcription or a combination of the two. **Transcriptions** enable us to study various speech acts and events in this book, and it is the method you will become most familiar with when you study speech in an examination situation.

Transcription

A method of writing down exactly what is said in a systematic way. The style of transcription used in the English Language and Literature specification is **phonemic**, with additional symbols to aid understanding of what is said. This style of transcription is sometimes called an **impressionistic** transcription. A second style of transcription is **phonetic**, which uses symbols for sounds, the most widely known symbols being the International Phonetic Alphabet.

Speech can be seen as falling into the following categories, depending upon the intended degree of permanency:

- face-to-face interaction such as conversations or interviews
- non face-to-face interactions such as telephone conversations
- broadcast materials such as live radio or television programmes
- recordings such as audio books or 'teach yourself' tapes.

Even though speech in all of the above situations can be either temporary or permanent, it does have the unique quality of being 'live' in all of them because, as listeners, we hear the voices of the speakers, whether they are recorded or not, and the voice has the ability, through the paralinguistic features we have already outlined, to convey a unique personality.

Beyond the categories listed above, speech covers a range of specific functions that are dependent upon the situation, or are bound by the context.

Context

The social circumstances and situation in which speech takes place; the context influences the nature of what is said and how it is communicated. External contexts must be considered and commented upon when you analyse any speech act.

The definition given above draws your attention to the importance of context in speech, which is slightly different from the contexts we have examined so far. The following activity focuses solely on this sense of context.

Activity

Look closely at the following examples of speech from a range of situations. The context is vital for our understanding of each speech act, but can be guessed from these particular examples.

- What is the context for each of the following pieces of speech?
- What information can you give about each of the people speaking?
- What function does each piece of speech have?

1 **Young girl:** Can you tell me the way to the bus station, please?

   Man: Take the next right and follow the road for about half a mile and it's on your left. You can't miss it.

2 **George:** How are yer Fred?

   Fred: Mustn't grumble y'know, although t'missus in't too well.

3 So what yer need ter do (.) er is (0.5) er click on the bl (.) the tab (.) which says blank publications an' (0.5) er find cust (.) erm (1.0) the custom page button.

4 What a great song that is. Well, it's almost half past eight and it's time for our regular look at the papers. Hmm. Some interesting stories to catch the eye this morning.

These examples all show that the context or situation in which speech has been produced is integral to our understanding of what is being said. We can now look at the range of situations where speech is used.

The functions of speech

The situation or context of speech helps us to understand its function more clearly and to distinguish the nuances of certain speech acts. The functions of speech are as follows, starting with the most obvious and most common:

Conversation

This includes any spoken situation where speech is exchanged between participants, although where they are not necessarily face-to-face. For instance, we often have telephone conversations without looking at the person we are talking to (with the advent of videophones and video conferencing, this is now not always the case). We can say that conversation is **interactional** in that it involves two or more participants. However, utterances within conversations have a number of sub-functions, which are outlined below:

- Making propositions. When we make conversation, we establish relationships with others, we co-operate and we keep channels open for further conversations. In order to facilitate these, we make propositions to each other where the things we talk about and discuss are linked to real or possible events in our own world, and where what we say can be either true or false. These are called **constative** (or **representative**) **utterances** since they are capable of being analysed as to their veracity or truthfulness. All of the following are examples of constative utterances:

  A: I've had a terrible day at school, Mum.

  B: It was lovely on Saturday.

  C: Coronation Street's on!

- Exchanging pleasantries. When we engage people in conversation, we do not launch straight into what we have to say without signalling that we want to open up a route of communication. These indicators, such as 'Excuse me' or 'Hello' are called **phatic utterances**, and usually precede the content of our conversations. We may also engage in phatic communication when it is not what is said that is important, more the fact that we are talking. When we meet one another and comment on the weather or ask how the other person is, it could be viewed as an exchange of simple pleasantries and nothing more; in other words, it is linguistically vacuous and serves only a social function.

- Expressing feelings. Another function of speech is to convey our feelings and emotions. Obviously, this depends upon how comfortable we feel about articulating our feelings and how confident we are as people. However, with people we know or are close to, we often use **expressive utterances** to transmit our innermost feelings.

  A: I feel awful about it.
  B: I really hate Pete Doherty.
  C: Oh, I love you so much!

- Doing something. There are certain times where we want someone to do something for us, so we will order, suggest or request a particular thing. This kind of utterance is a **directive**.

  A: A pint of beer and give me a bag of crisps, too.
  B: Shut the window for me, will you?
  C: Don't speak with your mouth full.

Pedagogic talk

It is sometimes difficult to draw the line between conversation and the kind of talk that takes place in the classroom. It is often said that educational talk is not only interactional but also **transactional**, since its function is to get something done.

The formality of the classroom has, to some extent, disappeared as teachers embrace the advantages of learning through informal means and differing teaching styles. Nonetheless, the classroom does not always allow the same degree of feedback in exchanges as everyday conversation, and the teacher often controls who can feed back. Similarly, when parents are talking to their children about appropriate behaviour, they adopt a position akin to a teacher and control the number of turns and amount of feedback from the child they are addressing.

Sub-functions of pedagogic talk are as follows:

* Conveying information. Speech is frequently used to communicate information and facts, as teachers do in many different ways. The talk is often informal, participatory and includes turn-taking and feedback. This type of conversation or speech produces **referential utterances**, having factual information as their basis; they can also be constative or representative in their nature, since they are based on truth.

  A: England won the World Cup in 1966.
  B: There are a number of different types of noun: common, proper, abstract, collective and so on.
  C: Copenhagen is the capital of Denmark.

* Ethical transmission. There is also an aspect of teaching and parenting that embraces the transmission of morality and ethics. This results in **ethical propositions**, that is, behavioural guides that usually embed values or moral codes within their main content. These types of utterance often have their foundation in civil law.

  A: You should not kill other people.
  B: Nice girls don't swear.
  C: Do not urinate in public places.

Accompanying performance

When people accompany certain actions in the real world with speech, a unique type of speech act takes place: the **performative** (or **declarational**) **utterance**. This includes ceremonies where certain procedures are followed, and formalized events that require certain accompanying actions. Events such as religious observances, marriage ceremonies and legal procedures can all be included here.

A: By the power invested in me in this court, I sentence you to sixty days of community service.
B: I take this woman to be my lawful wedded wife.
C: I name this ship the Bonnie Lassie.

This type of speech could also include those speech acts that require the speaker to undertake some future action. These are known as **commissive utterances** and include threats, promises, pledges and refusals.

A: I promise to meet you next week.
B: I'll come right back.
C: We will not be going to the shops today.

Entertainment

This includes talk on television, radio and the stage. These media all use speech in quite special ways. For instance, television and radio can include spontaneous, unscripted speech, as seen in interviews and chat shows, although these will usually have some kind of agenda or topic to guide the discussion. Obviously, the talk on television is supplemented by visual elements, but both television and radio base much of what is conveyed on speech.

Scripted speech plays a major part in such programmes as news bulletins (through the use of autocues), soap operas and documentaries. Scripted speech as seen in dramas and theatrical productions is another area that deserves separate consideration.

Rhetorical speech

Again this is a unique type of speech in that it is (usually) scripted and relies, to a great extent, on the use of rhetorical and persuasive devices, in order to influence listeners. Politicians are very adept at using rhetoric; advertisers often use persuasive techniques to boost sales of their products. Rhetorical and scripted speech will be examined later in this chapter.

Egocentric speech

When we are alone we sometimes talk to ourselves; children more so than adults perhaps. The purpose of this is unclear: are we articulating our thoughts, and if we are, then aren't thoughts a kind of silent speech in themselves? Whatever the purpose, we are certainly able to talk to ourselves and many of us do it, even if we might not admit it! Perhaps we should view egocentric speech as a kind of personal monologue for our own benefit.

Activity

Using a table set out like the one below, collect examples of your own that show:

- different usages of the range of utterances listed
- the context of each utterance.

Utterance type	Your example	Context
Constative utterance		
Phatic utterance		
Expressive utterance		
Referential utterance		
Directive utterance		
Commissive utterance		
Ethical proposition		
Performative utterance		

Difference in form between speech and writing

In comparison to speech, writing possesses a different range of functions. Writing can be circulated to millions of people who can read it simultaneously or at different times, together or across the globe. Because of this, it has taken on the function of cultural transmission, allowing potentially huge audiences to share the same written experience.

Because of the difficulty in remembering long tracts of language, written prose has also developed as the major literary form, used in the widest sense of the word. Fictional stories, biographies, news stories, history and religion all use the prose medium for recording details that could not be stored in the memory or transmitted orally with accuracy.

The following table may help to summarize some of the key differences between the functions of speech and writing.

	Speech	Writing
1	Speech is essentially a social activity. We use it for many different ends, from passing the time of day to the more formalized rituals of ceremony.	Writing is more suited to the recording of factual material, giving an accurate account of what has happened in printed form.
E.g.	*talking to a friend about what we did last night*	*an account of what happened at a political summit in the newspaper*
2	Speech is suited to the 'here and now', where we do not need to make records. It is more immediate and temporary.	Writing allows us to record more facts and material than we could remember for future reference. It is less immediate but has the advantage of permanency.
E.g.	*any conversation which is purely informal and not recorded in any way*	*a diary that is written every day over a sustained period of time*
3	Speech allows us to tell someone how we feel, how to behave or what should be done in certain situations. We can access these perceptions instantly.	Writing tends to give us the opportunity to explore the possibilities of ideas and theories. It also records laws formally, rather than suggesting codes of behaviour.
E.g.	*telling someone what you believe they should do, after they have asked you for advice*	*scientific theories as seen in periodicals; written local by-laws*
4	Since the brain allows retention of only a certain number of facts, speech allows us to verbalize only what we can recall; it can therefore be subject to inaccuracy.	Writing allows us access to reference material when we do not know something or are uncertain of facts. It often allows us to ascertain the truth about matters.
E.g.	*retelling a story where certain facts are misreported or muddled up*	*any reference book, e.g. an encyclopaedia or dictionary*

Speech

Some of the major characteristics of speech arise out of the fact that much speech is **unplanned** or **spontaneous**. Because a lot of speech is not thought out before its expression, we find that a number of unique features occur that give spontaneous speech its special quality.

One of the characteristics we have already noted, is that we do not speak in the carefully constructed, standard sentences which make up the prose of written English; we speak in non-sentences or **utterances**. This word is a much more accurate way to describe units of speech, since it reflects what we utter or say, and it would be quite misleading to say we speak in sentences. Indeed, if we did speak in sentences, we would find conversation boring and a trial to listen to and take part in. It is the fact that we use non-sentences, part-sentences, paralinguistics and kinesics that gives speech its distinctiveness and makes it such a useful tool in everyday life.

When we examine the form of spoken language, it is helpful to break down the component parts of the speech act itself: the relationship of the speakers, the manner of the speech, the topic or subject matter and, finally, the structure of the conversation.

Examine carefully the following piece of spontaneous speech, which occurred at the start of a conversation between four young people having a break at college: Sarah (S), Kris (K), Hannah (H) and Will (W).

Key

(.) micropause
(1.0) pause in seconds
<u>underlining</u> particular emphasis of a word
[overlap
:: elongation of sound

S: will you get us a coffee Kris
K: yea:::::h (0.5) okay *(goes to coffee bar)*
S: what've yer just 'ad
H: further maths (.) I <u>rea:::lly</u> wish I hadner taken it
S: why
H: it's <u>solid</u> (.) <u>absolutely</u> rock hard
S: I feel the same about film (.) there's so much a <u>analytical</u> stuff (.) as well as all the (.) the <u>theory</u> an' all that (0.5) hiya *(Will sits down)*
W: hi
H: hiya
S: how was English
W: s'allright (.) our teacher's a right sarky git though (.) he had a go about me teeshirt (.) then me hair (.) and <u>then</u> he made me read (.) <u>bastard</u> *(laughs)*
S: who is it
W: Rob Myers
H: oh I've got him as well (.) seems okay <u>actually</u>
W: yeah (.) well (.) 'f 'e says any thing else I'll be *(inaudible)*
S: so (.) we goin' out on Friday or what
H: could do (.) I'll've been paid by then (.) you up for it Will
W: suppose so (.) don't <u>think</u> I'm doin' anything else
                                                            [
H: great
                                                            [
W: where's Kris
S: gone to get me a coffee
W: I'll go an' see if he'll get me one too
S: so (.) where shall we go then
H: the Piper

- -

This is a typical example of an exchange that young people have, where they are known to one another, and see each other on a regular basis. The following list of points reveals how it is possible to derive these conclusions from the text.

1 **Relationship**: We can see immediately that the participants in the conversation are known to each other:

- the participants rarely use each other's names, certainly not when they are greeting each other
- the girls decide to discuss plans for Friday night
- they have common reference points (the teacher, the name of the club).

2 **Formality:** The conversation is quite informal, despite having a structure to it:

- the participants use many contracted forms (''f 'e' for 'if he')
- they also employ terms which are fairly exclusive to their peer group ('solid' and 'up for it')
- there are very few external constraints in terms of context, and it is obviously possible for others to join in (Will joins the conversation without any apparent difficulty and then leaves it to go and join Kris).

3 **Topicality:** Since this is part of a conversation that takes place during a break, a range of topics might come up:

- the need for a coffee; Sarah expresses this and Kris accepts the task of going to get one
- the way that their lessons are progressing
- their reactions to a member of staff
- the initial plans for a night out.

Once a topic has been exhausted, a new topic can be introduced and explored (Will does this by giving his opinion on a teacher); if a new topic is introduced before the present topic has worked out its natural course, then the new topic may be rejected or picked up later. A **topic shift** is when a new topic is taken up and is explored by the participants; we see this when Sarah asks if they are going out on Friday.

4 **Structure:** It is often easy to pick up the thread of what is happening in a conversation and discover what the participants are talking about if there are clues to help us. Sometimes the topic is the route into a conversation; here we have a number of references to lessons and teaching as well as socializing, which help us to work out the way in which the conversation develops. But it can sometimes be difficult to tune into a conversation when it is in full flow, as you have no doubt experienced yourself when you have come into a room where the participants are completely immersed in their talk. It takes a little while to work out what the parameters of the conversation are and what subject is being discussed; sometimes we pick up the wrong subject, and this can result in misunderstanding or confusion.

The next section looks at some of the strategies conversation in more detail.

Adjacency pairs

One vital organizational device we employ all the time in conversation, whether formal or informal, is the adjacency pair. This is where one type of utterance leads to another, always with a distinctive pattern that we have intuitively come to recognize through conversational practice. Adjacency pairs:

- are spoken by different people
- always have a rational link
- are characterized by the second utterance following on from an initial utterance.

Adjacency pairs allow conversation to progress in a structured, if unplanned, way. They are unplanned in the sense that we don't know what is going to be said next, even though the topicality has already been decided upon. Adjacency pairings can include the following, (although this is not an exhaustive list):

- greeting and returned greeting
- question and answer
- request and acceptance or refusal
- statement and corroboration
- compliment and reply (not necessarily accepted)
- complaint and apology
- leave-taking and farewell.

We can see that there is a structure to the conversation by examining the way that the pairings are linked. The first section of the conversation is broken down for you, to show how some of the adjacency pairs work:

S: will you get us a coffee Kris
K: yea:::::h (0.5) okay

- -

This is a request, where Sarah asks Kris to get a drink for her using an interrogative; he accepts the request, although his extended 'yea:::::h' indicates that he might not be too happy to begin with, especially since he seems to clarify his acceptance by confirming it through 'okay'.

S: what've yer just 'ad
H: further maths

- -

This is another question and answer adjacency pair, where Sarah simply asks for some information which is given by Hannah. She uses an interrogative utterance 'what've yer just 'ad' to elicit this information from her friend; Hannah gives a simple reply in the form of 'further maths'. However, the next adjacency pair starts with an opinion in the form of an expressive utterance, where her feelings are shown by the extended and emphasized intensifier '<u>rea:::lly</u>':

H: I <u>rea:::lly</u> wish I hadner taken it
S: why
H: it's <u>solid</u> (.) <u>absolutely</u> rock hard

- -

Here, Sarah asks Hannah to elucidate by use of the simple interrogative 'why', and Hannah gives her reply that the subject is 'solid', which she then builds on with the adjectival phrase 'absolutely rock hard'. This section can also be seen as a three-part exchange. This is where a particular section of conversation requires three distinct, ordered sections:

- an initiation or beginning utterance
- a reply
- a response to the reply or feedback.

> **Feedback**
>
> The process of receiving a reply to a piece of speech, which shows that the listener has understood the nature of the message sent by the speaker; a tool to show that the effectiveness of a piece of communication can be verified.

This applies to the part of the conversation we have just examined:

- the initial point about the difficulty of the subject: 'I rea:::lly wish I hadner taken it'
- Sarah's reply: 'why'
- and Hannah's response and feedback to the reply: 'it's solid (.) absolutely rock hard'.

The conversation continues with another adjacency pair, which chains from the last part of the three-part exchange:

H: it's solid (.) absolutely rock hard
S: I feel the same about film (.) there's so much a analytical stuff (.) as well as all the (.) the theory an' all that (0.5)

- -

Here Sarah seems to sympathize with Hannah's feelings about her problems with a new subject as she responds with one of her own, 'film [studies]'. We have here an example of a statement followed by a corroboration and example from Sarah, which is then exemplified through comment on the parts of the subject which are 'analytical'. There is some general and imprecise use of language, often a characteristic of young people, when she uses the noun 'stuff' and the rather general noun phrase 'the theory an' all that'.

The next part is purely phatic as Will enters and she greets him, which he then replies to:

S: ... hiya
W: hi

- -

Hannah also indulges in phatic communication as she takes Will's greeting to be a signal to reply herself, as the second part of an adjacency pair:

W: hi
H: hiya

- -

The linking of some of these adjacency pairs is called **chaining**, since each pair is attached to the previous one, usually in a linear fashion and rather like the links in a chain. This enables the participants to explore topics and work them out to their natural conclusion. As you can see from the example you have just looked at, we are fairly dependent on the notion of conversational chaining through adjacency pairs, as they allow conversation to flow unimpeded. When we violate the unspoken rules of adjacency pairing, conversation tends to break down. For instance, if we persistently fail to respond to a question we have been asked, then the questioner will assume that something is wrong and will either ask what the matter is or end the conversation.

Turn-taking

One of the skills we possess as conversational participants is taking turns when we talk. We 'pass' the conversation over to other group members, and it is taken up or refused by other participants as they see fit. Conversations are characterized by the fact that only one person speaks at a time: each is taking a turn, as it were. However, that turn may be relinquished, may be passed on to someone else or may even be 'stolen', especially if one speaker is monopolizing the conversation. As participants in a conversation, we are fairly certain that we will get a turn to say something at some point. But how do we know when a turn is 'up for grabs', or whether a certain person will speak as opposed to someone else? A number of signals occur in utterances to help us here. They include the following:

- The speaker **elongates** or **stresses** the final word of the utterance; there is a good example of this in the conversation we have already looked at, where Hannah says she feels that the teacher is 'okay <u>actually</u>', the stress on the adverb signalling the end of her utterance. Because this is the part of the utterance that she wants to stress, she does so by placing the adverb at the end of her utterance.

- The speaker may also indicate that his or her turn is ending by dropping the sound level, coupled with less emphasis. A good example of this in the conversation is where Sarah says she is also finding aspects of Film Studies difficult: 'the <u>theory</u> an' all that'. We can see that the three words after the stress on the noun 'theory' are much less important and almost seem throwaway. The fact that it also includes a clipped form of the connective 'and' probably indicates that it is less important too.

- Phrases such as 'you know', 'like' and 'or something' can sometimes indicate the end of a turn as these words are being used like fillers, thus showing that the speaker is running out of steam and it is time for someone else to take up the turn.

- Speakers may designate that their turn is over by making their utterance complete grammatically and syntactically. Questions are good examples of this, although the fact that they require an answer makes it doubly obvious that the turn is being handed over. Completed statements such as 'And that's the end of it' or 'That's all I have to say on the matter' are examples of syntactically complete utterances which show the speaker has finished.

- Finally, there are those signals that cannot be seen on the page, which are paralinguistic in nature: eye contact with another listener, sitting back in a chair or another similar relaxation of the posture, and use of the hands or head (nodding) could all signal it is another person's turn to speak.

Turn-taking is a vital part of conversational management and, in conjunction with adjacency pairings, it is one of the two major structures of spoken interaction. There are other features that are less frequent, but nonetheless important.

Insertion and side sequences

Once a conversation has been initiated, there can be interruptions from unexpected sources. People can come into the room or something might happen that requires the speaker's immediate attention, such as a knock at the door or a telephone ringing. The consequence of this is a **conversational insertion** or **insertion sequence**, where the original conversation is suspended and then resumes once the interruption has been dealt with. An example might look something like this:

X: so there we were an' then

           [

Z: 'scuse me (.) d'you want me to type that up for you ⎫
X: oh yes please (.) thanks   ⎬ Insertion sequence
Y: so what happened   ⎭
X: right (.) there we were an' the whole thing just (.) <u>exploded</u>

- -

Z's interruption is obviously important and so it takes precedence over the original utterance, where a story is being told. The insertion sequence is dealt with and then the original topic is returned to.

Side sequences, however, are much more obvious and sometimes last for a number of utterances. They act as an elucidation or explanation of something that has previously been uttered:

X: Let's go to the pub.
Y: Will Mike be there? ⎫
X: Nah.   ⎬ Side sequence
Y: What about Alan?   ⎪
X: Don't think so.   ⎭
Y: Oh all right then.

- -

In the snippet of conversation given above, we see that Y wants clarification of who will be in the pub before giving his affirmation in the final utterance that he will go; note that the first and last utterances form an adjacency pairing within which the side sequence is embedded.

Closing sequences

When we draw towards the end of a conversation, especially if we are standing talking in the street or some other public place, we signal that we wish the conversation to come to an end by a variety of methods. This is another form of conversational management; it can often take a number of utterances to achieve, and repetition is frequently used to sum up and then close the exchange. Look at this example, taken from the end of the conversation between the four students to whom you were introduced earlier:

S: so I'll see you at lunch then
K: yeah
S: are we goin' down town
K: yeah (.) see yer then
S: okay (.) see yer later Will
W: bye
H: bye
W: bye

This sequence has a number of distinctive features to it, including pre-closing signals which tell other people in the group that the closing ritual is about to commence ('so I'll see you at lunch then') and then some phatic utterances ('bye') which keep the channels open for further talk, at lunch time presumably. In much the same way that phatic utterances signal the opening of a conversation and open up avenues for discourse, closing sequences round off a conversation in a co-operative manner, and also allow those conversational avenues to be re-opened at a later date. This is the basis for co-operative discourse and we use it all the time.

Elision, ellipsis and other shortened forms

Because speech is often quick and characterized by informality among friends, **elision** often occurs. Elision is a characteristic of connected speech and often occurs when we put certain words together to make often-used phrases. A good example would be *fish 'n chips*, where the 'and' is contracted to 'n and the whole phrase sounds like one word. An example from the conversation we studied earlier is 's'allright', which is a contraction of 'it's all right'; there is also the phrase ''f 'e', which is an elided form of 'if he'. This last phrase also highlights some people's predilection for dropping the 'h' sound in speech, often through speed or laziness.

Whereas contraction also referred to as **elision** refers to the omission of certain letters in words and phrases, **ellipsis** refers to missing whole words, which are generally understood from the context of the speech. This can take a variety of forms:

- pronouns: Hope you can come *for* I hope you can come
- verb phrases: Wanna coffee? *for* Do you want a coffee?
- full phrase: Q: Where are you off to?
  A: To town. *for* I am off to town

In the conversation that we have looked at, a good example of an elliptical sentence is Hannah's utterance: 'could do (.) I'll've been paid by then (.) you up for it Will'.

In this utterance there are two elliptical sections. First, 'could do' is missing the personal pronoun 'I' as it isn't really needed; the original question has been directed at her only. Secondly, the question at the end of the utterance 'you up for it Will' has the verb 'are' missing from it, probably because of speed and the informality of the whole exchange.

Other contractions include shortened versions of things such as:

- **names:** shortening of names is often seen as an indicator of informality, for example Peter becomes Pete or Sarah becomes Sal
- **verbs:** in speech we often shorten negated verbs, so 'cannot' becomes 'can't', 'shall not' becomes 'shan't' and 'is not' becomes 'isn't'
- **pronouns and verbs:** as with the forms we have seen above, when some verbs are placed with pronouns, contraction occurs in speech: 'I will' becomes 'I'll', 'you will' becomes 'you'll' and so on.

Liaison

Liaison is another feature of speech that occurs when two words are spoken at speed and the running together or **liaison** of these two words produces a new sound. For instance, when a word starts with a vowel, there is sometimes a carry-over sound, from a previous word ending in a consonant.

'There is someone over there' might be heard as 'There ris someone over there', where the 'r' is sounded at the start of the verb 'is', resulting in a word that sounds like 'ris'.

Juncture

As we have already seen, when we speak we can merge words together so they become virtually indistinguishable. **Juncture** is the almost imperceptible gap that appears between words so we can distinguish them; it is most often characterized by a monentary pause, but it is not always clear in spontaneous speech. This can result in some interesting, and occasionally amusing, misunderstandings, which the comedians the Two Ronnies used in a famous sketch set in a hardware shop. A man enters the shop and asks for various items but the shopkeeper misinterprets his request, simply because of the juncture (or lack of it) between the shopper's words. For instance the shopper asks for 'fork 'andles' (his accent drops the 'h' at the start of the word 'handles') and the shopkeeper returns to the counter with four candles, as the lack of juncture between the shopper's words (as well as his accent) allows for this misinterpretation.

Non-standard forms and slang

The standard forms that are used in writing are often flouted in speech; no doubt those of you who use non-standard forms will have had some of your written English corrected before now! In the conversation we have been examining, a couple of non-standard forms are used: Will says, 'our teacher's a right sarky git though (.) he had a go about me teeshirt'. Here Will uses the non-standard intensifier 'right' for 'very' and then replaces the first-person possessive pronoun 'my' with 'me', which is technically not possessive at all. It can also be noted that the adjective 'sarky' is a non-standard, informal version of 'sarcastic'. Finally, the mildly derogatory term 'git' is certainly a feature of spontaneous speech, where slang, swearing and demotic forms often pepper informal conversations.

Informal speech is also characterized by use of slang terms, words that are acceptable in casual speech and understood by everyone; in writing, they would often be deemed inappropriate unless they were part of reported speech. Slang terms are often short-lived and sometimes recognizable only to the peer group who use them. An example within the conversation we have studied is 'solid' meaning 'difficult' or 'hard'.

Non-verbal aspects

We have already mentioned, and seen in the transcriptions, **overlaps** where two people speak at once; this is marked by the symbol '[' in transcriptions, with the overlapping speech being printed in alignment. Overlaps occur for various reasons: an end of turn may have been misjudged, someone may be keen to add to a point and wish to steal a turn, or there may be many participants who all hold equal status within the conversational group.

Pauses are self-explanatory: they indicate a gap in something said, and are marked by a parenthesis with a number inside, to indicate the number of seconds of time that elapsed between speech. For example '(1.5)' would indicate a pause of one-and-a-half seconds. Pauses allow thinking time, obviously quite important in spontaneous speech. Micropauses (.) are sometimes seen as the punctuation of speech, as they can indicate the boundaries of clauses and unitary pieces of information; at other times, they exist solely to allow the speaker the opportunity of taking a breath or considering the next part of the utterance.

Voice-filled pauses are gaps that are filled. Examples of voice-filled pauses are 'erm', 'er', 'um' and 'ah'. They help to indicate that the speaker's turn is not over yet and so prevent interruption as well as indicating that some thought process is taking place; there is also a school of thought that says that such pauses show our mouths do not move as quickly as our minds, so we get these little hiccups in speech. If they are words in their own right but carry no apparent meaning, these pauses are called **fillers**, because they fill a gap. Frequently used fillers include:

- you know
- sort of
- you see
- I mean
- kind of
- well.

Repetitions or **stuttering** can often be found in conversations: it is as if the speaker is searching for the right word and is unsure as to whether he or she has found it. It may be only a letter that is repeated, as in the conversation reported above, when Sarah says: 'there's so much a <u>analytical</u> stuff', where she is obviously searching for the correct word and makes a repair within her utterance.

False starts also occur periodically, especially if the speaker becomes muddled or has so much to say that he or she loses track of speech constructions. Sometimes, if we start an utterance and realize we have made a mistake and need to correct ourselves, we use a conversational **repair**, which can often be prefaced or coupled with the filler 'I mean'.

Remember that girl (.) er Stacey (.) er no (0.5) Tracy I mean

- -

Hedging is a feature that occurs when you don't necessarily want to make your feelings known or you are keen to fence-sit so as not to give your position away, often for fear of offending. An example of this kind of speech is the following:

X: what d'you think then
Z: we::::ll (.) I'm not sure really

- -

Here Z is hedging by using the interjection 'well' as a signal of hesitation, through the elongation of the word, and finally by directly stating uncertainty.

Discourse markers are words which often indicate that a speaker is about to take a turn or establish some sort of position in the conversation. Words such as 'right' or 'so' or 'okay then' as initial words in utterances are good examples of this. They have the effect of saying, 'I'm going to speak now. I want you to listen to me.'

Markers of sympathetic circularity and **backchannel behaviour** are 'words' often heard when someone is in full flow and the listener feeds back by making noises to indicate that he or she is listening to what is being said. Examples of this would be 'uh uh', 'yeah', 'I see', 'mm' and so on. Often these are delivered while the other speaker is speaking, so they provide examples of simultaneous speech.

Writing

It is not necessary to go into great detail about writing, as many of the differences should already be apparent. However, a brief outline of some of the features of writing will help you to understand speech more fully.

When we write, we have the opportunity to develop and organize our work, making amendments and revisions as necessary. We also have the ability to plan out documents prior to writing them; this enables us to use complex sentence structures, with subordination and intricacy of syntax. In speech, especially spontaneous unplanned speech, we do not often use intricacy and we tend to keep our utterances syntactically and grammatically simple.

Similarly, because writing does not have the visual clues that speech often does, the former tends to use unambiguous expressions and descriptions and avoid **deixis**. Deixis is the use of terms and expressions that rely on the context to give their meaning, such as 'that one', 'over there' and 'here'.

As you study literature, you will often see sophisticated patterning and elaborate use of literary techniques; these are, in many ways, characteristic of the written mode and allow the reader to reflect upon how construction and meaning both contribute to the overall effect intended by the writer. In speech, we are rarely faced with such complexity and we often find speech is shot through with vagueness and ambiguity.

Mistakes, revisions, and shortfalls in writing can all be rectified or removed, either immediately or at a later time; in the intervening period, no one need see the document, so once the mistakes have been corrected, only the writer is aware that they were present in the first instance. In speech, however, once a mistake is made it cannot be undone.

Finally, writing does not share the **prosodic** or auditory properties of speech such as stress, intonation, pace and volume. Perhaps the only features writing does have that relate to prosody are elements such as emboldening or underlining for emphasis, and exclamation or question marks to indicate degrees of astonishment or inquiry.

Differences in form and features

The differences between speech and writing are summarized in the following table:

	Speech	Writing
1	Speech is usually unplanned, with use of much repetition, hesitation and non-standard forms.	Writing can be planned and revised, and can easily conform to Standard English usage.
2	Pauses, fillers and simple syntactical constructions often mark out where utterances begin and end. However, this still does not ensure that all boundaries are clear.	Sentence boundaries are marked by the conventions of punctuation. Sentences often vary in their simplicity and complexity in a way that speech utterances do not.
3	Speech is more immediate and quicker, but it is less easy to pick up meaning through listening to someone else talking to you, since you need to work at the speaker's speed.	Writing is less immediate and has to be searched out, and is slower to access than speech, but it does allow the reader to work at his or her own pace.
4	Once a mistake in speech is uttered it cannot be erased or withdrawn, although it can be qualified — but the audience may well be suspicious of these qualifications.	Mistakes in writing can be altered at the writer's own convenience prior to the written matter being seen by its audience.
5	Speech relies heavily on deixis and the knowledge of immediate context.	Writing can often be free of context and needs to use detail and subordination for the sake of clarity.
6	Speech is enhanced by our ability to manipulate speed, volume and stress in what we say to facilitate meaning; this is difficult to replicate in the written mode.	In writing, if we wish to include prosodic features we need to resort to complex description or use punctuation to help us. This is not very efficient and can be cumbersome.
7	Speech is not conducive to recording and it is usually a matter of memory as to what has occurred in a conversation; it is therefore not a useful reference tool.	Writing allows easy and accurate reference to be made; it also allows easy recording of facts and data to enable us to have access to them at a later date; we do not need to rely on our own memory.

Different representations of speech

We now turn our attention to the different types of speech representation that you may be faced with. You will be asked to compare a particular speech representation with spontaneous speech in the examination. Obviously, both of these will be written representations of speech, including the spontaneous speech.

A good place to start is with planned speech, that is, speech that is meant to be heard as speech but has been composed beforehand for rhetorical purposes. Political speeches are a very rich seam to mine here, and you can gather many examples from the Internet to help you to examine some of the techniques used by politicians to influence a particular audience.

However, there are other valuable areas to examine. As you have already seen, both the prose and dramatic works that you have studied will provide you with evidence of speech representation. Also, there are semi-scripted situations on the television, with interviews and chat shows being the most common. You can also find examples of speech representation in the media such as, radio and television scripts. There are printed versions of speech in non-fiction sources such as magazine interviews, newspapers and comics. Finally, a new area which is very prevalent in modern life is electronic communication, where speech is emulated in e-mails, text messages and chat rooms.

The language and features of planned speech

Planned speech differs from spontaneous speech, in that it is thought out, considered, and perhaps scripted in some form prior to its delivery. We hear many examples of this on a daily basis, ranging from the broadly planned but unscripted delivery of a teacher or lecturer, to the formulaic rhetoric of political speeches.

> **Rhetoric**
>
> The art of speech making, with the express purpose of altering or affecting the listener's emotions, by conveying the individual viewpoint of the speaker and/or the speaker's logic or reasoning.

In planned speech, the speaker often makes use of an assortment of devices that are specifically intended to convey his or her message. In many instances, this is inextricably linked to the purpose of persuading the audience to adopt, or at least consider, the speaker's point of view. The devices are often supplemented by skilful use of **phonological features** such as sound and rhythm, thus enhancing the impact of what is articulated.

Look closely at the following piece of rhetoric. Gordon Brown made this speech when he was appointed as the next prime minister in June 2007, at a special Labour party conference. The following extract at the close of his speech, allows us to examine the use of a number of rhetorical devices first hand:

And I've learned something else about how we can change our country – how we can build a progressive consensus.

In the last ten years, from Make Poverty History to campaigns on disability, gay rights and the environment, Britain has changed for the better, not just because of government, but because of movements that have gone beyond traditional parties, captured people's imaginations and transformed people's lives.

As a party we have always known that we succeed best when we reach out to and engage the whole community. So here I stand proud of our Labour Party but determined that we reach out to all people who can be persuaded to share our values and who would like to be part of building a more just society.

So my message today is also to people who want to change from the old politics, who yearn for a public life founded on values, who are inspired by what we as a nation can now achieve together – join us. Join us in building the Britain we believe in.

And don't let anyone tell you the choice at the next election will be change with other parties and no change with Labour. Because when I take office on Wednesday I will, as our party has always done, heed and lead the call of change.

So for young people wanting the first step on the housing ladder to their first home, we will meet the challenge of change.

For families wanting their sons and daughters to get the chance of college or university, we will meet the challenge of change.

For parents wanting affordable child care, we will meet the challenge of change.

For families and pensioners who want an NHS there when they need it, we will meet the challenge of change.

For people wanting a stronger democracy, we will meet the challenge of change.

And we will govern for all the people of our country.

This week marks a new start.

A chance to renew.

And I say to the people of Britain:

The new government I will lead belongs to you.

I will work hard for you.

I shall always try my utmost.

I am ready to serve.

- -

There is no doubt that this piece of speech tells us much about the speaker's views and his reasoning: he constantly refers to the 'challenge of change' (the content that precedes this outlines the changes he wants for the country), and he underpins this by the use of the first-person singular pronominative form, 'I', and continues by including the audience in what he asserts, with a shift to the first-person plural pronominative form, 'we'. There is also an appeal to the emotions of those listening. It is here that we can begin to examine specific rhetorical features.

Emotive language

Rhetorical speech-making uses emotive language to appeal to the audience. Gordon Brown uses strong verbs in his powerful closing section:

- build
- change
- transform
- capture
- stand
- persuade

He supplements these by careful adjectival choice:

- traditional
- proud
- just
- stronger

There are also many abstract nouns, which makes the speech much more theoretical as it moves towards its conclusion:

- consensus
- environment

- imagination
- challenge

As well as the linguistic evidence, Brown also uses the following techniques:

Giving opinions

Brown offers his opinion on the position of the Labour Party at the moment he is speaking:

> So here I stand proud of our Labour Party but determined that we reach out to all people who can be persuaded to share our values and who would like to be part of building a more just society.

His use of the adjective 'proud' occurs early in the sentence, and he emphasizes common values by using the first-person plural possessive pronoun 'our', finally finishing his sentence with a reference to a 'just society', the implication being that his party have been instrumental in making society just as well as continuing to promote this goal.

Using exclamations

While Brown does not overtly use exclamatives in the speech, there is an exclamatory quality to the final section where he couples repetition with exclamation to finish each section with the same words: 'we will meet the challenge of change'. In particular, the following sentence is exclamatory in style:

> And don't let anyone tell you the choice at the next election will be change with other parties and no change with Labour.

The statement indirectly criticizes other political parties as well as claiming that the Labour Party will be at the cutting edge of change and that it would be a complete surprise if it wasn't; hence its exclamatory sense.

Exaggeration or understatement (respectively, **hyperbole** and **litotes**) may also be used to help add vigour to exclamatory statements.

Giving personal guarantees and surety

> So my message today is also to people who want to change from the old politics, who yearn for a public life founded on values, who are inspired by what we as a nation can now achieve together – join us. Join us in building the Britain we believe in.

Here Brown emphasizes his political assurance by foregrounding 'my message' and then using the first-person plural pronoun 'us' to add further power to his personal guarantee.

Use of summary

In rhetoric, one of the most effective devices is the use of a conclusive sentence that draws the whole of the speech together, while also leaving the listener with something memorable to take away, ponder on and digest. A famous example is by Winston Churchill:

> Let us therefore brace ourselves to our duties and so bear ourselves that, if the British Empire and its Commonwealth last for a thousand years, men will still say, 'This was their finest hour'.

Gordon Brown's ending to his speech is strong as it has a certain conclusiveness about it; he moves from the collective, through use of the pronoun 'we', to the personal 'I' and the use of the modal verbs of certainty, 'will' and 'shall':

> And we will govern for all the people of our country.
>
> This week marks a new start.
>
> A chance to renew.
>
> And I say to the people of Britain:
>
> The new government I will lead belongs to you.
>
> I will work hard for you.
>
> I shall always try my utmost.
>
> I am ready to serve.

Notice that some of his sentences are in very fragmentary form, and that this adds to the increasing pace of the piece. His final sentences are very similar syntactically and there is a simplicity and strength about his final utterance, where the infinitive verb 'to serve' is used. This is a verb that has all kinds of historical resonances.

Some of the emotive devices that Brown does not use in this speech are as follows. The speech would probably lose some of its strength if *all* these devices were used.

Threatening disaster

This is a tool often used in planned speeches, akin to saying, 'if you don't do this then something earth-shattering will happen that will have dreadful consequences for all!' Brown hints at this earlier in his speech, with the following reference to the economy, and there is a suggestion of potential disaster in the use of the verb 'safeguarding' as well as the negative adjective 'vulnerable':

> I believe in a British economy founded on dynamic, flexible markets and open competition. But for workers undercut by employers in this country who break the law by paying less than the minimum wage we will act – new protection for vulnerable workers. That's what I mean by safeguarding and advancing the British way of life.

Mocking opponents

Disparaging one's opponents is something that comes very readily to politicians. In one of his first speeches as prime minister, Gordon Brown's predecessor Tony Blair poked fun at the Conservative Party by making a comparison between the new Tory leadership and the fictional family of monsters, the Addams family:

> The only party that spent two years in hibernation in search of a new image and came back as the Addams family.
>
> Under John Major, it was weak, weak, weak! Under William Hague, it's weird, weird, weird! Far right, far out!

Among other things, this evokes an image of:

- their grotesqueness
- their dysfunctional nature
- the artificial nature of their relationships
- the comical way that they behave
- the reaction of horror they provoke in some people.

Along with the opinions given earlier in the speech, this helps to disparage and belittle the Tory Party, which is all part of Blair's agenda in this particular address.

Structural techniques

You have already seen the importance of structure in the way that pieces of writing are put together. Structure also plays an important role in planned speech. Some of these structural techniques are described below.

Patterning

Various types of pattern are often employed during planned speech. In the speech of Gordon Brown, we can see a very common technique: **patterns of three**. There is a certain cohesion to ideas packaged in threes, and the rhythm and completeness of the ordering can be clearly seen.

> campaigns on disability [1], gay rights [2] and the environment [3]

The three nouns or noun phrases suggest comprehensiveness in the way that Britain has embraced change. This is then further emphasized by the second part of the sentence, which has another three parts or sections, thus mirroring the first part:

> ... because of movements that have gone beyond traditional parties [1], captured people's imaginations [2] and transformed people's lives [3].

Repetition

Any repetition of words or phrases can highlight the central ideas of a speech, and has the cumulative effect of driving home the message. Many orators use this technique simply to emphasize a point; Brown does this effectively at the end of five consecutive sections of his speech where he finishes each section with the phrase 'the challenge of change', the key topic of his whole address.

At the end of the speech, he uses a similar method, this time repeating the second person pronoun 'you' at the end of two sentences while starting three of them with the first person pronoun 'I'. Once more, this helps the overall cohesive effect.

> The new government I will lead belongs to you.
>
> I will work hard for you.
>
> I shall always try my utmost.
>
> I am ready to serve.

Lists

The effect of listing is similar to that of using repetition, as the message is further emphasized simply through the accumulation of the list of words.

The type of listing that makes use of commas or semi-colons to link the ideas together, is called **asyndetic listing**. It has the effect of allowing idea after idea to pile on top of one another. Sometimes, conjunctions such as 'and' are used to link ideas into lists, again having a cumulative effect. This technique is known as **syndetic listing**.

Questions

The use of rhetorical questions; questions that do not require an answer, is another feature of planned speech. It has the effect of adding weight to the point being made, by implicitly providing an answer, but it can also help to move an argument on. In Brown's speech, he does not use questions, which indicates that he is certain and wants to show that his speech is not about asking questions, but rather to give solutions and answers.

Opposites

Use of antithesis, or balancing of opposite ideas, can also have a powerful effect when coupled with other devices.

Literary techniques

Metaphor, imagery and simile are terms you will be familiar with from your literary studies, and they are also something that you might identify in planned or sometimes unplanned speech.

Similes gain their effects by comparing one thing to another, whilst metaphors often offer a more immediate image, where the speaker refers to something as if it were something else. This is done as in writing, in order to highlight important characteristics of the object or theme that the speaker wishes to describe.

There may also be examples of **personification**, **symbolism** and **irony** in planned speech, terms you have already been introduced to in your literary studies; any effect they have will be similar to the effect when used in created literature.

Phonological techniques

Phonological techniques use the sound qualities of language to enhance its effects. Some of the most common phonologic techniques are as follows:

Alliteration and assonance

These are literary devices that you will have already come across: **alliteration**, the repeated use of the same consonant sounds especially at the begining of words, and **assonance**, the repeated use of the same vowel sounds. An example of alliteration is the 'ch' sound in 'the challenge of change'. Both techniques have the effect of making the words and phrases stand out and consequently help us to remember them later, something that Brown wants us to do with this speech, especially as the key idea in the speech is his appetite to embrace 'change'. Naturally, these techniques are often used in advertising and other forms of persuasive writing too.

Consonance

This technique is perhaps one that is often overlooked in planned speech but has, when used, a similar strength to alliteration and assonance. Consonance helps us to remember a phrase, through the repetition of a consonant in the middle or at the end of words, as in a phrase by Tony Blair from another part of the speech quoted earlier: 'the uneata<u>ble</u>, the unspeaka<u>ble</u> and the unelecta<u>ble</u>'. This is a type of repetition and also includes assonance in the use of 'un', but it has the added effect of drawing attention to the words through the repeated ending.

Rhyme

As with all other phonological techniques, the use of rhyme enhances the sound of the words and adds to the structural cohesion of the speech, particularly at the end of phrases or sentences. A good example of this in Brown's speech is:

> I will, as our party has always done, <u>heed</u> and <u>lead</u> the call of change.

The two underlined verbs help to emphasize Brown's actions.

Intonation and stress

The way in which words are intoned and the stress they are given can often help to convey the attitude of the speaker. It is often difficult to see this when the speech is printed on the page, but there are often syntactic clues as to which words are important. In the final line, for instance, we can imagine that the adjective and verb are the stressed words here as they carry the real sense and power of the line:

> I am <u>ready</u> to <u>serve</u>.

Sometimes words are elongated to accentuate their importance; you have already seen examples of this in the section on unplanned speech.

Volume and speed

Changes in volume can have a radical effect on any speech, whether planned or unplanned. The effect of raising one's voice is obvious: it carries with it associations of power, commitment, certainty, passion and possibly anger. It can also be used for dramatic effect, especially after a period of quiet and calm speech. This can help shock the audience and have the effect of waking them up to listen more intently to the speaker.

Speech in the broadcast media

In the media, speech is often very like spontaneous speech, but it has an agenda. A topic will have been decided beforehand, especially if it is some kind of interview or chat show, as shown below.

In the following piece of conversation, which is part of a longer interview that was conducted on television by Michael Parkinson (P), with the Scottish comedian, Billy Connolly (C), Parkinson appears to be simply chatting to Connolly. However, there is careful use of the following:

- topic management by the interviewer
- evidence of research having been done beforehand
- opportunities taken by the interviewee to seize the turn and say something funny.

Nonetheless, it still has the look of spontaneous speech, as Connolly probably doesn't know the questions that will arise.

Activity

Examine this interview transcript closely and pick out the features that suggest:

- the spontaneous nature of the conversation
- that specific exchanges have been selected beforehand to be used in the interview.

P: There's a there's a (.) kind of sense of vocation isn't there in a comic (.) I think I mean (.) you are driven to it aren't you

        [

C: It's vocational

P: It not (0.5) er really

[

C: Witho::ut (.) question

P: It has to be doesn't it

C: Aye (1.5) an' I think most k (.) things are (0.5) yours is vocational obviously (.) you've a great love of what you do (0.5) I have a love of what I do (.) an' we're very lucky because you find it (0.5) I think it's a question of bein' (0.5) try to be honest with yourself (0.5) what you a:ctually want to be (1.0) an be (.) eve even if it's embarrassin' (.) like yer wanna be a comedian (.) an' you say to yer dad (.) I'd like to be a comedian an' he goes (.) you're no funny (0.5) you're no very funny (0.5) w w what t d'y'wanna be a comedian for (0.5) are you daft (1.5) an' I became (0.5) a welder to escape the worst excesses of homosexuality actually (1.0) I

P: Wha'

C: I wanted (.) ter go to drama school (0.5) an' an' ma father said (.) O:::::h they're all homosexuals (.) you don't wanna go there (1.0) an' I said I'd like to be in the merchant navy (1.0) O:::::h for God's sake (1.0) they're all homosexuals (2.0) so I I became (.) this this welder guy

P: And this

C: an' it haunted me you know (1.0) u until (.) I er got

P: What what (.) er haunted you

C: Bein' bein' (.) what I thought I should be

P: Yes

Speech representation in prose fiction

When writers wish to present speech in prose fiction, they may build a range of characteristics into their speech representation in order to create a particular effect. This effect will have been carefully considered and the writer will have made a specific effort to ensure that it is clearly conveyed.

Look at the following extract, taken from the novel *Eden Close* by Anita Shreve. In this particular section, the main character's mother and a neighbour, Edith, look at a baby who has been left outside Edith's house; her husband Jim is away on business.

'Jesus God,' said his mother, stepping back quickly as if she'd seen something deformed.

The two women stood looking at each other for a moment and didn't speak.

'What is it?' his mother asked finally.

The other woman didn't understand the question. 'What is it ...?'

'A boy or a girl?'

Edith looked momentarily stunned. Then she tilted her head back and closed her eyes. 'Oh God, I wish Jim were here,' she suddenly cried. 'I don't know. I don't know.' She looked as though she were about to fall, with the bundle in her arms.

'We'll go inside,' said his mother quickly, clicking into gear in that way she had when there was a crisis or when he had fallen and hurt himself.

- -

This section is typical of the way that speech is represented in prose fiction, with the following features being evident:

1   Separate speakers are given separate lines to indicate who is talking.

'What is it?' his mother asked finally.

The other woman didn't understand the question. 'What is it ...?'

- -

The first speaker is the main character's mother, and the neighbour's reply to the initial interrogative 'What is it?' is met with another question, to indicate her flustered nature as well as her misunderstanding of the original question's purpose.

2   Use of speech marks around what is said to indicate the actual speech.

'Jesus God,' said his mother.

- -

The mother's involuntary outburst, in the form of a mild blasphemy, is shown with speech marks before and after it.

3   Use of punctuation to convey the particular utterance type, such as an exclamatory or interrogative utterance. In the following example, an interrogative is indicated by the question mark at the end of the utterance:

'A boy or a girl?'

- -

4   Use of reporting clauses to help indicate who the speaker is, especially when there are multiple characters within a particular scene.

'Oh God, I wish Jim were here,' she suddenly cried.

- -

In this example the reporting clause 'she cried' is qualified by the use of the adverb 'suddenly'.

Because there are only two characters, it is also possible to leave out reporting clauses, as the turn-taking is indicated by the use of separate lines.

5   Use of adverbs, adverbial clauses or subordinating clauses attached to the reporting clause to help convey the way that the speaker delivers the lines:

'We'll go inside,' said his mother quickly, clicking into gear in that way she had when there was a crisis ...

- -

Here the use of the adverb 'quickly' shows that the mother takes charge of the situation, followed by the subordinating clause 'clicking into gear in that way she had when there was a crisis ...' to convey that this character is used to dealing with tricky situations, perhaps because she is a parent herself while Edith is not.

Quite often, when there are only two characters, the speech can have more of a realistic feel to it since reporting clauses are missed out. When this occurs, there is more of a focus on the words that are spoken rather than the writer's interpretation through reporting clauses and subordination.

Breaking conventions

Very occasionally, novelists will go against convention and not use the accepted forms of delineation of speech between characters, and instead use other methods to make speech different from the prose narrative. In the following extract, taken from *The Heart of It* by Barry Hines, the main character Cal is talking to his mother (who calls him Karl) about his life and his girlfriend.

Because Hines uses no speech marks, the reader has to concentrate very hard to work out the following:

- what is speech
- what is thought
- who is speaking
- which parts are narration.

Activity

What do you think is the overall effect that Hines is looking for in this extract?

You're spoiling that cat. You'll never get rid of it now, you know.

Didn't you ever fancy having a family, Karl?

Cal stalled for a few moments by watching television and he was still looking at the screen when he answered her. Not really. I've moved round a lot. There's been one or two women along the way, but children never came into it.

What about Hélène?

What about her?

You've known her a long time.

Cal worked it out. Five, six years. Yes, I suppose that is a long time. For me.

Isn't she interested in children?

Hélène! His exclamation was loud enough to wake up the cat. No way. She's too interested in her career. Oh, by the way, I've got a little surprise for you tonight.

What is it?

Wait and see. If I tell you now it won't be a surprise, will it?

Why don't you stop for your tea then?

Cal tried to think of an excuse, but he couldn't come up with anything convincing. Yes. All right then. That'll be nice.

In the novel *A Prayer For Owen Meany* by John Irving, Irving puts all that Owen Meany says in capital letters. This has the effect of emphasizing everything that Owen says, and helps to make Owen's words inspirational. There is also some irony in the fact that Owen is small for his age, yet is very wise:

'YOU SEE WHAT A LITTLE FAITH CAN DO?' said Owen Meany. The brain-damaged janitor was applauding. 'SET THE CLOCK TO *THREE* SECONDS!' Owen told him.

'Jesus Christ!' I said.

'IF WE CAN DO IT IN UNDER FOUR SECONDS, WE CAN DO IT IN UNDER THREE,' he said. 'IT JUST TAKES A LITTLE MORE FAITH.'

'It takes more practice,' I told him irritably.

'FAITH TAKES PRACTICE,' said Owen Meany.

- -

These are just two examples of the creative ways in which some authors present speech in prose.

Lexical issues

You will have found that there are very obvious differences between the types of linguistic units used in written and spoken texts. This is mainly due to the fact that when we speak we tend to use many more **grammatical** (or **function**) words than **lexical** (or **content**) words. This means that speech has low lexical density; that is, when we calculate the proportion of grammatical words in relation to lexical words, we see that the latter are not as heavily represented. Writing, especially literary writing, has high lexical density.

When we speak we tend to use lexical words from a simple stock of core content words that we use day in, day out. Often these words are fairly concrete and simple in nature. The use of abstract terms can be fairly limited in speech, because the mode is more suited to concrete terminology. When abstracts are used, they are often formulated into verbs. For example, we could convert the abstract noun *hatred* into the form of a pronoun and verb such as 'I hate …' These words are in contrast to the more literary lexis used in written prose.

High-frequency and low-frequency lexis

Another specific lexical point of comparison is that of **high-frequency** and **low-frequency** lexis. High-frequency lexis is the occurrence of familiar and well-used words and this happens frequently in speech. There are many words that you hear often in speech, such as: *very*, *think*, *know* and *other*, for example. In writing, however, especially poetry, low-frequency lexis is much more prevalent, with less common words and a higher rate of synonyms, simply because poetry is a highly planned form of literature.

Similarly, in speech, there is a tendency for:

- less abstract vocabulary, for example, *stuff* and *things*
- more generalized, simpler vocabulary
- the use of fillers, such as, *I mean* and *y'know*

In writing, however, there is a leaning towards:

- more abstract vocabulary, for example, *she became a mighty personality*
- greater variety of vocabulary
- the use of overt stylistic devices such as metaphor and imagery.

Deixis

One final area of lexical comparison is that of **deixis**, which is a kind of linguistic pointing, in that it is word usage that relies totally on context. Deictic expression falls into two broad categories. **Proximal** terms are those expressions that refer to things near to the speaker, such as *this*, *here* or *now*. **Distal** terms relate to things that are away from the speaker, such as *that* or *then*.

The use of **reference** in both speech and writing can often be quite marked. Reference allows us to identify things, people, places and so on. The three major areas are **anaphoric**, **exophoric** and **cataphoric** reference.

Reference

Anaphoric reference is by far the most common. It allows us to refer back to something that was mentioned earlier in the conversation. This form of 'anaphora' should be distinguished from the literary term of the same names, which is used to describe the repetition of a specific word at the beginning of successive lines of text. The form of 'anaphora' referred to here is the linguistic term, that describes internal references, to matters discussed within a written text or extract of speech.

An example of this is demonstrated below:

> the food's rather (1.0) <u>bland</u> I feel (.) actually it's often <u>lukewarm</u> (.) an' a lot of it's the <u>bloody</u> same

The third-person singular pronoun 'it' is an example of anaphoric reference here, where the last noun mentioned was 'food'; the use of 'it' refers back to that word. We use anaphora all the time in speech, since it allows us to be speedier in communicating, as well as making speech less repetitive. When anaphoric reference is used in writing, it is done more thoughtfully, as shown below:

> Hilda was a Northumbrian princess who spent her childhood hiding from her father's enemies in the Kingdom of Elmet to the west. When at last her father was killed, poisoned by a neighbouring king, she became a nun and then the abbess of Hartlepool on the northern bank of the Tees.

This passage uses a number of anaphoric references to the original proper noun 'Hilda', including 'her', 'she', 'nun' and 'abbess'. The writer has been able to vary the use of anaphora in this case as well as introducing extra information.

Exophoric reference means referring to something that only the context or situation can identify, a kind of linguistic pointing or reference. For example if a speaker was to say 'it's a bit like this one here', we, as outsiders to the conversation, would have no idea what it is that is being referred to. The linguistic pointer 'here' gives no clue.

Cataphoric reference is less frequent in speech and is used as a stylistic device in writing; it is often used to withhold information, since it refers forward to something mentioned later on in the writing. It is often used to generate interest in an issue by grabbing the reader's or listener's attention but deliberately remaining vague about the detail behind the reference. An example of a cataphoric reference would be as follows:

> <u>Death-obsessed</u>, that is how residents have described the local music scene.

Grammatical issues

One of the key issues that you will be able to discuss when comparing the use of different modes is that a wide range of grammatical features are unique to speech, and can thus form an interesting and rich comparison to the grammatical complexities of writing.

Elliptical forms are very common in speech, such as 'typical of the place' for '*it is* typical of the place'. In a construction such as this, the subject, in the form of the third-person pronoun, is missed out, as is the verb 'is'. In contrast, writing largely uses complete sentences with far fewer elliptical constructions.

The clause structure of spontaneous speech can be examined further. Often, there is a high incidence of subject–verb construction, followed by a postmodifying object, complement or adverbial. These simple clauses are often connected by a variety of co-ordinating features such as fillers, relative pronouns, adverbs, determiners and elliptical forms.

Look at the following extract, where two people are agreeing about the lack of options for vegetarians in America.

Speaker B: dead right (.) I know exactly what yer mean (0.5) I mean I'm a veggie (.) so::: there's very little for me there

Speaker A: aw yeah (.) it's crap for veggies in <u>America</u> as a whole (.) everything's geared to eatin' meat

[

Speaker B: uhuh (.) yep

- -

If we break down just a small part of the conversation, we can see that there is a high incidence of simple clause structures, often starting with the pronoun 'I' and followed by a verb then an adverbial, object or complement.

Subject: I

Contracted verb: 'm

Complement: a veggie

Here it is easy to see where each clause ends and the next begins, but as a speaker becomes more animated or excited you will find that clauses become more complex in their construction, or there is a high incidence of co-ordination between the clauses, or the clauses become pared-down phrases – quite often noun phrases – which take the place of a full clause. It is fairly common in unscripted speech for the co-ordinating conjunction *and* to be used as an indication of continuation by the speaker, and as in the example given below, for a speaker to give quite long lists initially before using the co-ordinating conjunction as a signal that he has more to say:

> y'know it's burgers <u>an'</u> chicken 'n' fries 'n' pizzas (.) an' that's it really (2.0) 'n' after a while all I longed for was good ol' English food

This is also why so many children repeatedly use the word *and* in stories when they first learn to write; they are simply replicating a pattern they have heard and used in speech. The continuation markers in writing are so much more varied; for example:

> Out of the tops of refinery chimneys flames like lurid petals bend in the wind. The wind takes the fumes and smoke across the coastal plain, deep down into lungs, withering up gardens and struggling attempts at trees, and across to Scandinavia which it coats with bitter, orange dust.

In this passage, the writer uses a range of methods to link her sentences together, including subordinating clauses and other prepositions.

Issues of transmission

In speech, attitudes are often indicated by use of the following.

- **Prosody** (the way we utter words, including pitch, pace, rhythm and volume). Speakers use emphasis for certain words or phrases to give them precedence in the utterance. For example stress on an adjective might help to convey the speaker's feelings about the subject he or she is talking about. In writing however, the writer is likely to convey his or her values by use of carefully chosen adjectives: '*lurid* petals' and '*bitter, orange* dust.'

- **Standard and non-standard forms** (whether we conform to the accepted norms in our speech, or deviate and use non-standard words and constructions). Slang words are examples of non-standard forms, as are regional dialect words: such forms are more common in speech than in literary texts, although both can be found in literary texts as a method of characterisation.

- **Lexical choice** and use of **modifiers** (certain words chosen for emphasis or contrast). In speech, the use of modification can greatly influence the meaning of what is said. Consider the utterance: 'yer realize the food's rather (1.0) bland I feel (.) actually it's often lukewarm (.) an' a lot of it's the bloody same'. The first modifier he uses is the postmodifying adjective 'bland' followed by 'lukewarm' before descending into mild demotic language with the adjective 'bloody'. The mixture of fairly low-frequency lexis with the first two adjectives, followed by the high-frequency swear word, adds contrast and perhaps communicating the speaker's exasperation.

Studying prose in context

When we study a piece of writing we may initially give most of our attention to exploring and analysing the text we see in front of us. However, no literary text can exist in a vacuum, or entirely on its own. All kinds of factors influence the way authors write and affect the way we read their work. Becoming aware of this background information can enhance our understanding and enjoyment of texts by enabling us to see them as part of a wider picture. In other words, we place them in context.

For Section B of AS Unit F671, you need to think about your set novel in terms of context. This means that you will need to explore some of the factors surrounding the production and reception of the text.

There are several ways in which you can begin to place your texts in context. You might consider:

- how a text interrelates with the events of the **author's life**
- the place of a particular text in the **author's** *oeuvre* or **writings as a whole**
- how the text reflects the **historical period** and/or the **place** in which it was written
- the text as an example of its **genre** or of a particular **literary style** or **period**
- the ways in which the **language** of a particular time or place is reflected in the text
- how our reading of the text might be influenced by the way other readers or critics have reacted to it recently or in the past, that is, its **reception**.

Relevant contexts

Understanding contexts involves becoming familiar not only with the events, but also the beliefs, ideas and concerns that have influenced or inspired the writer you are studying. It works both ways, however. As you study the literary works, they themselves will reveal a lot about how society functioned at the time when they were written. You will be expected to recognize features that make a text typical – or atypical – of its context and to make your understanding clear by supporting it with example from your text.

The following section will consider ways to explore literature from a contextual point of view.

The author's biography

It can certainly be interesting and increase our enjoyment of texts if we learn something about the lives of the people who wrote them. Indeed, it can be difficult to make any sense at all of some writing without such knowledge. There can be two sides to this issue, however. Some critics believe that a text should stand alone and that as students of literature we should concern ourselves only with the words on the page, while others suggest that we should learn as much as possible about an author's life and times in order to understand the work fully. For AS and A2 level, you are aiming to achieve a balance between these two approaches.

Some awareness of a writer's biography may be invaluable for understanding what lies behind the work, but it cannot take the place of thorough knowledge of the text itself and it can create some pitfalls. For example, in essays or exam answers, it may be tempting to include more of the writer's life story than necessary, if you have spent time learning about it. Unless you have specifically been asked to write about the text in this way, too much biographical information can waste valuable time and words that would be better spent focusing on the text itself. It is more likely that you will want to demonstrate your understanding in more subtle ways, including facts or background details only when they are clearly relevant or when they support points you want to make about the text.

Finding biographical information

As a starting point, editions intended for study, particularly of classics or older texts, often include an introduction with some biographical material. The best way to gain a deeper understanding of an author's life and times, however, is to read a good biography, or if one exists, an autobiography.

Biographies can vary enormously. Some can be thoroughly researched and packed with information but very dry and dull to read, while others may be enjoyable – even scandalous – but less accurate. It is worth dipping into a few, if they are available. It can be particularly interesting to compare the different viewpoints found in biographies written by contemporaries of the author with those written more recently.

You could also try the following:

- **Encyclopaedias**
- **Diaries** or **letters** from the author, published in book form. Where available, these can give fascinating insights into a writer's life, and how and why he or she writes, as well as reflecting the events and concerns of the time.
- **Television documentaries** or **films** about the lives and times of famous writers.
- The **Internet**. Contemporary writers, and associations of people interested in particular authors, often have websites, although you may have to search carefully for genuinely useful information.

The author's *oeuvre*

It can be important to know not only about the lives of writers but about their other works, so that you can see whether the text you are studying is typical of its author or whether it stands out for some reason. You may be asked to show that you are aware that authors can have 'favourite' themes or features of style, which crop up regularly in their writings.

Activity

1 Choose a writer whose work you are currently studying. Arrange for each member of your group to research one possible source of information about this author and make notes to bring to your next session. Aim to cover a range of sources, past and present, if that is relevant.

2 Discuss what you have discovered, noting any differences in your findings. Combine your information and create a handout on the life, work and times of your chosen writer.

Time and place

When you are studying texts in context, knowledge of the historical period and the location in which they were written is an essential tool for understanding the literature. Different times and places or cultures have conventions, styles or variations of language which, with experience, we can learn to recognize.

Place can be as important as time. In recent decades there has been a surge of interest in the work of British writers who can trace their roots to other cultures, and in the literature of other English-speaking countries. Some of this is what we call 'post-colonial' writing, by authors from nations which were previously colonies under the rule of European powers like the British Empire. Writers from the West Indies like Jean Ryhs, India, and several African states, as well as from Canada and Australia, may fit this category. In a colony, the 'native' or indigenous culture may have been partly suppressed to make way for that which was imposed by the European invaders. With independence, there may be efforts to reassert the original culture. In any case, such societies are complex mixtures, often carrying the weight of the memory of oppression. The struggle to find a true sense of identity is therefore a frequent theme.

If you are studying texts from this background, find out as much as you can about the writer's cultural situation and the setting of the text. You will also need to be aware that some of these writers use non-standard forms of the English language.

Literary period

As well as relating texts to a historical period, we sometimes put them in the context of a **literary period** or style, which is not quite the same thing. Texts written around the same time are likely to have at least some similarities, but texts from a particular literary period are connected at a deeper level. Their authors are likely to share particular ideas about life, art and literature which are reflected in their work. They may be part of a 'movement' – a group of people who share a philosophy or belief system. Such groups tend to arise in response to political or social events, or out of a desire for change. For example, in the late eighteenth century, the Romantic movement was a reaction against the dry, formal, rather artificial styles of the previous decades. Writers embraced the spirit of revolution that was sweeping through Europe and America, and literature reflected a greater concern with nature, imagination and individual experience. A century or so later, in the years after the First World War, the Modernists experimented with artistic forms and styles. The old styles of art and writing no longer seemed appropriate in a world that had changed beyond recognition and had ceased to make sense in the way it had done in the past.

Language

Language evolves continuously over time. We can see enormous differences between the language of our time and that of Chaucer or Shakespeare, but even in relatively recent texts, vocabulary and usage may be unfamiliar.

Language also alters with place. Within the British Isles, there are many varieties of English and quite a number of writers have experimented with these, from Emily Brontë's representation of Yorkshire dialect in *Wuthering Heights* to James Joyce's Irish English, or from Lewis Grassic Gibbon's Lowland Scots in *Sunset Song* to the broad Glaswegian of Irvine Welsh's *Trainspotting*. Also, as already mentioned, writers from other cultures may use other forms of English. These are not 'wrong' or 'inferior', but are languages in their own right, with their own structures.

Working with extracts

The Examination question that you will answer for Section B of Unit F671 will ask you to compare your prose text to extracts, whilst also using them as a 'sample' to demonstrate your understanding of the literature of the period you have been studying. The extracts will be taken from non-fiction texts, such as biographies, essays, diaries or letters, which comment on some aspect of life and society or reflect ways of thinking particular to that period. Some of the extracts may also be multimodal.

To succeed in this task, you will need good close reading skills as well as a thorough understanding of the wider picture in order to be able to assess this 'sample' in relation to its context.

Selecting examples from your texts

When you write about context in the exam, it is important that you never lose focus of the question and also of your texts. This means that is important to support points that you make in relation to context by referring directly to examples from the novel that you have studied and the non-fiction extracts that you will receive in the exam.

You can prepare for this by using a table like the one below. This example is based on *The Great Gatsby* by F. Scott. Fitzgerald but you could create a similar table for the text that you are studying, replacing the listed contexts with those that are relevant to your novel. As you read your text and study it in class, you can add quotations to these categories and begin to accumulate a bank of references to the contexts that are evident in the novel.

The Great Gatsby	
Context	**Quotations from the text**
Legacy of the war	
Attitudes to wealth	
Role of women in the 1920s	
Modernism	
Fragmentation of narration	
Self-imprisonment	
New York	
Prohibition/attitude towards war	
Cinematic techniques	

3 AS and A2 coursework

For your AS and A2 coursework you need to demonstrate a number of skills quite different to those required of you in your examinations. For your AS coursework for example, you need to become familiar with analysing multimodal texts, understanding the factors involved in transforming texts into multimodal form and finally creating your own multimodal response to a text you have studied. The coursework folder itself consists of two sections and three elements. The first section is an analytical study of your chosen literary and related multimodal text. The second section is divided into a re-creative task and a supporting critical commentary.

Your A2 coursework is also divided into two sections. In the first section, you will need to write a comparative study of at least three texts, one of which may be a spoken language text and one of which must be non-literary. For the second part of this coursework you will also need to produce a piece of creative writing, and as with your AS coursework, this will need to be supported by a critical commentary, setting out and justifying the choices you made when fashioning your creative response. If you do not deal with spoken language in Section A, then you must consider it as part of your creative piece and work on you critical commentary.

What are the benefits of coursework?

The benefits that the coursework element can bring to your course and the breadth that it can give to your studies are well acknowledged, and that is the reason that it is used extensively as a means of assessment in English.

In particular, coursework can:

- offer you more of a say in the nature of the assignment you undertake
- provide you with opportunities to set your own tasks and goals and pursue particular literary interests, thus developing more independence in your learning
- allow you to produce work free of the constraints of exam conditions, so that you can present more carefully planned and considered responses and employ the drafting process
- develop skills that will help you perform more effectively in the exams
- help you to gain experience in undertaking research and wider reading in preparation for studying English at degree level.

Texts and multimodality

Multimodal texts are texts that combine different modes of communication to convey meaning. This could be a combination of speech, writing, sound, video or images. Multimodal texts have become a lot more prolific in today's society than they were in the past. The range of texts available to the consumer has increased dramatically in the last century, as a consequence of improvements in printing, multimedia technology and new methods of mass communication such as radio, television and the Internet. A consumer in today's society can now easily seek and receive information that may be comprised of numerous modes of communication. The following commonplace texts could all be described as multimodal:

- A newspaper article with text and photos

- A website containing video clips from a new film release, with a written review and photos of the cast

- A music video

- A film

- A TV documentary comprising video footage, interviews with witnesses, still photos and a narrated voiceover

- An illustrated book

- A revision guide CD-ROM with revision notes, audio clips and interactive revision games

For Task 1 of your AS coursework, you will study multimodality specifically in the context of the multimodal transformation of a written text already in existence. You will study one substantial written text, which can be of any literary genre, and one multimodal text based on the first. In some cases the multimodal text may be a version of the original text; in other cases it may simply be about, or written in reaction to the original text.

The following are examples of possible combinations:

Jane Austen – *Emma*	and	*Clueless* (1995 film directed by Amy Heckerling)
William Shakespeare – *Twelfth Night*	and	Animated Shakespeare (film version)
Robert Harris – *Pompeii*	and	Extracts on Pompeii from a Lonely Planet Country Guide
Virginia Woolf – *Mrs Dalloway*	and	*The Hours* (2002 film directed by Stephen Daldry)

- -

When reading your initial written text it may be useful to consider the following questions:

1. **What aspects of the original text lend themselves well to adaptation?**

   What parts of the text could be transformed? What aspects of the original text might be an attractive starting point for writers or producers wishing to adapt the text, by making it multimodal?

2. **What factors have shaped the multimodal version of the written text that you are studying?**

   What elements or attitudes differ in the multimodal text in comparison to the original text, and what effects do these changes have upon your overall impression of the text? Are both texts aimed at the same audience or different audiences? How can you tell?

3. **How does the multimodal text compare to your own interpretation of the original text?**

What would you have done differently if you had to produce a multimodal transformation of the original text? Do you agree with the way the producer of the multimodal text has read the original? What other interpretations might be possible?

These questions present some of the ways in which you might think about the links between the written text and the multimodal text that you are studying.

Activity

- Consider the pair of texts that you are studying. Draw a table with three columns as shown. Use the table to make notes on your texts. You can add extra points to the left-hand column if you need to.

	Written literary text	Related multimodal text
Title		
Mode/s		
Date of publication		
Purpose		
Intended audience		
Plot differences		
Setting		
Characters		
Language		
Point of view		
Aspects omitted from the original		
Aspects added to the original		

- Review what you have written in your table. Some of the points, such as the intended audience or the date each text was produced, may help you to understand the differences between the texts. Other points, such as changes to the setting, characters or plot may raise further questions. Pick two points from the table, and discuss with a partner, what they reveal about the relationship between the texts you are studying.

Re-creative production

One aspect of GCSE English that many students enjoy is writing creatively, whether it is under examination conditions and with a particular purpose in mind, or writing at length as part of a coursework folder. At Advanced level, the types of imaginative writing that you do will be more demanding and require more preparation.

This A Level Language and Literature specification has two opportunities for creative writing; both with exact yet quite different starting points. At AS Level, you will undertake a re-creative writing task based on your chosen literary text and connected multimodal text, which you will have compared as part of your analytical study for Task 1. The text that you produce must be multimodal and must make use of at least two different modes, such as writing, images, sound or spoken language. Your text might be complete in itself or a section of what could be a much larger work. You will also need to write a commentary about your production, explaining your chosen approach and the links between the original passage and your own work.

Any imaginative or creative writing of your own should always take careful note of, and vigilantly adhere to:

- audience
- purpose
- context
- style
- format.

As with any language production task, knowledge of different types of writing and familiarity with differing textual examples is very important.

The basics: purpose and audience

It is vital for you to recognize that any text that is produced always has a **purpose** and a particular **audience** in mind. These are two key terms, and they form the backbone of any framework for language production. The terms may be defined simply as follows:

Purpose

What the text is trying to communicate to its target audience and the responses it seeks from the reader(s) or listener(s).

Audience

Who the text is written for or aimed at; the audience can vary from the very general (such as adults) to the very specific (female twenty-somethings who work in the city).

To help you see at first hand the differences between these two, use the framework for textual analysis given on pages 1-3 when looking closely at the two texts printed on the next page.

Activity

The following extracts are taken from two versions of 'Julius Caesar'. The first is taken from Act 3, scene 2 of William Shakespeare's play and the second is taken from an illustrated version of the play by Marcia Williams. Both texts present Caesar's funeral, when Brutus and Antony stand up separately to address the crowd.

What does each writer concentrate on or aim to do (purpose) in each extract? How does the use of multimodal elements in the second extract help to achieve this aim? You should focus on matters such as the presentation of character, the structure of the narrative and the setting when you look at each writer's purpose in this way.

What clues are there that help you to see who the readership (audience) is intended to be for each of these extracts? You should concentrate on lexis (the words used), grammatical and syntactical issues (the way particular words are selected and then strung together) and phonological and stylistic features (sound and style devices).

Extract 1 William Shakespeare's Julius Caesar

Act 3 scene 2

Brutus Be patient till the last.
Romans, countrymen, and lovers! hear me for my
cause, and be silent that you may hear. Believe me
for mine honour, and have respect to mine honour that
you may believe. Censure me in your wisdom, and
awake your senses that you may the better judge.
If there be any in this assembly, any dear friend of
Caesar's, to him I say that Brutus' love to Caesar
was no less than his. If then that friend demand
why Brutus rose against Caesar, this is my answer:
not that I loved Caesar less but that I loved
Rome more. Had you rather Caesar were living, and
die all slaves, than that Caesar were dead, to live
all freemen? As Caesar loved me, I weep for him;
as he was fortunate, I rejoice at it; as he was
valiant, I honour him; but, as he was ambitious, I
slew him. There is tears for his love, joy for his
fortune, honour for his valour, and death for his
ambition. Who is here so base that would be a
bondman? If any, speak, for him have I offended.
Who is here so rude that would not be a Roman? If
any, speak, for him have I offended. Who is here so
vile that will not love his country? If any, speak,
for him have I offended. I pause for a reply.

All None, Brutus, none.

Brutus   Then none have I offended. I have done no more to
Caesar than you shall do to Brutus. The question of
his death is enrolled in the Capitol, his glory not
extenuated wherein he was worthy nor his offences
enforced for which he suffered death.

Enter Mark Antony *and others, with* Caesar's *body*

Here comes his body, mourned by Mark Antony, who,
though he had no hand in his death, shall receive
the benefit of his dying, a place in the
commonwealth, as which of you shall not? With this
I depart: that, as I slew my best lover for the
good of Rome, I have the same dagger for myself
when it shall please my country to need my death.

Comes down

All   Live, Brutus, live, live!

First Plebeian   Bring him with triumph home unto his house.

Second Plebeian   Give him a statue with his ancestors.

Third Plebeian   Let him be Caesar.

Fourth Plebeian   Caesar's better parts
Shall be crown'd in Brutus.

First Plebeian   We'll bring him to his house
With shouts and clamours.

Brutus   My countrymen –

Second Plebeian   Peace, silence, Brutus speaks!

First Plebeian   Peace ho!

Brutus   Good countrymen, let me depart alone,
And, for my sake, stay here with Antony.
Do grace to Caesar's corpse, and grace his speech
Tending to Caesar's glories, which Mark Antony,
(By our permission) is allow'd to make.
I do entreat you, not a man depart,
Save I alone, till Antony have spoke.

Exit

First Plebeian   Stay ho, and let us hear Mark Antony.

Third Plebeian   Let him go up into the public chair,
We'll hear him. Noble Antony, go up.

Antony   For Brutus' sake, I am beholding to you.

Goes into the pulpit

Fourth Plebeian   What does he say of Brutus?

Third Plebeian   He says for Brutus' sake
He finds himself beholding to us all.

Fourth Plebeian   'Twere best he speak no harm of Brutus here!

First Plebeian This Caesar was a tyrant.

Third Plebeian Nay, that's certain:
We are blest that Rome is rid of him.

Second Plebeian Peace, let us hear what Antony can say.

Antony You gentle Romans –

All Peace ho, let us hear him.

Antony Friends, Romans, countrymen, lend me your ears!
I come to bury Caesar, not to praise him.
The evil that men do lives after them,
The good is oft interred with their bones:
So let it be with Caesar. The noble Brutus
Hath told you Caesar was ambitious;
If it were so, it was a grievous fault,
And grievously hath Caesar answer'd it.
Here, under leave of Brutus and the rest –
For Brutus is an honourable man,
So are they all, all honourable men –
Come I to speak in Caesar's funeral.
He was my friend, faithful and just to me,
But Brutus says he was ambitious,
And Brutus is an honourable man.
He hath brought many captives home to Rome
Whose ransoms did the general coffers fill;
Did this in Caesar seem ambitious?
When that the poor have cried, Caesar hath wept:
Ambition should be made of sterner stuff;
Yet Brutus says he was ambitious,
And Brutus is an honourable man.
You all did see that on the Lupercal
I thrice presented him a kingly crown,
Which he did thrice refuse. Was this ambition?
Yet Brutus says he was ambitious,
And sure he is an honourable man.
I speak not to disprove what Brutus spoke,
But here I am to speak what I do know.
You all did love him once, not without cause;
What cause withholds you then to mourn for him?
O judgment, thou art fled to brutish beasts,
And men have lost their reason! Bear with me,
My heart is in the coffin there with Caesar,
And I must pause till it come back to me.

First Plebeian Methinks there is much reason in his sayings.

Second Citizen If thou consider rightly of the matter,
Caesar has had great wrong.

Third Citizen Has he, masters!
I fear there will a worse come in his place.

Extract 2 Mr William Shakespeare's Plays

Only Mark Antony, his friend and admirer, returned to grieve for Caesar.

Antony then begged the conspirators to kill him too, if they bore him any grudge.

But Brutus wanted no other bloodshed, and promised to explain his actions in full.

Then Antony asked to speak at the funeral and, against Cassius' advice, Brutus agreed.

Left alone with Caesar's lifeless body, Antony swore that he would avenge his death.

Brutus explained to the shocked citizens of Rome that Caesar had threatened their freedom.

But when Antony spoke with great passion of Caesar's love for them, the people were moved.

They turned against the conspirators and rioted through the streets, seeking revenge.

Now Antony was satisfied. With the citizens behind him, he could drive out his enemies.

Pursued by the angry mob, the conspirators fled the city. Brutus and Cassius both raised armies, intending to retake Rome.

Antony formed an alliance with Octavius, Caesar's lawful heir, taking money left by Caesar to the citizens of Rome to pay for their legions.

Marcia Williams

From the activity, you will no doubt come up with a variety of answers to each of the questions. You will have seen that the first extract provides two dramatic speeches from the play, whilst the second deals with various events from the plot from Caesar's murder to Antony's allegiance with Octavius. This shows that the text has been considerably condensed in the illustrated version, with the writer presenting selected events from the plot and cutting down the funeral speeches to just a few lines. You should also have noticed that the vocabulary and syntax has been modernized and simplified in the illustrated version. Together with the comic-book style illustrations and speech bubbles, the style of language suggests that the illustrated version of *Julius Caesar* is aimed at a young audience, whilst Shakespeare's text is much more adult in its appeal.

Context and topic

Any text must have a purpose, and the purpose may be a combination of a number of ideas. But many students make the mistake, when analysing texts, of thinking that the purpose stands alone and that there are no other elements to be considered. For instance, when students analyse texts, they commonly write that a text's purpose is 'to persuade' or 'to entertain'. However, they are missing a crucial point here – the text must have been written 'to persuade someone to do something' or 'to entertain a particular audience in some way'. In other words, it is a pointless exercise, to look at the different purposes a text might have without considering the audience the text is aimed at, and the context within which it is produced. Any text will also have a certain amount of content or a central topic, which can also be linked to the context. Answer the questions in the activity on the two texts that follow, and you will see how these features play a vital part in any text.

Adventure holiday advertisement

> ### NEVER A DULL MOMENT
>
> Abseiling, pony trekking, windsurfing, motorsports, canoeing, learning to drive, training to be a lifeguard – PGL offer over 60 different activities at 23 centres across the UK and France for 6–18 year olds.
>
> Whether you have a young child or a teenager, they won't experience a single dull moment on a PGL holiday!

Football commentary from BBC local radio

An' the ball goes out of play for another throw-in to Darlo (1.0) just over twenty minutes remainin' (1.0) Darlington nil (1.0) Wolverhampton Wanderers two (1.5) an' it looks as if Wolves (.) are headin' to south London (0.5) to play Charlton (.) in the fourth round (.) in ten days' time (2.0) unless we see a mighty comeback (1.0) from Darlington (1.0) in these remainin' minutes.

Key

(1.5) indicates a pause in seconds

(.) indicates a micropause

Activity

Examine the two texts above closely.

- What evidence is there that these two texts are dependent upon their context?
- What pointers are given as to the subject matter of each text?
- Having answered the previous two questions, can you say what purpose each text has? Remember to make your estimation of the purpose in terms of a particular audience), and give sufficient evidence to account for each of your answers.

As you will no doubt have noticed, the place of production of each of the above texts is all-important. If the first text were found in the middle of a recipe for lasagne, it would be totally inappropriate; but it is part of a leaflet advertising a holiday company, so it is contextualized and we accept its appropriateness. If we heard the second text in the middle of a dinner party, we would again consider the piece to be out of context; but if we switched on the car radio and heard it, we would readily accept it.

The subject matter of these two texts is also obvious. In the advert, we see a number of nouns that are all part of the semantic field of sporting activities: 'abseiling', 'windsurfing', 'canoeing'. In the second text, there are a number of terms that belong to the semantic field of soccer: 'ball', 'throw-in', 'Wolverhampton Wanderers', 'fourth round'. It is easy, therefore, to recognize what the texts are about and that in turn helps us to put them into context.

There is one other crucial difference that you will have noted about these two texts: one is written and the other is spoken (it is represented here in the form of a transcript). To add to our framework of the terminology used in analysing language production, we can define context and topic in the following way:

Context

The situation in which the text takes place, is used or is intended to happen.

Topic

What the text is about, its subject matter or 'topicality', which can be recognized by words used in a particular semantic field.

Form and style

As we have already noted, a number of other factors can affect textual production but do not always come into play. One of these matters is the **form** that the text takes, or the **representation** of the text. If we look at the following text, we can see simply by its appearance that it is an advertisement, despite the fact that there are no images. The layout, the use of words, the inclusion of a location, telephone number and website address, all help to convey this.

OVERCOME SHYNESS

BUILD SELF-ESTEEM

Combat fear, conversation blocks and physical symptoms
in a new group, led by a skilled psychotherapist.

Achieve success and build self-confidence. Proven results.

CALL FOR FREE CONSULTATION

THE SHYNESS CLINIC

Somerset Place, W1
Tel: 0797 000 0000

www.bashfulpeople.com

So we can define form in the following way:

> **Form**
>
> The way that the text is represented, seen or heard; the recognized format of textual representation that is applied by the writer to the whole of the text.

One vital area we must also consider is the style in which a text is written (or spoken). Since any stylistic issues will have been decided beforehand, this will be linked very closely to the purpose, and consequently to the audience. Style is a term you will also come across when you study literary texts; indeed, you should already have a good grasp of what constitutes a writer's literary style from your study of literature at GCSE. We can define it for textual production purposes by breaking it down into five major areas.

> **Style**
>
> The way that the text is written. It includes such matters as **lexis** and **semantics** (the words used), **grammar** (the ways in which single words are organized into meaningful chunks of text), **phonology and style** (the way sounds and stylistic devices are used and combined to help convey textual meaning), **cohesion** (the way the text is ordered and hangs together) and **graphology** (what the text looks like).

Language production

It is essential that you take all of the above areas into consideration when you plan and produce texts (as well as when you analyse texts), and you must always ensure that you are able to justify your choices in your commentary.

The chart below is a diagrammatic representation of the issues that we have discussed so far.

TEXT

What and who is it for?

↓

PURPOSE   **AUDIENCE**

What is it about?

↓

TOPIC

What form should the text take? Should it be written or spoken?

What lexical, semantic, grammatical, phonological, cohesive and graphological issues will there be?

↓

FORM   **STYLE**

Where might it appear or happen?

↓

CONTEXT

You can see that with this flow-chart model, each stage of production is dependent on the choices made in the preceding ones and also has implications for the next stage. But, as the model below shows, the decisions do not necessarily have to be made in a linear fashion. We can also consider the text as being at the centre of a production 'circle', where each stage of production is linked to the other stages and the text needs all of them in order to work.

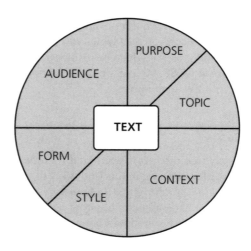

In the diagram we see that each segment must be suitable and all must be working together before the 'whole' can operate as a text.

Whichever of these models you feel is most appropriate and works for you is the framework you should use when you come to write texts of your own, whatever they may be, either as a creative response to themes you have studied or as a re-creative adaptation of an existing text.

In conclusion, you should be aware that no texts are produced in a vacuum; you should always assume that any writing you do on this course has a particular purpose and audience at its heart. Once these two areas have been identified, considerations can be given to topic, form, style and context. If texts are produced without these considerations, it is likely that they will not be effective.

Recasting texts

As part of Unit F672 you will need to produce a re-creative text. The focus of the recasting exercise will be to transform certain content and features from the texts you have studied into a multimodal text. Together with your re-creative work you will also produce a critical commentary, explaining the process of transformation and exploring how your text relates to the original texts.

Your multimodal creation must be **1000–1300 words in length** and must make use of at least **two** different modes of communication. It may include, for example, written content, images, spoken content, audio or video. The piece you produce might be a complete text or it could be presented as a section of a much larger work. While knowledge of your set text is vitally important, it is the principles of textual adaptation and recasting that are paramount to your success in this unit. When completing this particular question, it is extremely important that:

* you focus on the audience for your new text
* you focus on the task
* you reshape the original materials as necessary.

Obviously, you will remember that the reaction of the people for whom a text is written (or spoken) is very important. How a writer conveys attitudes, values and concerns in a text is paramount to its success or failure. In this unit you will need to consider which adaptations and changes you need to make when you construct your new text for a new audience.

The task

Adapting writing to a particular requirement could be compared with the job of a theatrical director. Theatrical productions of dramatic texts are given individuality and angled towards particular audience reactions by means of the interpretation that the director imposes upon the production. The notion of a play being given an interpretation by an individual director can be applied to this task. You are asked to take material you should be familiar with, and place your stamp of individuality on it by interpreting it through textual adaptation and recasting it in a multimodal form, so that a new audience can view it.

You will need to reflect on the knowledge you have about your source texts before you start planning your own text. Note down any ideas you have as you read the texts and other different types of texts, as this may help you take a particular stance later in the recasting process.

Activity

Look at the following list of forms of production. Think about what you know about each from your own experience. Note down, for each one, some of your ideas on possible form and style:

- an entry for a children's encyclopaedia
- an artical in a tabloid newspaper
- a website showcasing new sports cars
- a leaflet on the dangers of smoking for teenagers
- a documentary on the Falklands War
- a quick-start instruction sheet for computers
- an advertisement for high-quality wines in a magazine
- a snowboarding game on a games console
- an illustrated travel guide

Evaluating your source text

Having identified the main content that you wish to use in your new text, you need to evaluate the material in terms of its linguistic content, so that you can ensure that the changes you make are appropriate for the new target audience and purpose that you select. This allows you to focus on the kinds of changes you will make, and thus reflect on them in your commentary.

Use the following checklist to make a linguistic evaluation of your text, ensuring that this includes consideration of the particular features you wish to focus on in your adaptation.

Evaluate source texts		Decide changes for adapted text
Audience:	⇒	Determine:
• who?		• new audience
• how linked to style?		• new style
Mode:	⇒	Identify:
• speech		• new modes?
• writing		• how will different modes relate?
• mixed modes		• print or digital?
		• video and/ or audio?
Genre:	⇒	Identify:
• what?		• new genre?
		• same genre?
		• mixed genres?

Written style:	⇒	Identify:

Written style:

- use of lexis
- use of syntax
- use of grammar
- phonological features
- rhetorical features
- integration of modes

⇒ Identify:

- lexical changes
- syntactical changes
- grammatical changes
- phonological changes
- rhetorical changes
- use of multimedia
- integration of different modes

Structure and cohesion:

- order
- chronology

⇒ Identify:

- new order
- new chronology

Graphological features:

- any presentational device

⇒ Identify:

- new presentational devices

By focusing on the way you are to adapt your text at this stage and engaging in a hypothetical comparison, you will also save yourself time when planning the comparative commentary, since you will already have identified the major areas for analysis.

The commentary task will allow you to discuss some of the linguistic and stylistic choices that you have made as part of the process of transforming selected material from your source texts into a multimodal text. This will cover:

- how language and form have been used to suit audience and purpose
- how vocabulary and other stylistic features have been used to shape meaning and achieve particular effects.

It is wise to note down some of the key stylistic choices you make when you are planning out your re-creative task, as this means you will be able to deal with the commentary more effectively.

Adopting an approach

There are particular ways that you might choose to adapt your text, including how you select and integrate the multimodal elements of your adaptation. Examine some of the following ideas:

Use of narrators, characters or figures

- first-person pronominative form, adopting a persona through which you can deliver your material
- third-person narrative, constructing a particular character through which the information, based on the original text, can be channelled
- creation of a situation where characters interact, using material from the original text as a narrative base

Use of particular forms

- a graphic novel incorporating text and images
- a magazine article with an interview and illustrations
- a scene from a musical incorporating speech and audio

Use of the spoken mode

- dialogue between a number of characters
- a range of different narrators, each with his or her own distinctive speech style, accent or dialect forms
- an interview with an expert witness or character

Use of presentational features

- time-lines or chronological representations
- use of links in electronic materials and interactive features
- summaries, abstracts and synopses
- glossaries, word boxes and definitions
- bullet points and subheadings

Use of graphological devices

- illustrations, images and pictures (where appropriate)
- headlines, titles and captions
- use of audio, video or other multimedia content

Remember that your choice of strategy for delivering your new text is very important and will help to ensure the overall success of your work.

Structuring selected material to use in your new text

As with any piece of written work, planning is vital. Because you have been given word limits and parameters within which to write, it is best if you first prepare an outline of your text.

A paragraph plan is a simple way of doing this; but since you will be planning a multimodal text you may also find it useful to sketch out a draft layout or storyboard, where you can map out what kinds of texts your recasting will incorporate and how they will link together to form one text. You should consider cohesive details such as plot, story-line, sequencing and chronology here too.

The total word limit for your AS coursework is **3000 words** and, whilst you are free to divide this as you wish between the separate tasks within it, it is recommended that you allocate around **1000 to 1500 words** to your analytical study for Task 1 and between **1000 and 1500 words** to Task 2; your multimodal text and commentary. You can be flexible as to how you divide the word count for Task 2, but as a basic guideline the multimodal text should be the same length or longer than the commentary. The commentary however, should **not be less than 500 words**. If it is, you are unlikely to be able to develop the critical analysis sufficiently to gain good marks.

Marrying the outline with the style

Having established the approach you are to take with your material, you can now decide upon the ways in which you are going to write the verbal, or written component of your new text. At this point you need to reflect on the stylistic details that will enhance your new text, giving it the elements that will help it to succeed. Use the following framework to help you:

Lexical and semantic choices

- semantic field
- connotations and denotations of words
- formality
- jargon or specialist terms
- abstract ideas or concrete facts.

Grammatical choices

- pronouns and pronominative form
- noun types: abstract or concrete
- use of modifiers: adjectives (factual, emotive, descriptive and evaluative); adverbials (time, place, direction, situation and quality).

Sentence types

- statements, questions and commands
- simple, compound or complex
- co-ordination and subordination
- premodification and postmodification.

Verb usage

- tense
- voice.

Use of rhetorical and phonological devices

- repetition and patterning
- imagery and other literary devices.

Writing your new text

When you draft your new text, take the following points into consideration:

- double-space your text in case you want to amend or add to it when you re-read your work; you may also find it useful at this stage to draft your work on computer so you can alter it easily
- stick to the word limit – quantity does not necessarily equal quality in this section
- check back to your plan frequently to ensure consistency of style and delivery
- focus on those aspects of the adaptation that will be part of your commentary; underline or highlight them in another colour if necessary, to remind you to refer to them in the next task
- be prepared to redraft your work as many times as it takes to get it to a state you are happy with.

Recasting

Here is the recasting methodology in outline:

1 Study your chosen texts, analysing linguistic, literary, cultural and presentational features.

2 Determine the type of multimodal text that you wish to produce in response to the texts that you have studied.

3 Decide what multimodal features your text will contain and how they will interlink.

4 Reflect on your knowledge of the type of text you wish to produce, including the multimodal features within it.

5 Re-read your source texts or significant sections of them.

6 Evaluate content and appropriate stylistic changes.

7 Adopt an approach to the source material.

8 Structure the material you have selected to use in your new text.

9 Marry your text-outline with your chosen style.

10 Draft your new text.

11 Re-draft your text as necessary.

Writing your critical commentary

Your first step is to analyse the task so that you can build your own analytical framework that highlights the choices you made when writing your new text.

If you have done your planning and writing in a systematic way in the previous section, you should be able to tackle this as an extension of the recasting process. Remind yourself of the section where you evaluated the original text and decided on the nature of the changes you were going to make.

At the beginning of the recasting process, you will have examined the original text and determined how to respond to it. You should have noted:

• the purpose of your writing – what effect you intend it to have

• the intended audience of the piece – whom you are addressing

• the content from the source texts that you can usefully adapt.

Your next step was to identify the methods you needed to consider for effective textual transmission. You should have noted:

• how you intended to convey your information – careful consideration of viewpoint and style

• how issues of audience link to the purpose of the task – a reflection on any audience limitation

• how to use your subject matter – judgement of limitations and word limit, which elements of the original text have the relevant material, and possible multimodal features.

If these parts of the process have been addressed, the commentary should be easier to produce, since your framework for analysis will already be established in your mind.

Firming up your analytical framework

For your evaluation of your own writing, you can follow the same process as you used to plan your re-creative response, reflecting on whether any consideration of each particular point was needed before progressing on to the next:

- audience
- mode
- genre
- written style:
  - use of lexis
  - use of syntax
  - use of grammar
  - phonological features
  - rhetorical features
- structure and cohesion of the material
- graphological features.

Once you have reminded yourself of how you constructed your text, you can start to consider some of the details that characterize your own writing. Pick out some salient examples and explain them fully.

Fleshing out your analytical comparison

One way of putting flesh on the bones of your analysis is to consider the outline above in terms of a table, as below. This is an easy way of selecting the material you are to discuss.

Source texts		Adapted text	
Issues	**Intended effect and illustrative example**	**Issues**	**Intended effect and illustrative example**
Audience: – who? – how it is linked to style		**Audience:** – new – new style	
Mode		**Modes**	
Genre		**New genre**	
Written style – use of lexis – use of syntax – use of grammar – phonological features – rhetorical features – single or multimodal		**New style** – lexical changes – syntactical changes – grammatical changes – phonological changes – rhetorical changes – multimodal elements	
Structure and cohesion		**New order**	
Graphological features		**New Graphological features**	

You may find the table useful in the draft stages of writing your evaluative commentary. The advantage of using a table such as this is that it allows you to reflect on your processes of initial textual consideration and follow them up by selecting the most important changes you made in your adaptation. It may be the case that some of these areas will require little or no attention in your commentary; others may need only one example; while there will be some you want to emphasize by giving a couple of examples. Remember your word limit and use this to help you prioritize which points to emphasize in your response to this task and which ones to leave out.

Writing your commentary

When you begin your analysis, remember the analytical model you were given at the start of this book on page 3, which will help to keep your comparison focused on explanation and interpretation. You can chain your points together by using a three-point critical structure. In order to do this, you need to:

1   Identify the point you want to discuss from your own text in order to highlight the linguistic or stylistic point you wish to make.

2   Give a clear example from your text: quotation is necessary.

3   Explain and interpret how it works within your text in terms of purpose, audience and subject matter.

This will help you build up an effective commentary that will be systematic, through use of the outline above and also use of an analytical model that covers identification, description and explanation of linguistic issues.

It is vital that you cover the range of methods you have drawn on to help you make your adaptation. This is where your knowledge of other, similar texts you have read might help you. You should draw on your knowledge of the variety of literary and non-literary texts you have read and make reference to them wherever necessary. Try to relate this to your understanding of audience and purpose, by showing how language is used in targeting audience and helping to underpin the purpose of the text.

Be brief and focused in your analysis so that you are not using up too many words on one area when you could be discussing other issues. Remember, if your adaptation has been successful, there should be a range of areas to discuss; you can select the appropriate ones. However, don't make obvious points: use examples that highlight your writing skills and remember to use concrete examples.

A2 Coursework

For Task 1 of your A2 coursework you will produce an analytical study of the relationships between the substantial text and supporting texts. The substantial text must fall outside the accepted literary canon, but must still be considered influential or culturally significant. Many of the skills that are required for this task build on those that you will have already put to use in your AS coursework. This task expands upon these skills by requiring you to consider a greater number and greater range of texts.

The following table provides examples of possible text selections.

	Substantial text	**Supporting texts**
Example 1	Elizabeth David, *French Provincial Cooking*	Magazine feature on lifestyle influences Transcripts of TV programmes on national cookery
Example 2	Bill Bryson, *A Short History of Nearly Everything*	Charles Darwin, *The Voyage of the Beagle* Extract from *Guardian*, 'Bad Science' column Transcript of Year 7 students in science lesson
Example 3	Dale Carnegie, *How to Win Friends and Influence People*	'Business-speak' motivational training-course material Transcript of scene from BBC TV series, *The Office*
Example 4	Bob Dylan lyrics	Scholarly article by English Literature authority, arguing that Dylan is a major poet Transcript of an interview with Dylan
Example 5	Nelson Mandela speeches	Glossary of rhetorical terms and features used in political speeches Extracts from *Julius Caesar*, illustrating rhetorical skills Transcript of a TV or radio discussion of the significance of the speeches, at the time and in hindsight
Example 6	Irvine Welsh, *Trainspotting*	Transcript of discussion on recovering from addiction Material used in secondary schools for a drug-awareness campaign
Example 7	Book of Common Prayer, 1662	Website offering alternative (religious and secular) wedding and funeral ceremonies *Four Weddings and a Funeral*, 1994 film directed by Mike Newell

Coursework tasks

The type of coursework task that you face will depend on a number of factors. If your whole group is studying particular coursework texts, it is likely that you will have little input into the questions that you are set. You will probably be supplied with several appropriate titles and asked to choose one as the basis of your assignment. On the other hand, if you have chosen the texts you are writing on, you will probably negotiate an essay title with your teacher. If so, you will need to identify aspects of the texts about which you would like to write. Your teacher will discuss these ideas with you and will help you to formulate an essay title that is both suitable and phrased in the right way.

An essential difference between an exam essay and a coursework essay is reflected in the kinds of task set. Examination questions are specifically designed to be answered within strict time limits under exam conditions, whereas you might work on a coursework task for several weeks, using various research skills, reference to other writers, and critical works. This needs to be kept in mind if you have some input into creating your coursework question.

Choosing a title

Before you can begin your comparative analytical study, you will need to decide upon an appropriate title or question. This question should enable you to make links between your chosen texts, and these links should reveal your ability to approach your study from both a linguistic and literary perspective. Your teacher will be able to assist you in thinking through and formulating your title, and you should have a firm sense of what this is going to be before beginning on the first draft of your written study.

Appropriate titles for **Example 1** might include:

1. How important is 'voice' in the success of cookery writing and broadcasting, and how does it achieve its effect?

2. How does writing and broadcasting about food reflect specific periods and their wider attitudes and values?

3. How do the selected texts show changing attitudes towards cookery and household management?

Appropriate titles for **Example 5** might include:

1. How does rhetoric influence the opinions of listeners and audiences?

2. Do the effects of rhetoric make a lasting impact or are they bound by context?

3. Is rhetoric a noble art or a political tool?

Structuring your answer

Once you have selected your question, you can read and re-read your texts in the light of it and begin to formulate ideas for your answer. The following structure suggests how you might construct your response. You can use it to plan and organize your notes. Focusing your preparation at this stage will help you to ensure that you have considered all the important issues at stake, and also give you the opportunity to gather the examples and textual references necessary to build your answer.

Section A – Substantial text

- How would you classify your chosen text?
- How has it been classified in the past?
- What genre or genres does it incorporate?
- What is its cultural status and significance?
- What contexts have influenced the production of this text?
- What perspectives, values and attitudes does the text present?

Section B – Supporting texts

- What are your reasons for selecting the supporting texts?
- Why, when and by whom were the texts produced?
- How do they relate to the substantial text?
- How do they differ?

Section C – Comparative literary and linguistic study

- What have you identified by means of comparison in terms of:
    - register
    - tone
    - voice
    - lexis
    - semantics
    - syntax
    - grammar
    - rhetoric
    - features of spoken language
    - different ways of reading.

Section D – Creative comparisons with other areas of the course

- What other aspects of your AS and A2 Level studies might help to develop points in your comparison? For example:
    - voice
    - power and authority
    - mode.

Comparative writing

As part of A2 Unit F674 you will need to prepare and write a comparative study, exploring relationships between a substantial text that falls ouside the accepted literary canon and at least two other texts, one of which must be a spoken language text and one of which must be a non-literary text. When planning a comparison between three or more texts, your major task is to identify the way in which you will construct your analysis. There are two quite different methods of achieving this: the **anchor text** method or the **integrated text** method, both described below.

Whichever of the methods you choose, you must remember that it would be virtually impossible to cover all the areas that are listed in the analytical framework; you should concentrate on selecting an appropriate focus for your comparative analysis and ensuring that you cover the necessary linguistic and literary points.

The anchor text method

This is where you start by analyzing one text, and then compare parts of the other texts to it: this is called *using an anchor text*. What you are doing is using one text as the initial focus of your analysis, and then comparing the other two texts to it. The advantage of this method is that you can decide which text to start with, often the most 'substantial' or the one that you think is the most accessible to you, and then decide what other areas of comparison you might make. The disadvantage, of course, is that your initial analysis of your anchor text is not comparative; however, this can be offset by the close comparative analysis that you provide once you bring the other two texts into your analysis.

This is an outline of the way you might approach your analysis if you use this method:

- choose which text you are going to start with
- make notes on what you are going to say about it
- use your notes on the first text to help you find comparisons with the other two texts
- write about your anchor text first
- pick out relevant comparisons that help you to show meaningful differences between the texts
- use key comparative words to help you, for example, *however, but, in comparison to, though* and *similarly*
- remember to use the three-point critical structure throughout (*see page 3 for a description of this*)
- try to integrate comments about feelings as you make each comparative point.

The integrated text method

The difference between this method and the anchor text method is that with this method you compare your texts from the outset. This means that you can choose the types of focus that you feel will benefit your answer most. It is, however, still necessary to build your answer around a structure. Here is one way of approaching your integrated comparison:

- decide upon the ways you can compare the texts
- use a logical order
- compare audience, purpose and mode
- pick out examples of lexical comparisons, grammatical comparisons, style features, cohesive issues and graphological features
- use key comparative words to help you, such as, *however, but, in comparison to, though* and *similarly*
- remember to use the three-point critical structure throughout (*see page 3 for a description of this*)
- try to integrate comments about feelings as you make each comparative point.

Creative writing piece

For Task 2 at A2 Level, you will be expected to produce a creative piece of your own, based on your knowledge and understanding of your coursework text. The creative piece can take on any form, including the form of a spoken text, but it should arise from your study of the substantial and supporting texts for Task 1. This does not mean that your creative text has to be based on the texts, but it does mean that the creative study should put into practise some of the issues and observations that you have discovered through your analytical study of the texts. It could be a complete text, but it could also be presented as a section of a much larger work.

The following list suggests some of the creative responses that might be possible in relation to the example texts already mentioned:

Example 1

Elizabeth David, *French Provincial Cooking*

with

Magazine feature on lifestyle influences

and

Transcripts of TV programmes on national cookery

Creative piece: Introduction to article for on-line literary forum, investigating the significance of food in literature.

Example 2

Bill Bryson, *A Short History of Nearly Everything*

with

Charles Darwin, *The Voyage of the Beagle*

and

Extract from *Guardian,* 'Bad Science' column

and

Transcript of Year 7 students in science lesson

Creative piece: Promotional material for the Science Museum's launch of its forthcoming *Science Matters* exhibition

Example 3

Dale Carnegie, *How to Win Friends and Influence People*

with

'Business-speak' motivational training-course material

and

Transcript of scene from BBC TV series, *The Office*

Creative piece: Presentation by 'life-coach' to a specific audience

Example 4

Bob Dylan lyrics

with

Scholarly article by English Literature Authority, arguing that Dylan is a major poet

and

Transcript of an interview with Dylan

Creative piece: Literary and linguistic analysis of own choice of song lyrics, making a case for consideration as having serious literary merit

Writing the commentary

In order to gain satisfactory marks for the creative piece of writing, it is vital that you produce an effective commentary. The commentary for your A2 coursework should deal with the reasons for your choice of approach and how your creative piece relates to your analytical study for Task 1. You should then comment on the stages of the process of production, explaining how your combined understanding of linguistic and literary factors have helped to direct your approach.

As part of your commentary you should also deal with the implications of the act of production itself. What is the cultural, social and literary context of your own production? What linguistic differences exist between your own text and the texts you have studied, and how might these differences be explained by reference to audience, context and perspective? You should use this approach to explain the key differences between your text and your source texts. Whilst considering these factors, you should always maintain a linguistic perspective and be prepared to comment closely on the technical construction of the text that you have produced.

Presenting your coursework

When producing coursework it is important that, where you use secondary sources, you learn how to use and acknowledge them correctly. The primary source for the essay is the texts that you are studying. The secondary sources are any other materials that help you in your work, such as study aids, critical works or articles about the texts. Where you use secondary source material, you must make sure that you acknowledge it in the bibliography at the end of your assignment.

The bibliography

In order to acknowledge appropriately the books and other materials that you have read or consulted while writing your coursework essay, it is important to understand the conventions of bibliography writing.

Even if you have read only part of a particular book or article, it should be included in your bibliography. If you have used only the texts themselves, you should still include a bibliography simply consisting of relevant details about the editions used. This will clearly show the examiner that you have used nothing other than the texts and it will also give information about the particular editions that you have used.

Your bibliography should be arranged in the following format.

- The surname of the author or editor (listed alphabetically)
- The initials of the author or editor, followed by '(ed.)' in the latter case
- The title of the book (underlined or in italics) or article (in inverted commas) and source
- The publisher's name
- The date of publication (usually the date when first published).

Here is an example of a student bibliography:

Bibliography

The Wife of Bath's Prologue and Tale

Anderson, J.J. (ed.), *The Canterbury Tales: A Selection of Critical Essays*. Macmillan Casebook Series, 1974

Lisowska, P.S., *The Wife of Bath's Tale*. Hodder and Stoughton, 2000

Marsh, N., *The Wife of Bath's Tale*. Macmillan Master Guides, 1987

Martin, P., *Chaucer's Women: Nuns, Wives and Amazons*. Macmillan, 1990

Tasioulas, J.A., *The Wife of Bath's Prologue and Tale*. York Notes Advanced, 1998

Hamlet

Baker, S., 'Hamlet's Bloody Thoughts and the Illusion of Inwardness' in *Comparative Drama* (Vol. 21. No. 4) Winter, 1987–88

Bradley, A.C., *Shakespearean Tragedy*. Macmillan, 1904

Brooks, J., *Hamlet*. Macmillan Master Guides, 1986

Dover Wilson, J., *What Happens in Hamlet*. Cambridge University Press, 1935

Holderness, G., *Hamlet: Open Guides to Literature*. The Open University Press, 1987

Jump, J. (ed.), *Shakespeare: Hamlet*. Macmillan Casebook Series, 1968

Rossiter, A.C., *Angel With Horns*. Longman, 1961

Potential weaknesses

Overall, examiners report that a high standard of work is produced by students through coursework. However, here are some points that they have highlighted as weaknesses or problem areas in some of the work they have assessed:

- ineffective use of evidence and quotation to back the argument
- tasks that centre on a general discussion of themes or character studies; these tend to lack interest and focus
- evidence of poor time management during the exam, such as too much time spent on the first question
- work that is limited to a personal response and lacks analysis
- including too much biographical or historical background.

4 Analysing drama

You will study two set drama texts as part of Unit F673 at A2 Level. One of the drama texts must be a pre-1800 text and the other must be a modern piece. The unit consists of two sections, Section A and Section B. Section A requires you to write a comparison of the drama texts based on extracts from **both** texts, focusing on how a specified theme is presented, and Section B will present you with a critical proposition, which you must explore through study of either **one** of the texts.

The example questions below demonstrate the format in which the drama questions will appear on your exam paper for Unit F673. Each question will relate to one pair of texts from the list of set texts for this unit. In Section A, you will answer the question in relation to two supplied extracts, one from each of your set texts, drawing on your wider knowledge of them. In Section B you will choose one of the texts from the specified pair in order to answer the question. In this section you will not be presented with an extract, but you may be given a short quotation as illustrated in the second example below. By referring back to the quotation and picking out key words from it in your answer, you will be more able to form a focused response.

Section A

John Webster: The Duchess of Malfi

Caryl Churchill: Top Girls

Using the following two passages as a starting point, and applying what seem to you relevant approaches from your combined linguistic and literary study, examine ways in which the situation of women in relation to male dominance is presented in the two plays.

Shakespeare: Hamlet

Tom Stoppard: Rosencrantz and Guildenstern Are Dead

Using the following two passages as a starting point, and applying what seem to you relevant approaches from your combined linguistic and literary study, examine ways in which acting and role-play are explored and presented in the two plays.

Section B

Christopher Marlowe: Doctor Faustus

Arthur Miller: The Crucible

Making close reference to the language, action and context of one of your chosen plays, examine ways in which an individual's struggle to assert and maintain a sense of self is presented.

Shakespeare: Hamlet

Tom Stoppard: Rosencrantz and Guildenstern are Dead

After his return from England, Hamlet believes that he has been saved by

> ' … a divinity that shapes our ends,
>
> Rough-hew them how we will.' (V. ii. 10–11)

Making close reference to relevant aspects of the language, action and context of one of your chosen plays, examine ways in which ideas of human destiny shaped by forces beyond the individual's control are presented.

In order to succeed in this part of your course you must demonstrate a detailed critical understanding in analysing the ways in which structure, form and language shape meaning. You will also need to understand literary concepts such as the linguistic and literary features of Elizabethan and Jacobean drama. You will need to recognize the features of drama as a genre, and learn about literary tradition and the context of culture and society at the time the plays were written.

This chapter will focus on how language is used in drama texts, and the interrelationship between that language and the effects created on the audience. In looking at the language of drama, both linguistic and literary issues will be examined, and the aim of your studies will be to develop a full understanding of the ways in which dramatists use language in their plays to create a whole range of effects, which in turn provoke particular responses from the audience.

The nature of drama

Drama is different from other forms of literature that you have studied in a number of respects. One key difference is that, by its nature, drama focuses on the spoken word rather than the written word. Sometimes we lose sight of this, because very often in studying drama for examination purposes the focus is on the written text of a play rather than the spoken performance of it. It is important, even when sitting at a desk with only the written text in front of you, that you consider the 'performance' aspect of drama. In many respects a play can be fully appreciated only when seen in performance, and this is why it is so important to try to see a live performance of the play or plays you are studying. If you cannot see the play on the stage, try to get hold of a video or film performance of it. Sometimes it is impossible to see any kind of performance of a play, in which case you will need to imagine what a performance might be like.

Another difference between drama and other literary forms is the fact that drama relies upon certain conventions – it has distinct rules of structure, format and presentation. This chapter will look at these conventions in more detail later.

As a drama text presents the core for a 'performance', it is often a more 'public' form of literary communication than other forms. As such, its audience is a particularly important element. When seen live on stage, the experience of a performance is a shared activity and there is a direct relationship between the way the dramatist writes, the way that this is put into performance, and the response of the audience.

If a dramatist's work is to survive, his or her works must be performed, and therefore the expectations of the audience need to be taken into account. Sometimes, when presented with something that doesn't meet their expectations, audiences can make their feelings felt and this can lead the dramatist to make alterations to the text. For example, when *The Rivals* was first performed in 1775, the audience response to it was so hostile that Sheridan withdrew it after the first night and substantially re-wrote a large proportion of it.

Shakespeare often deliberately includes things in his plays that he knows will appeal to and gain the approval of his audience. Although a dramatist does write about and explore themes and ideas that he or she is interested in and wants to present to the audience, no dramatist can afford to lose sight of the fact that plays must appeal to a particular audience.

Features of drama

Many types of drama exist from Shakespeare's texts, to modern plays and television or radio scripts. Despite the huge variety of forms of drama as well as subject-matter, a number of themes are common throughout this genre. Some of these are summarized below.

Conflict

At the centre of all drama is a sense of conflict, in one form or another. This could consist of conflict in the conventional sense where characters fight one another. Equally, conflict could be between individual characters and their ideals or values. The conflict could stem from within a character, perhaps torn between certain courses of action, or it could be spiritual or moral in nature. Whatever form it takes, this conflict will be ever-present throughout the text and form the basis for sustaining the dramatic tension and the interest of the audience.

Of course this is explored in different ways by different dramatists. In Shakespeare's *Othello*, for example, emotional conflicts exist within Othello himself as a result of Iago's interference with Othello's personal affairs. A more subtle use of conflict can be found in Shakespear's comedy *As You Like It*, in the opposition between court and countryside. In a more modern drama such as David Hare's *Murmuring Judges*, conflicts operate in different ways. We have the conflict of views about the role of the barrister as represented by the attitudes of Irina and Sir Peter, or the conflict of views on the right way of policing as seen through the characters of Sandra and Barry.

Activity

Think about any plays that you have studied in the past or are currently studying. Draw up a table for each of them showing what conflicts occur within each drama and how important each is to the overall effects of the play.

Realism

The question of realism is one that is often raised in relation to drama and it has provoked much debate. One view of realism in drama is that put forward by the poet and philosopher Samuel Taylor Coleridge, who felt that when watching a play the audience is prepared to 'willingly suspend disbelief' and believe in the reality of the characters and the action on the stage. Some drama does work like this, and in the 1950s a whole style of drama, including plays such as *Look Back in Anger* by John Osborne, became known as 'kitchen-sink dramas' because of their portrayals of 'real life' in the colloquial language of everyday speech.

It's quite clear, though, that not all drama sets out to be 'realistic' in that sense, and some dramatists deliberately present a different picture from the world we know. In Shakespeare's *Hamlet*, for example, the starting point for the action is the appearance of a ghost, and in *The Tempest* Prospero deals in magic, and spirits of the air do his bidding. In the plays of Samuel Beckett all kinds of strange things happen, such as in *Endgame* where the characters live in dustbins, or *Waiting for Godot* where two men wait for a character they know nothing about and who never arrives.

In reconciling these apparent opposites we come to the understanding that there are two kinds of realism – one is surface or physical realism where the characters, the things they say and do, the language they use and so on are immediately recognizable as representing 'real life'. The other kind of realism is psychological realism, in which the dramatist focuses on the feelings, thoughts, emotions, fears, inner desires and life of the characters. Both kinds of drama, or varying degrees of each, are open to the dramatist, depending on what impression they would like to make on the audience.

The theatre

Another consideration when studying a play, as opposed to other kinds of literature, is the fact that, as we have said, a play is meant to be seen on the stage. The dramatist will have given thought to the mechanics of performing the play in the theatre. Some dramatists give little guidance in this respect, while others give detailed stage directions to do with aspects like the set and lighting. These features are integral to the play and are generally designed to enhance the performance, the visual effect or the impact of the language of the play. The language of the play is still at the heart of the drama, but you need to be aware of how it interrelates with the other elements of drama that bring the language to life.

Plot and structure

The plot is obviously of central importance to most plays, although there are certain kinds of plays (those of Samuel Beckett, for example) where the lack of a conventional plot is essential to the overall effect of the drama. However, in much of the drama you have encountered, you will probably have found that the plot is a key element. The plot, however, is much more than simply the 'story' of the play; the way plot develops is an essential part of its structure. From a dramatist's point of view this structure is something that needs careful thought and planning, because ultimately it can influence whether the play is successful or not.

Here are some points you might have thought about. An effective plot should:

Activity

From an audience's point of view, what features do you think a successful play should have in terms of plot?

- capture the audience's interest and attention right from the start
- maintain the interest of the audience throughout
- move the action on from one episode to the next
- arouse the interest of the audience in character and situation
- create high points, or moments of crisis at intervals
- create expectation and surprise.

Generally speaking, if a play contains most or all of these features, it is likely to be well received by the audience.

When studying plays you will see that most follow a particular pattern in the way that they are structured, and it is possible to identify the following key elements:

1 **Exposition:** This opens the play, often introduces the main characters and provides background information.

2 **Dramatic incitement:** This is an incident that provides the starting point for the main action of the play.

3 **Complication:** This usually forms the main action of the play – the characters respond to the dramatic incitement and other developments that stem from it.

4 **Crisis:** This constitutes the climax of the play.

5 **Resolution:** This is the final section of the play, where things are worked out and some kind of conclusion is arrived at.

This is how the above pattern applies to Shakespeare's *As You Like It*:

1 **Exposition:** The play begins with the audience being given the information that a good duke has been usurped by his ruthless brother, Frederick, and has taken to the forest with a few faithful courtiers. There they live simply but happily. Rosalind, the good duke's daughter, has stayed behind at court to be with her friend and cousin, Celia, who is Frederick's daughter.

2 **Dramatic incitement:** Frederick becomes suspicious of Rosalind and banishes her from court.

3 **Complication:** Rosalind disguises herself as a boy and leaves to search for her father, taking with her Celia and the court jester, Touchstone. Another character, Orlando, leaves home to escape his brother, having heard from his servant that he is planning to kill him.

4 **Crisis:** Rosalind having fallen in love with Orlando, realizes she must find a way to reveal her true self to him.

5 **Resolution:** The exiles meet together and the love interests are happily resolved. Duke Frederick resigns his usurped position and repents, and everyone gets what is rightfully theirs.

Activity

Examine the structure of the plays you are studying. For each play, draw a diagram to represent the way the action develops and the way it fits into the pattern outlined above. Make a note of the 'key elements' in the development of the plot in each play.

The language of drama

The type of language used in a play – formal, serious, colloquial or slang – will depend on the kind of effects that the dramatist wants to achieve. For example, we can learn about characters through their language, or language can add colour to a scene, create atmosphere, and alter the tone and mood of a play.

Dialogue

The most obvious way in which dramatists use language in their plays is in dialogue, through which the characters convey information and interact with each other. There are dialogues of all kinds in plays and the language the dramatist uses will be chosen carefully to reflect the tone, atmosphere and content of the particular scene. Dialogue is a verbal exchange between two or more characters but it can take many forms. For example, it could present the tender exchange of love between two characters, it may involve characters plotting an evil deed together or it could be an argument.

Read the following extracts carefully. Extract 1 is from *The Rivals* by Richard Brinsley Sheridan. The servant, Fag, talks to Captain Jack Absolute about meeting the officer's father Sir Anthony, in Bath. Extract 2 is from *Hamlet* by Shakespeare. In it Hamlet talks to Ophelia as they prepare to watch the play that Hamlet has arranged in order to determine whether Claudius is guilty of his father's murder. Extract 3 is from *Rosencrantz and Guildenstern are Dead* by Tom Stoppard. Rosencrantz and Guildenstern are aboard a boat taking Hamlet to England, but Rosencrantz begins to doubt the purpose of their journey.

Extract 1 The Rivals

Act 2 scene 1

Captain Absolute's *lodgings.* Captain Absolute *and* Fag

Fag: Sir, while I was there, Sir Anthony came in. I told him you had sent me to inquire after his health, and to know if he was at leisure to see you.

Absolute: And what did he say, on hearing I was at Bath?

Fag: Sir, in my life I never saw an elderly gentleman more astonished! He started back two or three paces, rapped out a dozen interjectural oaths, and asked, what the devil had brought you here!

Absolute: Well, sir, and what did you say?

Fag: Oh, I lied, sir. I forget the precise lie; but you may depend on't, he got no truth from me. Yet, with submission, for fear of blunders in future, I should be glad to fix what *has* brought us to Bath, in order that we may lie a little consistently. Sir Anthony's servants were curious, sir, very curious indeed.

Absolute: You have said nothing to them?

Fag: O, not a word, sir, not a word. Mr Thomas, indeed, the coachman (whom I take to be the discreetest of whips) –

Absolute: 'Sdeath, you rascal! You have not trusted him!

Fag: O, *no*, sir – no, no, not a syllable, upon my veracity! He was, indeed, a little inquisitive; but I was sly, sir, devilish sly. 'My master', said I, 'honest Thomas' – you know, sir, one says 'honest' to one's inferiors – 'is come to Bath to *recruit*' – yes, sir, I said 'to *recruit*' – and whether for men, money, or constitution, you know, sir, is nothing to him, nor any one else.

Absolute: Well, '*recruit*' will do. Let it be so.

Fag: O, sir, 'recruit' will do surprisingly. Indeed, to give the thing an air, I told Thomas that your honour had already enlisted five disbanded chairmen, seven minority waiters, and thirteen billiard-markers.

Absolute: You blockhead, never say more than is necessary.

Fag: I beg pardon, sir; I beg pardon. But, with submission, a lie is nothing unless one supports it. Sir, whenever I draw on my invention for a good current lie, I always forge endorsements as well as the bill.

Absolute: Well, take care you don't hurt your credit by offering too much security. Is Mr Faulkland returned?

Fag: He is above, sir, changing his dress.

Absolute: Can you tell whether he has been informed of Sir Anthony's and Miss Melville's arrival?

Fag: I fancy not, sir; he has seen no one since he came in, but his gentleman, who was with him at Bristol. I think, sir, I hear Mr Faulkland coming down.

Absolute: Go, tell him I am here.

Fag: (*going*) Yes, sir. – I beg pardon, sir, but should Sir Anthony call, you will do me the favour to remember that we are '*recruiting*', if you please.

Absolute: Well, well.

Extract 2 Hamlet

Act 3 scene 2

Gertrude: Come hither, my dear Hamlet, sit by me.

Hamlet: No, good mother, here's metal more attractive. (*Turns to Ophelia.*)

Polonius: (*Aside to the King*) O ho! do you mark that?

Hamlet: (*Lying down at Ophelia's feet*) Lady, shall I lie in your lap?

Ophelia: No, my lord.

Hamlet: I mean, my head upon your lap.

Ophelia: Ay, my lord.

Hamlet: Do you think I meant country matters?

Ophelia: I think nothing, my lord.

Hamlet: That's a fair thought to lie between maids' legs.

Ophelia: What is, my lord?

Hamlet: Nothing.

Ophelia: You are merry, my lord.

Hamlet: Who, I?

Ophelia: Ay, my lord.

Hamlet: O God, your only jig-maker. What should a man do but be merry? For look you how cheerfully my mother looks, and my father died within's two hours.

Ophelia: Nay, 'tis twice two months, my lord.

Hamlet: So long? Nay then, let the devil wear black, for I'll have a suit of sables. O heavens, die two months ago, and not forgotten yet! Then there's hope a great man's memory may outlive his life half a year. But by'r lady, 'a must build churches then, or else shall 'a suffer not thinking on, with the hobby-horse, whose epitaph is 'For O, for O, the hobby-horse is forgot'.

Extract 3 Rosencrantz and Guildenstern are Dead

Act 3

Guil: (*leaping up*) What a shambles! We're just not getting anywhere.

Ros: Not even England. I don't believe in it anyway.

Guil: What?

Ros: England.

Guil: Just a conspiracy of cartographers, you mean?

Ros: I mean I don't believe it! (*Calmer*) I have no image. I try to picture us arriving, a little harbour perhaps … roads … inhabitants to point the way … horses on the road … riding for a day or a fortnight and then a palace and the English King …That would be the logical kind of thing … But my mind remains a blank. No. We're slipping off the map.

Guil: Yes … yes … (*Rallying*) But you don't believe anything till it happens. As it has all happened. Hasn't it?

Ros: We drift down time, clutching at straws. But what good's a brick to a drowning man?

Guil: Don't give up, we can't be long now.

 Ros: We might as well be dead. Do you think death could possibly be a boat?

Guil: No, no, no … Death is … not. Death isn't. You take my meaning. Death is the ultimate negative. Not being. You can't not-be on a boat.

 Ros: I've frequently not been on boats.

Guil: No, no, no – what you've been is not on boats.

 Ros: I wish I was dead. (*Considering the drop.*) I could jump over the side. That would put a spoke in their wheel.

Guil: Unless they're counting on it.

 Ros: I shall remain on board. That'll put a spoke in their wheel. (*The futility of it, fury*) All right! We don't question, we don't doubt. We perform. But a line must be drawn somewhere, and I would like to put it on record that I have no confidence in England. Thank you. (Thinks about this) And even if it's true, it'll be another shambles.

Activity

Examine each of these examples of dialogue and compare the ways in which language is used in each one, bearing in mind the following features:

- the lexis
- the tone created
- metaphorical and rhetorical features
- the overall effects created.

Here are some points you might have noted:

Extract 1 This exchange between Fag and his master Absolute is direct and the short-question-and-response format appears naturalistic, but it is carefully contrived to provide the audience with information. The language contains the mannered formality typical of drama of the eighteenth century.

Extract 2 The dialogue in this extract reveals a breakdown in understanding between Hamlet and the other characters. Hamlet's short remarks are enigmatic, whilst Ophelia's are tentative as she struggles to understand what Hamlet means. The clipped exchange creates a sense of tension in the scene, and Hamlet's focus on wordplay and innuendo emphasises the emptiness of the dialogue and the difficulty the characters experience in relating to one another.

Extract 3 Tom Stoppard uses bold statement and exclamation to suggest Rosencrantz's mounting frustration and outbursts of exasperation. He also inserts pauses between words and clauses to create the impression that his characters are thinking out loud, as they try to make better sense of their situation. The tone of the dialogue shifts rapidly between optimistic speculation, decisive action and moments of hopeless dejection. The frequent shift adds to a sense of despair in the scene and reflects the ineffectiveness of the characters' efforts to influence the course of the plot.

Activity

For each of the plays you are studying, pick three examples where the dramatist uses dialogue in different ways to create different effects. Analyse the language use closely in each example.

Presenting character

A key element in the overall effectiveness of a play is the extent to which the dramatist is successful in creating interesting and convincing characters. Although characters on the stage can be revealed through what they do, language has a key role to play in developing our perceptions of them. Some dramatists make extensive use of stage directions to tell us how they intend a character to appear to the audience. Of course, when watching a play on stage you will be seeing these directions translated into actions, rather than reading them.

Other dramatists, including Shakespeare, tend to provide little information about characters through stage dirrections, but rely almost entirely on the other methods of revealing characters to the audience that dramatists can use. These methods include:

- what characters say
- how characters speak
- how characters are described by others
- how characters behave.

Characters in plays usually have distinctive voices, which the dramatist creates in order to shape the kind of response he or she wants from the audience. In simple terms this can present a single dimension of a character. For example, read the following extract from *Othello*, which reveals things about the characters of both Iago and Roderigo.

Activity

Examine how Shakespeare uses language in the extract to give an impression of the characters of Iago and Roderigo. What kind of impression of each character do you get?

Othello

Act 1 scene 3

Roderigo: Iago.
Iago: What say'st thou, noble heart?
Roderigo: What will I do, think'st thou?
Iago: Why, go to bed and sleep.
Roderigo: I will incontinently drown myself.
Iago: If thou dost, I shall never love thee after. Why, thou silly gentleman?
Roderigo: It is silliness to live, when to live is torment: and then we have a prescription to die, when death is our physician.
Iago: O villainous! I have looked upon the world for four times seven years; and since I could distinguish betwixt a benefit and an injury, I never found a man that knew how to love himself. Ere I would say I would drown myself for the love of a guinea-hen, I would change my humanity with a baboon.
Roderigo: What should I do? I confess it is my shame to be so fond, but it is not in my virtue to amend it.
Iago: Virtue? a fig! 'Tis in ourselves that we are thus or thus. Our bodies are our gardens, to the which our wills are gardeners. So that if we will plant nettles or sow lettuce, set hyssop and weed up thyme, supply it with one gender of herbs or distract it with many, either to have it sterile with idleness, or manured with industry, why the power and corrigible

authority of this lies in our wills. If the balance of our lives had not one scale of reason to poise another of sensuality, the blood and baseness of our natures would conduct us to most preposterous conclusions. But we have reason to cool our raging motions, our carnal stings, our unbitted lusts, whereof I take this, that you call love, to be a sect or scion.

Roderigo: It cannot be.

Iago: It is merely a lust of the blood and a permission of the will. Come, be a man. Drown thyself? Drown cats and blind puppies. I have professed me thy friend, and I confess me knit to thy deserving with cables of perdurable toughness. I could never better stead thee than now. Put money in thy purse. Follow thou these wars; defeat thy favour with an usurped beard; I say, put money in thy purse. It cannot be that Desdemona should long continue her love to the Moor – put money in thy purse – nor he his to her. It was a violent commencement, and thou shalt see an answerable sequestration – put but money in thy purse. These Moors are changeable in their wills – fill thy purse with money. The food that to him now is as luscious as locusts shall be to him shortly as acerb as the coloquintida. She must change for youth; when she is sated with his body, she will find the error of her choice. Therefore put money in thy purse. If thou wilt needs damn thyself, do it a more delicate way than drowning. Make all the money thou canst. If sanctimony and a frail vow betwixt an erring barbarian and a super-subtle Venetian be not too hard for my wits and all the tribe of hell, thou shalt enjoy her – therefore make money. A pox of drowning thyself! It is clean out of the way. Seek thou rather to be hanged in compassing thy joy than to be drowned and go without her.

Immediately the contrast between the two is apparent and there is no doubt that Iago is the dominant character. Roderigo appears weak and feeble as he talks childishly of drowning himself. Iago clearly has little patience or sympathy for him and mocks him, calling him 'silly'. Iago's cynical view of life and of love is clear from the views he expresses to bolster up Roderigo. Notice the imagery he uses to describe Othello's love for Desdemona; it is expressed in terms of physical appetite – 'the food that to him now is as luscious as locusts'. The vocabulary he uses in connection with love – 'carnal stings', 'unbitted lusts', 'sated' – emphasizes the contempt and cynicism he feels towards the notion of love.

Most major characters in drama have different sides to their personalities and behave in different ways in different situations. In *Othello*, for example, the changes that come about in Othello's personality are reflected in his language, as he changes from a noble and assured leader with a rich and poetic language to a character eaten up with jealousy.

Activity

Think about the plays you are studying. Choose one of the main characters from each play and find two speeches he or she makes, where language is used differently in each one. Analyse the ways in which language is used in each speech, and describe the effects created.

Soliloquies

The soliloquy is another way that the dramatist can develop character through the language of the play. The soliloquy is a speech that a character delivers when alone on the stage or regardless of hearers. Through this device the dramatist has much scope for allowing characters to express their thoughts and feelings aloud, and therefore to let the audience know what is going on in their minds. It is often used to allow characters to reveal their true feelings, plans or motives.

In *Doctor Faustus*, Christopher Marlowe gives Faustus a number of soliloquies throughout the play, which allow the audience to witness the moral battle that Faustus undergoes before renouncing God completely in his relentless pursuit of power and greatness.

Activity

Look carefully at the following two soliloquies. The first is from *Doctor Faustus* by Christopher Marlowe, and in it Faustus reveals his intentions to the audience. The second is from *Murmuring Judges* by David Hare, and in it Sandra speaks about the nature of policing.

What do you learn from the first soliloquy about:

- the character of Faustus
- his attitude towards God?

Think about the tone of the soliloquy. Do you detect any shifts of tone here?

What do you learn from the second soliloquy about:

- Sandra's view of police work
- Her attitude towards her job?

Think about the tone of the soliloquy. What do you think the dramatist's purpose was in including this soliloquy?

Extract 1

Doctor Faustus

Act 2 scene 1

Enter Faustus *in his study*

Faustus: Now, Faustus, must thou needs be damned,
And canst thou not be saved.
What boots it then to think of God or heaven?
Away with such vain fancies and despair!
Despair in God and trust in Beelzebub.
Now go not backward. No, Faustus, be resolute.
Why waverest thou? O, something soundeth in mine ears:
'Abjure this magic, turn to God again!'
Ay, and Faustus will turn to God again.
To God? He loves thee not.
The god thou servest is thine own appetite,
Wherein is fixed the love of Beelzebub.
To him I'll build an altar and a church,
And offer lukewarm blood of new-born babes.

Extract 2

Murmuring Judges

Sandra Bingham *has appeared. She is in a uniform, a WPC, in her mid-twenties, with neat, dyed-blonde short hair. She is quite small and tidy. She speaks directly to us. As she does so, the gaol is replaced by the charge room of a large inner-London police station. A long desk dominates the room, and opposite it is a self-locking door, which gives on to the outside world. To one side of the long room is a passage which leads to the cells; to the other, the front desk of the police station. You are aware of the activity in the room behind as* Sandra *speaks to us, but the emphasis of the light is on her.*

Sandra: You see, it's all mess. That's what it is, mostly. If you take the charge room, for instance, there's maybe thirty or forty people arrested in a day. Most of them are people who simply can't cope. They've been arrested before – petty thieving, deception, stealing car radios, selling stolen credit cards in pubs. Or not even that. Disturbing the peace. Failing to appear on a summons. Failing to carry out conditions of bail. Failing to produce a current car licence. Failing to fulfil Community Service. Getting drunk. Getting drunk and going for a joyride. Getting drunk and then driving home. Attacking your wife. Who then won't testify. Trying to cash a stolen cheque, only being so stupid you don't even try to make the signatures match. Opening telephone boxes. Fifty-fifty fights in clubs which are nobody's fault. Crimes of opportunity. Not being able to resist it. Then going back, thinking I got away with it last time. Possession. One acid tab. One Ninja Turtle sticker containing LSD. One smoke. One sniff. One toke. One three-quid packet. *(She smiles.)* That's the basic stuff. It's the stuff of policing. All you have to do with it is be a ledger clerk. You fill in bits of paper. Every officer carries thirty-six bits of paper about their person at any one time.

*(*Sandra *starts to move round the room to collect the boy she has just arrested. She stops a moment, before the scene begins.)*

Policing's largely the fine art of getting through biros. And keeping yourself ready for the interesting bits.

> ## Activity
>
> **Now think about the plays that you are studying. Make a list of the soliloquies in each play, and for each one note down the following details:**
>
> - who is speaking
> - the context of the soliloquy
> - what is being said
> - why the dramatist uses a soliloquy at that point in the drama.

Asides

Asides are used to reveal character and motivation. The aside is a kind of stage whisper, or behind-the-hand comment. Sometimes it is directed at another character, but often it is aimed at the audience or the character appears to speak to himself or herself. For example, in Act 2 scene 2 of Shakespeare's *Hamlet*, asides are used to comical effect as they reveal Polonius's lack of wit. Polonius does not realize that Hamlet is deliberately making fun of him, and he speaks to Hamlet politely whilst secretly insinuating that he is love-sick for Ophelia.

Hamlet

Act 2 scene 2

Hamlet: Let her not walk i' th' sun. Conception is a blessing, but not as your daughter may conceive – friend, look to't.

Polonius: (*Aside*) How say you by that? Still harping on my daughter. Yet he knew me not at first; 'a said I was a fishmonger. 'A is far gone. And truly in my youth I suffered much extremity for love, very near this. I'll speak to him again. – What do you read, my lord?

Hamlet: Words, words, words.

Polonius: What is the matter, my lord?

Hamlet: Between who?

Polonius: I mean the matter that you read, my lord.

Hamlet: Slanders, sir. For the satirical rogue says here that old men have grey beards, that their faces are wrinkled, their eyes purging thick amber and plum-tree gum, and that they have a plentiful lack of wit, together with most weak hams – all which, sir, though I most powerfully and potently believe, yet I hold it not honesty to have it thus set down. For yourself, sir, shall grow old as I am – if like a crab you could go backward.

Polonius: (*Aside*) Though this be madness, yet there is a method in't. – Will you walk out of the air, my lord?

Hamlet: Into my grave?

Polonius: Indeed, that's out of the air. – (*Aside*) How pregnant sometimes his replies are – a happiness that often madness hits on, which reason and sanity could not so prosperously be delivered of. I will leave him and suddenly contrive the means of meeting between him and my daughter. – My lord, I will take my leave of you.

Activity

In the drama texts you are studying, find three or four examples of the use of the aside.

In each case make a note of:

- who is speaking
- what is being said
- what the purpose of the aside is.

Creating atmosphere

Until recent times, the theatres in which plays were first performed obviously did not have the sophisticated technology and elaborate sets that are available to modern dramatists. Much of the creation of scene, atmosphere and mood was done through the language of the play. In the Elizabethan theatre, for example, the plays were performed in daylight with no sets, and so all effects were created in the imagination of the audience through the words of the play.

Look at the following example from *Hamlet*. Barnardo arrives to relieve Francisco of his watch outside the castle of Elsinore at midnight. There have been sightings of a ghostly figure stalking the battlements and the watchmen are ill at ease. Read it carefully.

Hamlet

Act 1 scene 1

Enter Barnardo *and* Francisco, *two sentinels*

Barnardo: Who's there?
Francisco: Nay, answer me. Stand and unfold yourself.
Barnardo: Long live the king!
Francisco: Barnardo?
Barnardo: He.
Francisco: You come most carefully upon your hour.
Barnardo: 'Tis now struck twelve. Get thee to bed, Francisco.
Francisco: For this relief much thanks. 'Tis bitter cold,
          And I am sick at heart.
Barnardo: Have you had quiet guard?
Francisco: Not a mouse stirring.
Barnardo: Well, good night.
          If you do meet Horatio and Marcellus,
          The rivals of my watch, bid them make haste.
Francisco: I think I hear them.

          Enter Horatio *and* Marcellus.

          Stand, ho! Who is there?
Horatio: Friends to this ground.
Marcellus: And liegemen to the Dane.
Francisco: Give you good night.
Marcellus: O, farewell honest soldier, who hath reliev'd you?
Francisco: Barnardo hath my place. Give you good night. (*Exit*)
Marcellus: Holla, Barnardo!
Barnardo: Say, what, is Horatio there?
Horatio: A piece of him.
Barnardo: Welcome, Horatio. Welcome, good Marcellus.
Marcellus: What, has this thing appear'd again tonight?
Barnardo: I have seen nothing.
Marcellus: Horatio says 'tis but our fantasy,
          And will not let belief take hold of him,
          Touching this dreaded sight twice seen of us.
          Therefore I have entreated him along
          With us to watch the minutes of this night,
          That if again this apparition come,
          He may approve our eyes and speak to it.
Horatio: Tush, tush, 'twill not appear.

Activity

Analyse the ways in which Shakespeare's language creates the impression of a cold dark night.

Here are some things you might have thought about:

- The lexis creates a vivid impression of the cold: ''Tis bitter cold', and eerie stillness: 'Not a mouse stirring', 'watch the minutes of this night'.

- The use of short clipped lines and simple phrases creates a sense of tension in the scene. The characters appear too watchful of their surroundings to engage fully in conversation.

- Shakespeare creates an impression of the darkness, through the way the characters ask each other to identify themselves: 'Who's there?', 'Stand and unfold yourself', 'Say what is Horatio there?'. Francisco hears the approach of Horatio and Marcellus before he sees them, 'I think I hear them'.

Activity

Select two contrasting passages from the plays you are studying and examine how language is used to create a sense of atmosphere and mood. Remember to use specific examples from each passage to illustrate your comments.

Opening scenes

Plays usually begin with some kind of exposition, which sets the scene and gives the audience information. This can be important in order for them to understand what is going on, or to inform them of events that happened before the play starts. One way of doing this is to start the play with a soliloquy in which a character gives the audience information indirectly; another way is for information to be disclosed at the begining through conversation between two or more characters. Very often, the seeds of later action are sown in the opening scene.

In whatever way dramatists choose to begin their plays, it is vital that the drama captures the interest and imagination of the audience from the start. The central conflict must be introduced quickly, and the audience must become eager to know what happens next. In creating this atmosphere of expectancy and anticipation, the dramatist's use of language is central.

Activity

Look at the opening of each of the plays you are studying. What kind of openings do the dramatists create in each case? How does each dramatist:

- hold the attention of the audience?
- create atmosphere?
- convey important information?
- create a sense of character?

Themes

Plays address particular themes that the dramatist is interested in exploring and presenting to an audience. Although dramatists may make use of visual effects to examine these themes, the language of the play is the key element through which they are drawn to the attention of the audience. As plays usually contain more than one theme, the language can become a complex structure in which various thematic strands are woven together to present a unified whole.

The following extract is taken from *The Duchess of Malfi* by John Webster. Read it through carefully.

The Duchess of Malfi

Act 4 scene 1

Ferdinand: Excellent; as I would wish; she's plagued in art.
These presentations are but framed in wax,
By the curious master in that quality,
Vincentio Lauriola, and she takes them
For true substantial bodies.
Bosola: Why do you do this?
Ferdinand: To bring her to despair.
Bosola: Faith, end here,
And go no farther in your cruelty.
Send her a penitential garment to put on
Next to her delicate skin, and furnish her
With beads and prayer-books.
Ferdinand: Damn her! That body of hers,
While that my blood ran pure in 't, was more worth
Than that which thou wouldst comfort, called a soul.
I will send her masques of common courtesans,
Have her meat served up by bawds and ruffians,
And, 'cause she'll needs be mad, I am resolved
To remove forth the common hospital
All the mad-folk, and place them near her lodging;
There let them practise together, sing and dance,
And act their gambols to the full o' th' moon:
If she can sleep the better for it, let her.
Your work is almost ended.
Bosola: Must I see her again?
Ferdinand: Yes.
Bosola: Never.
Ferdinand: You must.
Bosola: Never in mine own shape;
That's forfeited by my intelligence,
And this last cruel lie. When you send me next,
The business shall be comfort.
Ferdinand: Very likely.
Thy pity is nothing of kin to thee. Antonio
Lurks about Milan; thou shalt shortly thither,
To feed a fire, as great as my revenge,
Which ne'er will slack, till it have spent his fuel:
Intemperate agues make physicians cruel.
(*Exeunt*)

Activity

From this extract, what key themes do you think the play might deal with?
Give reasons for your answer.

Metaphorical techniques

Like other writers, dramatists make use of imagery, metaphor, simile and symbolism to create effects through the language of their plays. Sometimes dramatists use the technique of repeating similar images in order to build up a theme or a particular effect. For example, read the following two extracts from Shakespeare's *As You Like It*. In the first Duke Senior speaks to other Lords in exile with him in Forest of Arden. He speaks about the corruption of court life and how the adversity they face in the wilderness is a lesser evil than deceptive councillors at court. In the second extract Amiens, one of the exiled Lords, sings a song which highlights the cruelty of mankind by comparing it to nature. Read the extracts through carefully.

Activity

Examine the ways in which Shakespeare uses imagery to emphasise the contrast between court life and life in exile. What does the contrast reveal about each character's attitude towards the life he led at court?

You should pay particular attention to the use of:

- metaphor
- simile
- symbolism
- repetition.

As You Like It

Extract 1

Act 2 scene 1

The Forest of Arden: enter Duke Senior, Amiens, *and two or three* Lords *dressed as foresters*

Duke Senior: Now, my co-mates and brothers in exile,
Hath not old custom made this life more sweet
Than that of painted pomp? Are not these woods
More free from peril than the envious court?
Here feel we not the penalty of Adam,
The seasons' difference, as the icy fang
And churlish chiding of the winter's wind –
Which when it bites and blows upon my body
Even till I shrink with cold, I smile and say,

'This is no flattery' – these are counsellors
That feelingly persuade me what I am.
Sweet are the uses of adversity
Which like the toad, ugly and venomous,
Wears yet a precious jewel in his head,
And this our life exempt from public haunt
Finds tongues in trees, books in the running brooks,
Sermons in stones, and good in everything.

Extract 2

Act 2 scene 7

(Song)

Amiens: Blow, blow, thou winter wind,
Thou art not so unkind
As man's ingratitude;
Thy tooth is not so keen,
Because thou art not seen,
Although thy breath be rude.
     He-ho, sing he-ho
     Unto the green holly,
     Most friendship is feigning,
     Most loving mere folly.
     The hey-ho, the holly,
     This life is most jolly.
Freeze, freeze, thou bitter sky,
That dost not bite so nigh
As benefits forgot;
Though thou the waters warp,
Thy sting is not so sharp
As friend remember'd not.
     He-ho, sing he-ho
     Unto the green holly,
     Most friendship is feigning,
     Most loving mere folly.
     The hey-ho, the holly,
     This life is most jolly.

Activity

Now think about the plays you are studying. For each play, make a list of images the dramatist uses and find specific examples. Remember to make a note of where these come from (Act, scene and line number).

Rhetorical techniques

Dramatists also make use of rhetorical techniques in their writing, and give to their characters the kind of language that can be used to persuade the audience or shape their responses in a particular way. Here are some of the rhetorical features that you will find in the language of plays:

- repetition of sounds, words and sentence structures
- listing
- alliteration
- onomatopoeia
- assonance
- antithesis
- hyperbole
- puns.

For example, in the following scene from Tom Stoppard's *Rosencrantz and Guildenstern Are Dead*, Stoppard uses **repetition** to highlight the way in which the characters reach a kind of semantic dead end. Rosencrantz and Guildenstern are trying to discover the cause of Hamlet's madness, but since they have run out of evidence to fuel their reasoning they begin to lose momentum and ultimately the point of their discussion.

Rosencrantz and Guildenstern Are Dead

Act 2

Ros: Hamlet is not himself, outside or in. We have to glean what afflicts him.
Guil: He doesn't give much away.
Player: Who does, nowadays?
Guil: He's – melancholy.
Player: Melancholy?
Ros: Mad.
Player: How is he mad?
Ros: Ah. (*To Guil.*) How is he mad?
Guil: More morose than mad, perhaps.
Player: Melancholy.
Guil: Moody.
Ros: He has moods.
Player: Of moroseness?
Guil: Madness. And yet.
Ros: Quite.
Guil: For instance.
Ros: He talks to himself, which might be madness.
Guil: If he didn't talk sense, which he does.
Ros: Which suggests the opposite.
Player: Of what?

(*Small pause*)

Guil: I think I have it. A man talking sense to himself is no madder than a man talking nonsense not to himself.
Ros: Or just as mad.
Guil: Or just as mad.
Ros: And he does both.
Guil: So there you are.
Ros: Stark raving sane.

(*Pause*)

Player: Why?
Guil: Ah. (*To Ros.*) Why?
Ros: Exactly.
Guil: Exactly what?
Ros: Exactly why.
Guil: Exactly *why what*?
Ros: What?
Guil: *Why*?
Ros: Why what, exactly?
Guil: Why is he mad?!
Ros: I don't know!

(*Beat.*)

Note how with each repetition of the word 'mad', the speakers become less certain of both the implications and validity of Hamlet's diagnosis.

Listing can also be used to accumulate words or phrases, to add impact, as in this example from *The Merchant of Venice*:

The Merchant of Venice

Act 3 scene 1

Shylock: Hath not a Jew eyes? Hath not a Jew hands, organs, dimensions, senses, affections, passions? Fed with the same food, hurt with the same weapons, subject to the same diseases, healed by the same means, warmed and cooled by the same winter and summer as a Christian is?

- -

Antithesis is a technique very commonly used in drama; it involves contrasting ideas or words balanced against one another. Some of Shakespeare's most famous lines are examples of antithesis:

To be, or not to be
(*Hamlet*)

Fair is foul, and foul is fair
(*Macbeth*)

My only love sprung from my only hate
(*Romeo & Juliet*)

The opposition of words in antithesis often reflects the oppositions or conflicts at the centre of the drama.

Hyperbole is another rhetorical technique you are likely to find used in drama. Hyperbole is a from of exaggerated language, used to create impact. For example, the passage recited in Act 2 scene 2 by Hamlet from one of his favourite plays, is full of hyperbole.

Hamlet: One speech in 't I chiefly loved – 'twas Aeneas' tale to Dido – and thereabout of it especially when he speaks of Priam's slaughter. If it live in your memory, begin at this line – let me see, let me see –

The rugged Pyrrhus, like th' Hyrcanian beast –
'Tis not so. It begins with Pyrrhus –
The rugged Pyrrhus, he whose sable arms,
Black as his purpose, did the night resemble
When he lay couched in the ominous horse,
Hath now this dread and black complexion smear'd
With heraldry more dismal. Head to foot
Now is he total gules, horridly trick'd
With blood of fathers, mothers, daughters, sons,
Bak'd and impasted with the parching streets,
That lend a tyrannous and a damned light
To their lord's murder. Roasted in wrath and fire,
And thus o'ersized with coagulate gore,
With eyes like carbuncles, the hellish Pyrrhus
Old grandsire Priam seeks.

- -

Puns were particularly popular with Elizabethan audiences, but it is likely that you will find some in any pre-twentieth-century text that you study. A pun is a play on words; when a word has two or more different meanings, the ambiguity can be used for a witty or amusing effect. For example, Mercutio in *Romeo & Juliet*, although mortally wounded by Tybalt, keeps up his reputation for word-play to the end by telling his friends:

> Ask for me tomorrow, and you shall find me a grave man.

Activity

Look through the plays you are studying and make notes on the use of rhetorical techniques such as repetition, listing, antithesis, hyperbole and punning. Identify what these elements add to the drama.

Irony in drama

A dramatist might use two types of irony. Both forms work on the basis that the audience knows something that a character or characters on stage do not.

Dramatic irony occurs when what is said by a character contrasts with what happens elsewhere in the action.

Verbal irony occurs when a character says one thing but means another.

Activity

Look at the plays you are studying and find three or four examples of the use of irony. Explain what the irony consists of, and its significance.

Drama and contextual variation

In terms of studying a drama text for A Level, **contextual variation** can refer to two quite separate elements of the play. First, the language of the play can vary depending on the **context of the particular scene**, groupings of character, and so on. For example, in Sheridan's *The Rivals*, Sir Anthony Absolute uses language in different ways according to the context in which he is speaking such as whom he is speaking to, and for what purpose.

The **context** of the play is also the **larger cultural frame of reference** within which the play came about – for example, the kind of society and the historical period within which the work was produced. When studying Shakespeare's plays it can be useful to have an understanding of the kind of theatres the plays were originally performed in or the kinds of beliefs the people of that time held. Similarly, in studying a play like *The Rivals*, an understanding of the life style and social etiquette of late eighteenth-century England can be useful in helping you gain a full understanding of the play.

Producing a comparative literary study

For Section A of A2 Unit F673, you are required to produce a comparative analysis of an extract from each of a chosen pair of set texts. One of those texts will be a piece of modern drama and the other will be a piece of drama written before 1800. Your comparison will focus on a particular theme concerning changing representation of power relationships through the genre of drama.

The unit will test your ability to:

- display a critical understanding of drama as a literary form and appreciate its dynamic possibilities
- understand the significance of contextual factors in both the creation and reception of drama texts
- recognize how writers use form, structure and language to create meaning
- produce accurate, fluent and coherent written work.

The texts

You will be required to answer one passage-based question on two extracts from your two set texts.

The text choices are as follows:

January 2010 – January 2013

Christopher Marlowe – *Doctor Faustus*
with Arthur Miller – *The Crucible*

William Shakespeare – *Hamlet*
with Tom Stoppard – *Rosencrantz and Guildenstern Are Dead*

John Webster – *The Duchess of Malfi*
with Caryl Churchill – *Top Girls*

The set plays for this specification will change from June 2013; please consult the specification for information after this date.

Do's and don'ts when making your response

The following checklist will help you to ensure that you make the most out of the time available in your exam.

Do

- read the question and extracts carefully and make sure that you respond directly to them in your answer
- focus on **how** or **in what ways** writers use language, form and structure in order to create effects
- show awareness of contextual factors that help to explain interpretations of the texts
- make sure that you present an integrated comparison, in which you move fluently from one text to the other and back again throughout your essay
- make sure that your work is technically accurate in all respects, including use of terminology; leave time at the end of the exam to check this.

Don't

When tackling the question make sure that you do *not*:

- describe what the text says or what it is about – remember – the examiner will be looking for analysis, not description

- become too involved with historical or social contextual factors, unless they are significant to the analysis of the texts in terms of their language and effects, and to your comparison

- spend too much time describing general critical responses to the text or broad literary theories

- write broadly on general themes, ideas, characters – remember, detailed analysis and comparison should be at the heart of your essay

- include biographical detail unless it is important in terms of your analysis of the texts

- write about the texts separately – remember, your objective is to produce a piece of **comparative analysis**.

Approaching the comparison

Before you can really get to grips with the passage-based comparison, you must study each of your texts carefully, looking at all the relevant features that we have previously discussed. When you have developed a sound knowledge of the texts you are studying, you will need to begin to think carefully about them as a pair. As you have been reading and studying them it is likely that you will have been noting possible links, similarities or differences between them, but in order to compare them fully it is useful to have some kind of framework to help structure your thoughts. The following model is one way in which you could approach the comparative study:

Framework

- identification of comparative areas and issues in the texts.

Analysis and explanation

- identification and exemplification of central features of the texts, using contextual and structural frameworks

- description and comparison of the features of the text, for example exploration of ideas, themes, character and linguistic issues

- consideration and comparison of meanings and effects created in each text

- consideration of different levels of analysis.

Evaluation

- consideration and comparison of the success of each text with reference to explanatory frameworks.

5 Preparing for assessment

Set texts

You will need to revise set texts for the following units:

AS Level

- Unit F671. Section A: the construction of voice in prose fiction and in transcripts of real speech
- Unit F671. Section B: the creation of meaning in texts of different types and the relationships between them

A2 Level

- Unit F673. Section A: analytical comparison of extracts from a pair of set texts
- Unit F673. Section B: an essay based on one set text exploring a proposition that raises an issue central to the integrated study of language and literature

Analytical questions linked to set texts

In AS Unit F671, you will have two set prose fiction texts to study; you will need to prepare both so that you are able to answer both questions in this unit. One text will form the basis of the first section and the second text will form the basis for the second.

Before your examination it is vital that you carry out the following key revision tasks. You need to re-read or skim-read your text to remind yourself of what happens. You will not have your text with you in the examination and should therefor use it as much as you can as part of your revision, to help create a mental picture of the text and keep yourself refreshed in terms of quotations and plot details. You should also practise writing essays without your text to help you build up your confidence.

In A2 Unit F673 you will also study two set texts, which will both be drama texts. One text will be modern drama and the other will be pre-1800 drama. Section A requires you to produce a comparative analysis based on an extract from each text, and Section B asks you to explore either one of the texts in the light of a critical proposition. This proposition will raise an issue that is integral to the study of both language and literature.

Here are a few ideas to help you revise your set texts.

- Make a summary or time-line of what happens in the novel or play, so that you are absolutely certain of the intricacies of the plot.
- List all the important characters and their characteristics.
- Write down appropriate quotations, that help to illustrate the disposition or personality of the characters you have listed.
- Know where these quotations appear in relation to the plot, since you will not have the text to refer to.
- List all the relevant themes that are explored and link them to characters and key events in the books.

- List all the different stylistic techniques that the writers or dramatists use, with an example of each to help you remember how they work.
- Integrate these with linguistic terminology too, so that you remember to use this terminology in your answers.

Some students find it useful to put their notes on small cards rather than on paper; some like to have an exercise book dedicated to the revision of each set text, and some students like to use technology and put notes on their computer, laptop or PDA. Use whatever method works best for you: the important thing is that you complete some form of revision notes, that are easily accessible and are useful to you.

The fact that you will not have your set texts to hand in the exam means that you must:

- Know and learn the plot structure.
- Learn some key quotations from the texts for each of the characters and themes, but note that in Unit F673 you will also be provided with extracts in the exam that you should focus on and quote from.
- Remind yourself of the key features of speech and then learn them, so that you can use them to help analyse texts in line with the questions on the exam paper.

Once you have made appropriate notes, you should revise them by reading them, learning them and testing yourself as appropriate. You should also keep practising the writing skills that you need: use past papers and the exercises in this book to help you.

The chief examiner's perspective

Reflecting carefully on the aims of English Language and Literature study at AS and A2 Level will serve to highlight what you should be achieving in your integrated studies. All the specifications aim to encourage you to study language and literature as interconnecting disciplines in particular ways that will help deepen your understanding and enjoyment. More specific aims are detailed below.

The specification encourages you to:

- Select and apply relevant concepts and approaches from integrated linguistic and literary study, using appropriate terminology and accurate, coherent written expression.
- Demonstrate detailed critical understanding in analysing the ways in which structure, form and language shape meanings in a range of spoken and written texts.
- Use integrated approaches to explore relationships between texts, analysing and evaluating the significance of contextual factors in their production and reception.
- Demonstrate expertise and creativity in using language appropriately for a variety of purposes and audiences, drawing on insights from linguistic and literary studies.

Having studied all the units, you are now in a position to reflect upon these aims and contextualize them, observing how the course has enabled you to fulfil each one. The objective of this chapter is to give you some practical advice on how you can build these aims into your everyday studies, and how you can use them as hints to ensure your success in exam situations.

Recommended reading

The simple maxim that can enable you to target these aims is: read widely and discriminatingly! Students often limit their reading to the texts on which they will answer questions in the examination and those that their teachers introduce them to in the classroom. But other students are in a better position. It is becoming increasingly obvious to examiners that the most successful students are those who take responsibility for their reading and can show a breadth of reading when analysing texts. If you want to succeed you have to do the same – otherwise you put yourself at an immediate disadvantage.

The following list shows a range of the types of text with which it is useful to become familiar. Keep a reading journal and make notes on the key textual discriminators: genre, purpose, audience, form and context.

- A range of contemporary and classical literature covering all the genres, using your set texts as a good starting point, especially in contemporary writing
- A range of non-literary materials including:
  - journalistic writing, including 'quality' and popular daily newspapers
  - magazines (covering subjects such as: female issues, male issues, science, sport, business, music, media, specialist hobbies or interests, household issues or new technology)
  - periodicals (for example, historical, economic, scientific, political, literary, linguistic and medical)
  - comics (adult and children's)
  - advertisements
  - reports
  - manuals and instruction sheets
  - catalogues
  - forms and applications
  - legal and governmental literature
  - essays
  - diary forms
  - travel writing
  - encyclopaedias, reference and text books
  - children's books and literature

- A range of speech events, to include:
  - spontaneous speech
  - scripted speech and rhetoric
  - dramatized speech
  - representations of speech in literature
  - screenplays
  - interviews

- Use of new technologies, to include:
  - the Internet
  - e-mails
  - on-line discussions
  - chat rooms
  - messaging services.

It would be admirable to familiarize yourself with examples of all of these, but there is a limit to your time and resources, so dip into the list. You will begin to recognize common forms and styles, which can then be replicated or analysed in your responses. If you read widely, you are more likely to develop confidence and accuracy of written expression in all your answers, and your language will become more cohesive and organized.

In the examination

When you are in the examination room and under pressure, there are various pointers that you can always count on to help you.

- Always use the prompts in the questions to guide you, especially if you are in any doubt as to what is required in terms of frameworks.

- Highlight key words when planning out your answer.

- Plan your response, and never use pre-prepared answers: they rarely hit the pass mark and they stand out like sore thumbs!

- Use the terminology you have learned accurately and naturally, as an aid to enhance your critical responses.

- When answering questions on set texts, familiarize yourself with the assessment objectives at the beginning of the paper to ensure you know what the focus of your answer needs to be. You will need to have an understanding of the interplay between plot, character and textual issues and their representation in terms of language use, form and structure; you must then communicate this in your analysis.

- Write about authorial or speaker's intentions, methods, values and attitudes, and how they are communicated.

- Ensure that your responses are informed (by background reading), logical (through the use of frameworks), critical (by the use of correct literary and linguistic terminology), realistic (within the bounds of the question), and that they represent your personal voice.

In preparation for the exam, reflect on your present level of performance by looking at the mark schemes for past papers, especially those you have used as trial papers or as practice in class. These can often help inform you about those areas you have missed or misunderstood.

Pitfalls to avoid

There are certain things that you should avoid at all costs; examiners complain regularly about these issues and they usually show that a student suffers from lack of awareness about the subject and insecurity about writing examination responses.

Never:

- simply retell the story in the hope that it will do you some good: it won't!

- start writing immediately; always take five minutes to formulate and plan out your response

- panic: take a minute, scribble your ideas down if necessary, then crystallize them and finally plan your answer

- quote at length; be economical with textual reference and quotation, and always show why you have used a quotation by interpreting it

- ignore the question and write an answer to a question that was set last year, or by your teacher: you will fail!

It is perhaps appropriate to finish off this section with a mnemonic, which spells out those aspects of integrated literary and linguistic study you need to concentrate on to ensure you are as well prepared as anyone else:

D evelop your ability to produce interesting, informative and fluent examples of your writing

E xpand your critical vocabulary so that your answers are informed, logical and represent your own personal voice

P ractise timed essays including planning, drafting and evaluating

E xplore different approaches to answering questions until you have mastered techniques that you are confident with

N ever go into an examination situation unprepared: it is essential you are familiar with all aspects of each unit, including texts and frameworks

D o read widely! Read for meaning and always consider texts as a whole.

Glossary

Accent: A distinctive manner of pronunciation that marks a regional identity.

Adjacency pairs: A term relating to the structure of spoken language, indicating a sequence of utterances that form a recognizable structure. Adjacency pairs follow each other, are produced by different speakers, have a logical connection, and conform to a pattern. Questions and answers, commands and responses, greetings and returned greetings, all form adjacency pairs. For example: *A: Hurry up. B: I'll be out in a minute. A: Are you well? B: Very well, thank you.*

Adjective: A word that describes a noun, such as: the *wooden* table; the *red* balloon. They can also indicate degree. For example: the *tallest* girl was the *slowest*. Adjectives are also sometimes known as **modifiers**.

Adverb: A word that describes the action of a verb, such as: the cat jumped *swiftly*; the boy ate *hungrily*. Adverbs are sometimes known as **modifiers** and they can also act as **intensifiers.** For example: the man became *very* angry.

Allegory: A story or a narrative, often told at some length, which has a deeper meaning below the surface. *The Pilgrim's Progress* by John Bunyan is a well-known allegory. A more modern example is George Orwell's *Animal Farm*, which on a surface level is about a group of animals who take over their farm, but on a deeper level is an allegory of the Russian Revolution and the shortcomings of Communism.

Alliteration: The repetition of the same consonant sound, especially at the beginning of words. For example, 'Five miles meandering with a mazy motion' (*Kubla Khan* by S.T. Coleridge).

Allusion: A reference to another event, person, place or work of literature. The allusion is usually implied rather than explicit, and often provides another layer of meaning to what is being said.

Ambiguity: Use of language where the meaning is unclear or has two or more possible interpretations. It could be created through a weakness in the writer's expression, but often it is deliberately used by writers to create layers of meaning in the mind of the reader.

Ambivalence: The situation where more than one possible attitude is being displayed by the writer towards a character, theme or idea.

Anachronism: Something that is historically inaccurate – for example, the reference to a clock chiming in William Shakespeare's *Julius Caesar*. The Romans did not have chiming clocks.

Anapaest: A unit of poetic metre made up of two unstressed syllables followed by a stressed syllable. For example, there are four anapaests in:

ˇ ˇ / ˇ ˇ / ˇ ˇ / ˇ ˇ /
The Assyrian came down like the wolf on the fold
(*The Destruction of Sennacherib* by Lord Byron)

Anaphora: When used as a literary term, anaphora is the repetition of a word or phrase at the begining of successive lines or clauses for emphasis. For example, 'Cannon to right of them,/ Cannon to left of them,/ Cannon in front of them' (*The Charge of the Light Brigade* by Alfred Lord Tennyson).

Anaphoric: See **referencing**.

Antithesis: Contrasting ideas or words that are balanced against each other, such as: 'To be, or not to be' (*Hamlet* by Shakespeare).

Antonyms: Words that are opposite in meaning, such as: *dark/ light, fast/ slow*.

Archaism: Use of language that is old-fashioned; words or phrases that are not completely obsolete, but no longer in current usage.

Assonance: The repetition of similar vowel sounds. For example, 'There must be Gods thrown down, and trumpets blown' (*Hyperion* by John Keats). This shows the paired assonance of *must, trum* and *thrown, blown*.

Attitude: A particular stance or viewpoint adopted by a writer or speaker.

Audience: The people addressed by a piece of writing or speech. This is closely associated with the idea of **purpose**. Language (either written or spoken) is used in various ways, depending on the audience that it is aimed at and its purpose.

Ballad: A narrative poem that tells a story (traditional ballads were songs) usually in a straightforward way. The theme is often tragic or contains a whimsical, supernatural or fantastical element.

Bias: Language used in such a way as to express a prejudice against someone or something, or which favours a particular point of view.

Blank verse: Unrhymed poetry that adheres to a strict pattern in that each line is generally set in iambic pentameter (a ten-syllable line with five stresses). It is close to the natural rhythm of English speech or prose and can be seen in the works of many writers, including Shakespeare and John Milton.

Caesura: A conscious break in a line of poetry. For example: 'While the dew dropped, while the dark hours were cold' (*Despised and Rejected* by Christina Rossetti)

Caricature: A character described through the exaggeration of the features that he or she possesses.

Cataphoric: See **referencing**.

Catharsis: A purging of emotions such as takes place at the end of a tragedy.

Chaining: The linking together of adjacency pairs to form a conversation.

Clause: A group of words, usually with a finite verb, which is structurally larger than a **phrase**. Clauses are made up of elements, each of which expresses a particular kind of meaning. There are five types of clause element:

- the *subject* – identifies the theme or topic of the clause
- the *verb* – expresses a range of meanings, such as actions, sensations or states of being
- the *object* – identifies who or what has been directly affected by the action of the verb
- the *complement* – gives further information about another clause element
- the *adverbial* – adds information about the situation, such as the time of an action or its frequency.

All five elements appear in the above order in the sentence: *The teacher/ had told/ me/ to listen/ three times*.

Cliché: A phrase, idea or image that has been over-used so that it has lost much of its original meaning, impact and freshness.

Cohesion: Links and connections that unite the elements of discourse or text.

Coinage: The creation and addition of new words to the existing word stock.

Collective noun: See **noun**.

Collocation: Two or more words that frequently appear together as part of a set phrase. They are often well known and predictable, so many could also be described as **idioms** or **clichés.** For example: *safe and sound, loud and clear, here and there.*

Colloquial: An everyday or non-formal style of speech or writing, often characterized by the use of slang or non-standard features.

Comedy: Originally, simply a play or other work that ended happily. Now we use the term to describe something that is funny and makes us laugh. In literature, comedy is not necessarily a lightweight form. Shakespeare's *Measure for Measure,* for example, is for the most part a serious play, but as it ends happily it is described as a comedy.

Command: The type of sentence in which someone is told to do something. For example: *Stand up immediately*!

Common noun: See **noun**.

Complex sentence: See **sentence**.

Compound: A word made up of at least two free **morphemes**, such as: *babysitter, skateboard, mother-in-law.* (See also **morpheme**.)

Compound sentence: See **sentence**.

Conceit: An elaborate, extended and sometimes surprising comparison between things that, at first sight, do not have much in common. This can be seen in John Donne's poem *A Valediction: Forbidding Mourning,* where he compares the souls of himself and his lover with the legs of a draughtsman's compasses.

Conjunction: A word that connects words or other constructions. There are two kinds of conjunctions – co-ordinating and subordinating.

- *Co-ordinating* conjunction, such as, *and, but* and *or,* are the most common. These can join single words as in fish *and* chips or they can join phrases: Loved by the poor *but* hated by the rich. They can also join sentences by replacing full stops: He agreed to come. He did not speak. He agreed to come *but* he did not speak.

- *Subordinating* conjunctions also join but they use a different process. Co-ordinating conjunctions join two equal parts and they remain equals. Subordinating conjunctions join statements by making one less important than the other. One statement becomes the main statement and the other a subordinate supporting one, as in this example, where *although* becomes the subordinating conjunction: *Although* John was clever, he did not do enough work to pass his exams. Other subordinating conjunctions include *because, unless, whenever, if, that, while, where* and *as.*

Connotation: The additional associated meanings of a word beyond its dictionary definition.

Constative utterances: An utterance, or piece of spoken language, that can be judged in terms of whether it is true or false. For example: *I really like oranges,* or, *There is nowhere to sit down in there.*

Context: The social circumstances in which speech or writing takes place.

Contextual framework: The application of a particular socio-historical standpoint in order to analyse a text.

Consonance: The repetition in the middle or at the end of words of a particular sound, such as: 'When I had *ripped*, and *search'd* where hearts should lie.' (John Donne)

Contraction: A shortened word, such as: *isn't, don't.*

Convergence: A process of linguistic change in which accents or dialects become more alike.

Conversation analysis: A study of the key features of informal, spoken interaction.

Couplet: Two consecutive lines of verse that rhyme. For example: 'Had we but World enough, and time,/ This coyness, lady, were no crime.' (*To His Coy Mistress* by Andrew Marvell)

Dactyl: A unit of poetic metre consisting of a stressed syllable followed by two unstressed ones. For example, there are three dactyls in:

/ ˘ ˘ / ˘ ˘
Half a league, half a league,
/ ˘ ˘ / ˘
Half a league, onward.
(*The Charge of the Light Brigade* by Alfred Lord Tennyson)

Declarative: A grammatical mood that expresses a statement, such as: *I am a hard-working student.*

Degree: Comparison of adjectives or adverbs. Most adjectives or adverbs can be compared in one of three ways. The thing they express can be related to a higher degree, to the same degree or to a lower degree. For example, John is *tall* (*absolute* form). Kate is *taller* (*comparative* form). David is *tallest* (*superlative* form). Some examples adopt an irregular form such as *good/ better/ best/ bad/ worse/ worst.*

Deixis: Words that can be interpreted only with reference to the speaker's position in space or time. These are known as *deictic forms* and fall into three main types. *Personal deixis* includes the use of such pronouns as *you* or *I*, which identify who is taking part in the discourse. *Spatial deixis* shows the speaker's position in relation to other people or objects, such as: *this, that, here, there. Temporal deixis* relates the speaker to time using words such as *tomorrow, now, yesterday.*

Demonstrative: A term used to describe determiners or pronouns that distinguish one item from other similar ones. For example: *this, that, these* and *those.*

Denotation: The dictionary definition of a word. (See also **connotation**).

Denouement: The ending of a play, novel or short story where all is revealed and the plot is revealed.

Determiner: Words that 'determine' the number and definiteness of the noun. There are three kinds of determiners: *central determiners, predeterminers* and *postdeterminers.*

- *Central determiners* consist of the definite article (*the*) and several other words that can take its place, such as: *this, that, each, every, some* and *any*. Words like this are called determiners only when used before the noun. If they are used alone instead of the noun, they are being used as a pronoun. For example: I need *some* paper (determiner), or, I need *some* too (pronoun).

- *Predeterminers* can be used before the central determiners. They can include words such as *all*, *both*, *half*, *double*. For example: *all* this money.
- *Postdeterminers* follow the central determiners but come before any adjectives. Cardinal numbers (*one*, *two*, *three*), ordinals (*first*, *second*, *third*), and quantifiers (*much*, *many*, *several*) can be used in this way. For example: *ten* green bottles.

Diachronic: A term used to describe language change that occurs over a period of time.

Diacritics: Marks added to text, or phonetic symbols, to specify various sound qualities such as syllabus stress, length and tone. These are often used in literature to indicate poetic metre.

Dialect: A language variety marked by a distinctive grammar and vocabulary, used by people with a common regional background.

Dialogue: Language interaction between two or more people.

Diction: The choice of words that a writer makes. Diction is another term for **vocabulary** or **lexis**.

Didactic: A term describing a work that is intended to preach or teach, often containing a particular moral or political point.

Direct speech: The actual words spoken by a person or character, recorded in written form using quotation marks.

Discourse: Any spoken or written language that is longer than a sentence.

Divergence: A process by which accents or dialects move further apart and the differences between them increase.

Double negative: A part of speech or writing in which more than one negative is used in one verb phrase, frequently used in certain dialects. For example: *I haven't done nothing*. In Standard English it has the effect of creating an opposite meaning to that intended.

Dynamic verb: A verb that expresses an action rather than a state, and can be used in the progressive form, such as: *jump/ jumping*; *clap/ clapping*.

Elegy: A meditative poem, usually sad and reflective in nature. It is sometimes, but not always, concerned with the theme of death.

Elision: The omission of an unstressed syllable so that the line conforms to a particular metrical pattern, such as: *o'er* (over) and *e'en* (even).

Ellipsis: The omission of a part of a sentence, which can be understood from the context. For example: *I'd like to go to the concert but I can't* (*go to the concert* is omitted because the repetition is not necessary).

End-stopped: A verse line with a pause or stop at the end of it.

Enjambment: A line of verse that flows on into the next line without pause.

Etymology: The study of the history and origins of words.

Euphemism: A word that replaces a word or term that is considered unpleasant, or is a taboo word. For example: *to pass away*, meaning to die.

Exophoric: See **referencing**.

Fabliau: A short comic tale with a bawdy element, akin to the 'dirty story'. Geoffrey Chaucer's *The Miller's Tale* contains strong elements of the fabliau.

Farce: A play that aims to entertain the audience through absurd and ridiculous characters and actions.

Feedback: The reaction speakers receive from their listeners or the information speakers gain from monitoring their own speech.

Field: An area of meaning (for example, education) that is characterized by common lexical items (for example: *teacher*, *classroom*, *headteacher*, *caretaker* and *examination*.)

Figurative language: Language that is symbolic or metaphorical and not meant to be taken literally.

Foot: A group of syllables forming a unit of verse: the basic unit of metre.

Formality: A scale of language use relating to the formality of the social context within which it is used. Language can be used formally or informally depending on the context.

Formulaic: A term to denote language that is patterned and always appears in the same form. For example: *Yours faithfully*, *Bye for now*.

Framework: A critical skeleton that could be applied to analyse texts in various ways to suit the purpose of the analysis. A literary framework could be applied for example, or a linguistic or contextual framework.

Free verse: Verse written without any fixed structure (either in metre, rhythm or form).

Genre: A particular type of writing, such as, prose, poetry or drama.

Heptameter: A verse line containing seven feet.

Hexameter: A verse line containing six feet.

Homograph: A word with the same spelling but different meanings. For example the word *fair* has various meanings: *The girl had fair hair. The children went to the fair. The result was not fair.*

Homonym: A word with the same sound or the same spelling as another but with a different meaning, such as: *maid* and *made*; *May* (the month) and *may* (is allowed to). The term *homograph* can be used for words with the same spelling, *homophone* for words with the same sound, but *homonym* covers both.

Homophone: A word that sounds the same as another but has a different meaning, such as: *rode*, *road* and *rowed*.

Hyperbole: A deliberate and extravagant exaggeration.

Hyponymy: The relationship between specific and general words where the meaning of one form is included in the meaning of another. For example, *dog* is an hyponym of *animal*. *Yew*, *oak*, *sycamore* are hyponyms of *tree*.

Iamb: The most common metrical unit in English poetry, consisting of an unstressed syllable followed by a stressed syllable.

Idiom: A sequence of words that is a unit of meaning. For example: *kick the bucket*, *put your foot in it.*

Imagery: The use of words to create a picture or 'image' in the mind of the reader. Images can relate to any of the senses – not just sight, but also hearing, touch and smell. The term is often used to refer to the use of descriptive language, particularly to the use of **metaphors** and **similes**.

Imperative: A grammatical mood expressing a directive, such as a command, warning or request. For example: *Get out my house*

Incompatibility: A linguistic feature that defines one item and thereby excludes others. For example, it would not be possible to say *I am writing in one colour of ink and it is red and blue*. As it has to be either red or blue, one term excludes the other.

Indirect speech: The words of a speaker that are reported rather than being quoted directly. For example: *David said that he was going out.* **Direct speech** would be *'I am going out,' said David.*

Infinitive: A non-finite verb in the base form, such as: *they might see.* The word 'see' as used here, is an example of a non-finite verb. Often the verb is preceded by the preposition *to*, for example: *to see.* A split infinitive, which is often considered grammatically incorrect, is where another word is placed between the preposition and the base form of the verb. Perhaps the most famous example is Star Trek's *To boldly go ...*

Insertion sequence: A feature occurring in spoken discourse where the original conversation is suspended because of an interruption caused by a speech sequence from another source. When the interruption has been dealt with, the original speech sequence resumes.

Intensifier: A word or phrase that adds emphasis. For example: *very, unbelievably, awfully* and *terribly.*

Internal rhyme: Rhyming words within a line rather than at the ends of lines.

Interrogative: A grammatical mood expressing a question.

Inter-textual: Having clear links with other texts through the themes, ideas or issues explored.

Intonation: The tone of voice in speech.

Inversion: Reversing the order of clause elements, so that subject and verb appear in the reverse of their normal order. For example: *here is the milkman*, instead of: *The milkman is here.*

Irony: At its simplest level, irony means saying one thing whilst meaning another. It occurs where a word or phrase has one surface meaning but another, contradictory and possibly opposite meaning is implied. Irony is frequently confused with sarcasm. Sarcasm is spoken, often relying on tone of voice, and is much more blunt than irony.

Lament: A poem expressing intense grief.

Language acquisition: The process of learning a first language as a child.

Language change: The process of change in a language over a period of time.

Language of speech: Spoken language of any kind.

Lexis: The vocabulary of a language or particular use of language.

Litotes: A rhetorical means of stressing something by stating that the opposite is not true. For example: *It was no small feat*, meaning it was a large feat or, *they lost no time getting to the scene of the crime*, meaning that they got to the scene quickly.

Loan word: A word borrowed from another language.

Lyric: Originally a lyric was a song performed to the accompaniment of a lyre (a stringed harp-like instrument), but now it can mean a song-like poem or a short poem expressing personal feeling.

Main clause: A clause that is not dependent and makes sense on its own. See **clause**.

Malapropism: A mixing up of words that sound similar. Made famous by Mrs Malaprop, a character in Richard Brinsley Sheridan's *The Rivals*, who says, 'He is the very *pineapple* of politeness' (for *pinnacle*) and 'She is as headstrong as an *allegory* on the banks of the Nile' (for *alligator*).

Manner: An adverbial answering the question 'How?', such as, *slowly.*

Metalanguage: The language used to talk about language.

Metaphor: A comparison of one thing to another in order to make description more vivid. Unlike a **simile**, a metaphor states that one thing *is* the other. For example, a simile could be *The wind went through me like a knife*, whereas the metaphor might state *The wind cut through me*. (See **simile** and **personification**).

Metonymy: A feature where an attribute of the thing being described stands for the whole thing. For example, the term *crown* could be used to mean the monarch. *the turf* could stand for horse racing; and *Fleet Street* could mean the Press.

Metre: The regular use of stressed and unstressed syllables in poetry.

Modal: An auxiliary verb that cannot be used as a main verb. For example: *can, may, will, shall, must, could, might, would* and *should*.

Mode: A particular medium of communication, such as, speech or writing.

Modification: The use of one linguistic item to specify the nature of another. Adjectives act as modifiers, such as, *the blue sky* – as do adverbs. For example: *he ducked quickly to avoid being seen*.

Modifier: A word that specifies the nature of another word or tells us more about it. **Adverbs** and **adjectives** act as modifiers.

Monologue: Speech or writing produced, and often performed, by one person.

Monometer: A line of verse containing only one unit of metre, known as one 'foot'.

Monosyllabic: Having only one syllable.

Mood: Main clauses can have one of three moods: the *declarative* mood is used to make statements; the *imperative* mood is used to issue orders, commands or make requests; and the *interrogative* mood is used to ask questions.

Morpheme: A unit of a word, such as a prefix (like, *un-, dis-, Pre-*), or a suffix (like, *-ment, -ing, -ly*). A morpheme may also be a word in its own right, such as 'cup' and 'board' in the **compound**, 'cupboard'. (See also **Compound**.)

Narrative: A piece of writing or speech that tells a story.

Neologism: Sometimes called a nonce-word or **coinage** – a new or invented word or expression. Usually they are made up of adaptations of existing words, although the term nonce-word was originally applied to words that had a 'one-off' use such as the combination of *fair, fabulous* and *joyous* to give *frabjous*, used by Lewis Carroll in *Jabberwocky*. Examples of more modern neologisms are *zeroized, shopaholic* and *computerate*. Of course, when a word has been in use for a while or becomes common, it ceases to be new and is no longer considered a neologism.

Non-standard English: Any variety of language use that does not conform to the standard form of English accepted as the 'norm' by society. See **Standard English** and **received pronunciation**.

Noun: A word class with a naming function, which can be used as a subject or an object in a clause. Nouns can be grouped in several ways. Here are the main kinds:

- *Proper nouns*: the names of specific people, places, times, occasions, events, publications and so on. For example: *London, Lulu, the English Magazine, July* and *Christmas Day*. They are usually written with an initial capital letter.

- *Common nouns*: general objects or ideas, such as *table, window, book, pen*.

- *Abstract nouns*: qualities or states that exist only in our minds. For example: *cleverness, courage, justice, loyalty* and *mercy*.

- *Collective nouns*: groups of people, or collections of things as a whole. For example: *crowd, flock, regiment, convoy, forest* and *crew*.

Octave: The first eight lines of a sonnet.

Octometer: A verse line consisting of eight feet.

Ode: A verse form similar to a lyric but often more lengthy and containing more serious and elevated thoughts.

Onomatopoeia: The use of words whose sounds copy the sounds of the thing or process they describe. On a simple level, words like *bang, hiss* and *splash* are onomatopoeic, but the device also has more subtle uses.

Oxymoron: A figure of speech that joins words of opposite meanings together. For example: *the living dead, bitter sweet.*

Paradox: A statement that appears contradictory, but when considered more closely is seen to contain a good deal of truth.

Parallelism: The patterning of pairs of sounds, words or structures to create a sense of balance in spoken or written discourse, such as, 'I am the way, the life and the truth'.

Parody: A work that is written in imitation of another work, very often with the intention of making fun of the original.

Participle: The non-finite form of verbs that can occur after an auxiliary verb. For example: *was running* (present participle); *had run* (past participle). This form can also occur before a head noun as in the *running man*, or the *completed task.*

Particle: A grammatical function word that never changes its form, such as, *up, down, in, after.*

Pastoral: Generally, literature concerning rural life with idealized settings and rustic characters. Often pastorals are concerned with the lives of shepherds and shepherdesses, presented in idyllic and unrealistic ways.

Pathos: The effect in literature that makes the reader feel sadness or pity.

Patterning: Language used in such a way as to create discernible patterns, perhaps through **imagery**, a repeated symbol or motif, or use of **parallelism**.

Pentameter: A line of verse containing five feet.

Periphrasis: A round-about or long-winded way of saying something.

Personification: The attribution of human feelings, emotions, sensations or physical attributes to an inanimate object. Personification is a kind of **metaphor**, where human qualities are given to things or abstract ideas.

Phatic: A term describing language used to make social contact, which is intended more to convey general sociability than to communicate meaning. For example: *Nice morning, isn't it?*

Phonetic alphabet: Symbols and **diacritics** designed to represent exactly the sound of spoken language.

Phonetic transcription: A detailed transcription, using phonetic symbols, concentrating on the details of pronunciation.

Phonetics: The study of spoken sounds and the way in which they are produced.

Phonological features: Features of the sound of speech such as rhythm, stress, pronunciation, volume and pace.

Phrase: A group of words smaller than a **clause**, which forms a grammatical unit, but does not contain a finite verb and therefore does not make complete sense on its own.

Pitch: The auditory level of sound.

Pleonasm: The unnecessary use of words. For example: *here and now, this present day and age*. Also called **tautology**.

Plot: The sequence of events in a poem, play, novel or short story that make up the main story line.

Polysyllabic: Having more than one syllable.

Preposition: A word expressing a relationship of meaning between two parts of a sentence, most often showing how the two parts are related in space or time. For example: *we had a meal in a restaurant. I'll take you to the cinema.*

Pronoun: A word that stands for a noun. For example: Kate went to the cinema and *she* bought an ice cream. The word 'she' stands for Kate. *My car is red but my friend has a maroon one*, where the word 'one' stands for car. Pronouns include words such as: *he, she, they, we, her, him, all, both* and *each*.

Prose: Any kind of writing that is not verse – usually divided into fiction and non-fiction.

Protagonist: The main character or speaker in a poem, monologue, play or story.

Pun: A play on words that have similar sounds but quite different meanings. For example, in Shakespeare's *Romeo & Juliet*, Mercutio says, after he has been mortally wounded, 'Ask for me tomorrow, and you shall find me a grave man.'

Purpose: The reason why a piece of writing has been written or why a speech has been made. For example: *to entertain, to explain, to persuade* or *to argue*.

Quatrain: A stanza of four lines, which can have various rhyme schemes.

Received pronunciation: Sometimes known as RP, the British accent that has a high social status and is not related to a specific region or influenced by regional variation.

Recursive: Said of a grammatical rule that is capable of repeated application.

Referencing: References point to something else in the discourse. Pronouns are often used to make these references, although comparative structures that express certain similarities or differences can also be used. In this sentence the pronoun 'she' is used: *The student worked hard, so she had little spare time*. In this sentence comparative structure, 'the first one', is used: *The second team was good but the first one was better*.

There are three main kinds of reference:

- *Anaphoric* references point *backwards* in a text. The reader or listener must refer to a previous reference to make sense of the pronoun or noun phrase that points back to something mentioned earlier.

- *Cataphoric* references point *forwards* in a text. In other words the reader or listener must refer to a future reference in order to understand the structure used. For example: *those were the days my friend*.

- *Exophoric* references point *beyond* the text so the reader or the listener has to make a connection with something outside the text. For example: *the fish was this big*. Some kind of context or sign is needed here so that the statement makes sense.

Refrain: Repetition throughout a poem of a phrase, line or series of lines, as in the 'chorus' of a song.

Repetition: A device that emphasizes an idea through repetition.

Representational features: Language use where one thing is used to represent another, as in **symbolic language** or the use of **imagery**.

Rhetoric: Originally, the art of speaking and writing in such a way as to persuade an audience to a particular point of view. Now it is often used to imply grand words that have no substance in them. There are a variety of rhetorical devices such as the rhetorical question – a question that does not require an answer, as the answer is obvious or implied in the question itself.

Rhyme: Corresponding sounds in words, usually at the end of each line of verse, but not always.

Rhyme scheme: The pattern of the rhymes in a poem.

Rhythm: The 'movement' of a poem as created through the metre and the way that language is stressed within the poem.

Satire: The highlighting or exposing of human failings or foolishness within a society, by ridiculing them. Satire can range from light to extremely bitter in tone. For example: Jonathan Swift's *Gulliver's Travels* or George Orwell's *Animal Farm*.

Scansion: The analysis of metrical patterns in poetry.

Semantic features: Features that provide speech or writing with a linguistic meaning.

Semantic field: Areas of meaning identified by a set of mutually defining words. For example, *red*, *blue*, *green* and *yellow* are all words identified with colour. *Regiment*, *soldier*, *battalion*, *barracks* and *parade* are all identified as describing military things.

Semantics: The study of the meaning of language.

Sentence: A grammatical structure made up of one or more clauses. Usually in written language it begins with a capital letter and ends with a full stop (or a feature that performs the function of a full stop, such as a question mark). In analysing spoken language, **utterances** are often referred to rather than sentences.

In terms of purpose, there are four kinds of sentences.

- Command – *Get up, now!*
- Question – *How are you?*
- Statement – *I am going out tonight.*
- Exclamation – *Look out!*

There are also three kinds of sentences in terms of their structure.

- *Simple sentence* – A simple sentence has just one finite verb (a finite verb is a verb that has a subject).
- *Compound sentence* – consists of two or more simple sentences joined together by a co-ordinating conjunction. For example: *I hope to pass my exams and then go on to university.*
- *Complex sentence* – has one main clause and any number of subordinate clauses joined to it by subordinating conjunctions. For example: *The strikers will continue to hold their demonstrations because their concerns have not been addressed.*

Septet: A seven-line stanza.

Sequencing: The rules governing the succession of utterances in discourse.

Sestet: The last six lines of a sonnet.

Side-sequence: In spoken discourse, an explanation of something that has already been uttered.

Simile: A comparison of one thing with another in order to make a description more vivid. Similes use the words *like* or *as* to make the comparison.

Slang: Distinctive words and phrases associated with informal speech. Very often used within certain social groups or age groups.

Soliloquy: A speech in which a dramatic character, alone on stage or regardless of hearers, expresses his or her thoughts and feelings aloud for the benefit of the audience.

Sonnet: A fourteen-line poem, usually with ten syllables in each line. There are several ways in which the lines can be organized, but they often consist of an **octave** and a **sestet**.

Spondee: A unit of poetic metre containing two stressed syllables.

Standard English: The form of English considered to be and accepted as the norm in society, and used as the medium of government, education and law. Language that differs from this standard is known as **non-standard**.

Stanza: The blocks of lines into which a poem is divided. Sometimes these are referred to less precisely as verses, which can lead to confusion as poetry is sometimes called 'verse' too.

Stream of consciousness: A technique whereby the writer puts down thoughts in a 'stream' as they come to mind, without imposing order or structure.

Structure: The way that a poem, play or other piece of writing has been put together. This can include the metre pattern, stanza arrangement, the ways the ideas are developed, etc.

Style: The individual way in which a writer has used language to express his or her ideas.

Stylistics: The study of lexical and structural variations in language according to use, audience and purpose.

Sub-plot: A secondary story-line in a novel or play. Often, as in some plays by Shakespeare, the sub-plot can provide some comic relief from the main action, but sub-plots can also relate to the main plot in complex ways.

Sub-text: Ideas, themes or issues that are not dealt with overtly by a text but exist below the surface-meaning.

Syllable: A word or part of a word that can be uttered in a single effort of the voice. Patterns of stressed and unstressed syllables make up the rhythm-pattern of the language.

Symbolic language: The use of words or phrases to represent something else.

Synecdoche: A device in which a part is used to represent the whole. For example: *There were several new faces at the meeting.* In this sentence, the word 'faces' is used to represent 'people'.

Synonyms: Different words with the same or nearly the same meanings, such as: *shut* and *close* or *ship* and *vessel*.

Syntax: The study of the structure of sentences.

Tag question: An interrogative structure added to the end of a sentence that requires a reply. For example: *Terrible weather, isn't it?*

Tautology: Saying the same thing twice over in different words. For example: *The visitors arrived one after the other in succession.*

Tetrameter: A verse line of four feet.

Text: A piece of spoken or written language with a communicative function.

Theme: The central idea or ideas that a writer explores through his or her text.

Tone: The tone of a text is created through the combined effects of a number of features, such as **diction**, **syntax** and **rhythm**. The tone can be a major factor in establishing the overall impression of a piece of writing.

Topicality: The topic of a spoken encounter is directly related to its **manner** and its participants. The topic can determine the level of **formality**, and topic shifts can occur when speakers move from one topic to another. These mark key points in the discourse.

Transcription: A written record of spoken language, which may use symbols to represent the distinctive features of speech.

Trimeter: A unit of poetic metre containing three feet.

Trochee: A unit of poetic metre containing a stressed syllable followed by an unstressed syllable.

Turn-taking: Organization of speakers' contributions in a conversation. Turns may be fairly equal, or one of the participants may dominate.

Utterance: A piece of spoken language. The term is also used to describe a spoken 'sentence', since it can be difficult to apply the normal rules of a written sentence to speech.

Verb: A word that expresses actions, states of being or processes. There are three types of verb that can occur within a verb phrase.

- *Full* (or *lexical*) verbs have a clearly stateable meaning. These act as main verbs, such as *run*, *jump*, *go* and *look*.

- *Modal auxiliary verbs* express a range of judgements about the likelihood of events. These function only as auxiliary verbs, such as: *will*, *shall*, *may*, *might* and *can*.

- *Primary* verbs can function either as main verbs or auxiliary verbs. There are three of them: *be*, *have* and *do*.

Vernacular: The native language a community uses for speech.

Vocabulary: The words of a language – the same as **lexis**.

Zeugma: A device whereby two nouns are joined by a single verb or adjective. For example: *The lights and my spirits are fading.*